The Agile Virtual Enterprise

The Agile Virtual Enterprise

Enterprise

Cases, Metrics, Tools

H. T. Goranson

Q

QUORUM BOOKS
Westport, Connecticut • London

Library of Congress Cataloging-in-Publication Data

Goranson, H. T., 1947–
    The agile virtual enterprise : cases, metrics, tools / H. T.
Goranson.
      p. cm.
    Includes bibliographical references and index.
    ISBN 1–56720–264–0 (alk. paper)
    1. Flexible manufacturing systems.   2. Virtual corporations.
3. Production planning.   4. Business logistics.   5. Organizational
change.   I. Title.
TS155.65.G66   1999
670.42'7—dc21   99–13619

British Library Cataloguing in Publication Data is available.

Library of Congress Catalog Card Number: 99–13619
ISBN: 1–56720–264–0

First published in 1999

Quorum Books, 88 Post Road West, Westport, CT 06881
An imprint of Greenwood Publishing Group, Inc.
www.quorumbooks.com

Printed in the United States of America

The paper used in this book complies with the
Permanent Paper Standard issued by the National
Information Standards Organization (Z39.48–1984).

10 9 8 7 6 5 4 3 2 1

For Susan, my wife of 30 years

Contents

Preface: Why Study the Agile Virtual Enterprise?   xi
    Agility and the Virtual Enterprise   xiii
    How the Project/Book Was Put Together   xiv
Chapter 1: Introduction   1
    Agility Is Different   3
Chapter 2: An Historical Example   11
    Military Research "Can" Do's and Don't's   11
    A Review of Best Agile Practices   12
    Some Lessons Learned   17
Chapter 3: The Social Factor   21
    Waterworld   21
    Role of Culture as an Agent   23
Chapter 4: Cultural Memes   29
    The English and French Engineering Paradigms   29
    Lessons for Management Metrics   34
    Law Follows Engineering   35
Chapter 5: Empirical Principles of AVEs   37
    High Concept in the Virtual Enterprise   37
    High Concept in Organizing the Virtual Enterprise   41
    Feature-Based Manufacturing   44

Three Visions of the Future   46
The Bottom Line   51

Chapter 6: Agility and the Defense Industry   53

ManTech, Movies and the *Spruce Goose*   53
The Need for Agility   55
Necessity of Government Investment   56
The Advanced Research Projects Agency   58
Why We Were Sponsored   59
The Story So Far   63

Chapter 7: Definitions   65

Virtual Enterprise   65
Agility   68
Types of Change   73
Metrics   74

Chapter 8: What Agility Is Not   85

Lean Manufacturing and Agility   85
The Agile Virtual Enterprise and Electronic Commerce   87
Flexible Manufacturing   90
Static Business Practices   91
Techie Solutions   93

Chapter 9: Issues   99

A Tool Strategy   99
Summary of the Method   100
Limits of Our Approach   102
Agility Forum and A3 Agility   106

Chapter 10: The Agile Virtual Enterprise Reference Model   109

The Reference Model   114
Infrastructure Elements   126
Infrastructure Observations   132
Best Agile Practice Examples   144

Chapter 11: Communicative Acts and Information Theory   157

Leveraging Information Theory   158
Communicative Acts   159
Modeling by Communicative Acts   161
Parallel Trends in Theory   171
Bottom Line   173

Chapter 12: Examples   175

Use of the Metrics   175
An Example   180
Application in the Real World: A Case Study   186
Deeper into a Case Study   197
Cost and Benefits   203
Costs   203

Chapter 13: Trust 211

An Example of the Problem 211
Inductive and Deductive Trust 213
Mitigated Inductive Trust 215
Truth 219
Agents and Channels 221
Trust Metrics 223

Chapter 14: Summary and Tools 227

Strategy ("Threat" and Options) 227
Complexity 234
Softness 239
State 241
Dooley Graph Calculator 242
Conclusion 247

Bibliography and References 251

Index 257

Preface: Why Study the Agile Virtual Enterprise?

Until very recently, the primary developer of new technology in both the computer and manufacturing arenas has been the U. S. Department of Defense. On the computer side, essentially everything one can identify as a technology has benefited from such investment. But few people are aware of the profound influence the defense establishment has had on managing the manufacturing enterprise.

The computer aided design revolution and the ability to control machine tools by computer are largely the result of defense research. Robotics is almost exclusively a child of the military. But the parent of all modern management techniques is *modeling*. In the late 1950s and early 1960s, it became clear that one should be able to engineer—to design and optimize—a shop floor (the part of the enterprise that actually makes something) the same way you design and optimize any other product.

Although product design has an engineering discipline that allows factors to be represented and analyzed, the same was not always true for plant design. The Air Force Manufacturing Practices group in Dayton, Ohio, decided to create such a discipline. The central component was the representation or modeling language that allowed managers to see what went on in an unambiguous way and then make reasoned decisions. The result of this research, originally called the Intelligent Computer Aided Manufacturing (ICAM) program, is a collection of modeling methods and the metrics that result from them.

The research initially focused on the shop floor, and there *were* solid results. In fact, pretty much the entire discipline of industrial engineering depends on this research. Those results also were a major component of the U.S. military industrial strategy early in the cold war, allowing the U.S. to beat the Soviet block in advanced weapons. But the whole system made some assumptions:

- The whole product, in this case the weapons system, was designed and manufactured completely within a single firm or an enterprise.
- One could model the requirements for the product, while the world, in effect, stood still, and neither the requirements nor the implementing technology would change.
- The hard part of everything was on the engineering side, not the business process side.

These assumptions all proved false. Modern weapon systems are assembled by a systems integrator of components that are designed and manufactured by thousands of suppliers. In fact, the trend has been to artificially decompose the system (say an aircraft) into more parts than is natural so almost every congressional district can get its due share.

It can take 15 or more years to design and test a major system, and the world changes radically in that time. The assumptions guarantee that systems will meet an obsolete mission with obsolete technology, or need to be modified at great expense after being delivered. Worst of all, the bigger problem is not on the engineering side, but rather on the business side. As the problems, systems, and nature of change become more complex, most large firms still insist on managing that complexity with traditional, top-down management. But that ponderous system is no longer sufficient. There's just too much going on and too quickly.

In Chapter 4, a detailed example of a problem faced by the military industrial establishment is presented, a problem so huge that almost any level of research investment could have been justified. For now it is enough to know that, generally, major weapons systems cost twice what they should, with the extra dollars going to a poor infrastructure for managing complexity. (The same, incidentally, is true of cars, software, and commercial airliners; this problem is not just confined to military products.) Moreover, there are several novel weapons that we cannot be built at all, at any cost, until things are fixed, even though the individual pieces that comprise the weapons could easily be produced.

In recognition of these problems, the Defense Department responded with several targeted research programs, at the cost of two or three hundred million dollars. Some were focused on trying to keep the old paradigm going. A few looked to build a modern paradigm of how to manage dynamism and complexity.

Sirius-Beta, a research firm in Virginia Beach, Virginia—played a key role in all these important research programs. These programs evolved first from a focus on *concurrent engineering,* which worried about many distributed simultaneous designers. The next problem was how to coordinate this under the rubric of *enterprise engineering*. Finally, it all evolved into a focus on *agile manufacturing.*

These three areas and related programs represent over a half billion dollars in pure research. In the last few years, the central effort has been in the *agile manufacturing program*, which looks at new ideas and formal underpinnings for managers. This book is the result of that research.

AGILITY AND THE VIRTUAL ENTERPRISE

The agility program started life in the early 1990s with a roundtable of senior business executives. These were chartered by the Department of Defense and the National Science Foundation (NSF) and came from the full spectrum of manufacturing concerns. They reported that the number one problem was the lack of management tools to manage the problem of responding to unexpected change (Nagel and Dove, 1991).

A few bright, patriotic Senate staffers seized on this information to arrange the funding (approximately $120 million) for the agile manufacturing program. The Defense Department did not request the money; it already had several initiatives to maintain the status quo, for example a major initiative in lean manufacturing in the aircraft industry. Nonetheless, the money and charter appeared on the doorstep of the Advanced Research Projects Agency (ARPA), which is the Pentagon's premier center for high risk, high payoff projects. ARPA created a program that was managed by the three military services and the NSF. An Agility Forum was established at Lehigh University under the auspices of the Iacocca Institute. Three NSF-managed university research centers were established, and about thirty new research contracts were issued.

Unfortunately, much of the research twisted the original, novel idea to different agendas, and many preexisting projects were repurposed so that they could be funded under the new umbrella. For instance, some "agility" proponents used the term to describe doing things fast, or flexibly. Agile and lean manufacturing became rationalized as being the same, so as to avoid bloody political battles which the research community often shuns at all costs. There were electronic commerce, supply chain management, and activity-based costing projects which may have been worthy, but which had nothing to do with the original, useful vision of agility.

But a core of projects, mostly under the management of the Air Force, were able to focus on the original idea of agility: The ability to engineer your enterprise to *respond well to unexpected change,* to even *leverage* that ability as a competitive strategy. *Engineering* is a key term here, since it implies formal management principles rather than vague concepts.

Based on early discovery by our technical advisory committee, Sirius-Beta merged the goal of agility with the strategy of a virtual enterprise. This came from the idea that agile systems are facilitated by enterprises that are federations of components which encourages diversity in those components. This is contrary to the current way of doing things, which binds components in an enterprise by forcing them all to be the same in important ways; for example, often a large company will force all of its suppliers to conform to the same quality assurance practices it uses.

But there are a vast number of visions of what constitutes a virtual enterprise, from a conventional supply chain to the radical idea of small components opportunistically and temporarily bound for a short-term purpose. While the focus remains specific to the new strategy of agility, it can also encompass broad scope of virtual enterprises. As a result, the tools and methods described here can be used in whatever enterprise view you use; for example, either to make an automotive supply chain more agile as a strategy of the prime contractor, or to make the automotive prime contractor obsolete by managing the complex systems integration task by other, distributed means.

Incidentally, when the Republican Congress took over in 1996, the fifty-year heritage of investment in manufacturing technology as a matter of policy came to an end, and agility research with it. No matter, the important research has been done.

HOW THE PROJECT/BOOK WAS PUT TOGETHER

Since Sirius-Beta (as Senior Scientist for the firm, hereafter I will also use the pronoun "we") had been involved in managing many research projects, we had already developed our own ideas about how to do them properly. When the agility project came up, an "open research" strategy was devised, which involved every relevant expert regardless of where they were, and allowed many people to be involved in the details. We were convinced that with such a powerful and, in some applications, radical idea, exposure was the best guarantee of soundness.

Some years earlier, Sirius-Beta had led a Suppliers' Working Group of major information infrastructure suppliers acting under a special antitrust dispensation to conduct a $40 million investigation into the technical needs for this business problem of integrating the enterprise. As the White House-designated Action Officer, we managed a set of international workshops and a reporting conference which was cosponsored by the U.S. government and the European Strategic Program for Research in Information Technology (ESPRIT). The culmination was the International Conference on Enterprise Integration Modeling Technology (ICEIMT), involving virtually every important technical expert active in the field.

The published proceedings of the conference (Petrie, 1992) laid out the technical agenda for the Agile Virtual Enterprise. Incidentally, much of this research involved documenting the business case and therefore influenced the reorganizations of IBM, Digital, and NCR. The group's research was also the business and technical motivator for two important technical developments: Java and the Object Management Group's Object Request Broker. Java is a new programming language that facilitates federation among diverse sites, and the Object Request Broker is a standard protocol for integrating programming units called objects to support a similar goal.

For the research, Sirius-Beta established a guiding body which was administered by the Agility Forum. This group, the Agile Virtual Enterprise Focus Group met 25 times over three years around the country. The two-day meetings were free and open, involving representatives from 150 firms, large and small. There was also a core group of eight or nine. The Focus Group developed the mission definition for our research and the important Agile Virtual Enterprise Reference Model, which is described in detail beginning in Chapter 10. The Focus Group also directed case studies and reviewed the progress of the effort for business practicality. Organizations participating in the group are listed in Table 1.

Table 1 Participants in the Agile Virtual Enterprise Focus Group

Small Manufacturers	Large Firms	Consultants, Services, Infrastructure
Agile Web	AT&T	
Associated Fiberglass	Boeing Commercial Airplane Group	2 Technologies, Inc.
Ceco Corp.	Boeing Military and Space	Agility Forum
Contemporary Design	Boeing Rocketdyne	Andersen Consulting
Hehr Power Systems	Deere & Co.	Arthur D. Little, Inc.
HighTech Marketing	Dupont Advanced Material Systems	Ben Franklin Institute
Kavco Industries		Center for Manufacturing Competitiveness
Lider and Associates	Eastman Kodak	CommerceNet
Process Consulting	Ford Motor Company	Competitive Technologies Inc.
Rheaco Inc.	Goodyear Tire and Rubber	Conduit, Electronic Delivery Systems
Tex Direct	Hughes Missile Systems Co.	
Sherpa Corp.	H. R. Textron	D'Ancona & Pflaum
Symbiotic Resources	IBM	EDS
Web Pipeline, Inc.	Lockheed Martin	Enterprise Agility International
	Lockheed Martin Vought Systems	Executive Action Group
Researchers	Lockheed Missiles and Space Co.	FKW Incorporated
	Mack Truck	Gemini Industries
Aerospace Agile Manufacturing Research Center	Martin Marietta	Gaudiouse and Associates
Arizona State University	Metropolitan Edison Company	Global Strategic Solutions
Consortium for Advanced Manufacturing International	Newport News Shipbuilding	Gunneson Group International, Inc.
Cornell Theory Center	Northrop Grumman	
Georgia Institute of Technology	Raytheon	Hall & Associates
Illinois State University	Sikorsky	IBM
Industrial Technology Institute	Steelcase	Intelligent Systems Technology Inc.
Institute of Advanced Manufacturing Sciences	Texas Instruments	Institute of State and Regional Affairs (PA)
National Center for Manufacturing Sciences	U. S. Steel	Jim Bronson
National Institute of Standards and Technology	Westinghouse Electric	Knowledge Based Systems Inc.
Pennsylvania State - Harrisburg		Lockheed Martin Palo Alto Research Center
Sandia National Labs		Manufacturing Application Center
Sirius-Beta		Mantech International
University of Indiana		Menlo Park Ass.
University of South Dakota		Pennsylvania MILRITE Council
University of Texas - Arlington		Schnader, Harrison, Segal & Lewis
University of Texas - Austin		Society for Manufacturing Engineers
Western Kentucky University		Strategic Business Management
Work and Technology Institute		Symbiotic Resources
		Telart Technologies
		The Schraff Group
		VFD Consulting
		Virtual Learning Center

In many areas, we were moving in territory that had not been previously explored, nor studied rigorously, so we maintained special partnerships with a few world-class research organizations:

- The Agility Forum at Lehigh University, Bethlehem, Pennsylvania was the NSF-supported center for promoting the idea of agility. It served as the center for sharing results among many government sponsored projects and therefore cross-fertilization of business practices with our project. They chartered and financially supported the Agile Virtual Enterprise Focus Group, our official monitoring group. The Forum kindly hosted our web site for interim results and our email discussion group on outstanding issues. (The web address is www.agilityforum.org).
- The Automation and Robotics Research Institute of the University of Texas at Arlington (near Dallas, Texas) provided support for the huge local manufacturing base and performed basic research on enterprise engineering from the industrial engineering side. They provided a continuous enterprise user view and practicality filter for our research. Also, their NSF-funded Aerospace Agile Manufacturing Research Center audited our case studies. (arri.uta.edu).
- The Center for the Study of Language and Information at Stanford University, Palo Alto, California, is the eminent research center for the study of logic and information in a mathematical context. It supported some workshops and provided key formal foundations for the research. (www-csli.stanford.edu/csli/).
- The Industrial Technology Institute of Ann Arbor, Michigan was originally established by the automakers to explore advanced ideas, but has since become expert in a few areas of general applicability. One unique expertise is the study of language constructs to support autonomous agents in the enterprise. They provided key insights which supported the development of the agility tools. (www.iti.org).
- The Work and Technology Institute of Washington, D.C., focused on workforce issues in the context of technology and had the involvement of key futurists in the union sector. They understood the cultural and social issues in the context of novel business environments perhaps better than anyone and provided key anthropological insights. (www.wti.org).
- The Steelcase company, was a key investigator to the project and cosponsored the CSLI workshops. Steelcase provides office furniture and is deeply involved in modeling collaborative environments from the physical perspective, so we shared an agenda. (www.steelcase.com)
- Sirius-Beta's address is www.sirius-beta.com

The project to develop models and metrics for agility progressed over five years. First, we would develop an idea or identify a possibility or controversy. Next, we would take it to our Focus Group meetings and our email discussion group. This email discussion group involved most of the relevant key researchers worldwide (approximately 300). Finally, with partners, we would formulate a position, or at least a crisp statement of the alternatives. This would be posted on the project's web site. This site logged thousands of hits from interested parties, about 17% of whom made suggestions. With this feedback, the content on the site matured into coherent positions. This book is evolved from the section on the web site concerned with management users. (There were also sections for policymakers, tool developers, and academics.)

Over the years, we presented interim results in a couple dozen conferences, which was less useful than we had expected. This may have been because we already had the heavyweights otherwise involved. Of course the aforementioned ICEIMT workshops differed in being singularly helpful. Two other workshops are worth noting: A study on manufacturing challenges for 2020 by the National Research Council and a more detailed technical study by Oak Ridge National Labs, called the Integrated Manufacturing Technology Roadmap. Both were sponsored by The U.S. Departments of Defense, Commerce (in the form of the National Institute of Standards and Technology), and Energy to devise a meaningful vision of the future. The ideas you will see here are a prominent part of those studies.

Chapter 1

Introduction

The pendulum has swung too far; management trends today are predominantly based on the idea that you can fully understand your customer and your business including its processes and strategic goals. The idea that is misapplied here is that business is a predictable game, that you can and should know precisely what you are about, and only then can you act deliberately. But business is like everything else in life. Life is dynamic, unpredictable, and sometimes is inscrutable. Many things shift, and you are constantly being hit by surprises. Negotiating through life involves a certain amount of acting under unknown conditions, by recognizing and adapting to change. Just imagine someone telling you that to be a successful spouse, or parent, requires a reliable ability to scope everything out first—no one would ever get married or choose to be a parent!

In real life, you do all the planning you can, all the learning you feel is worthwhile and then, you dive in. You do this because you have confidence in your ability to adapt and develop strengths in areas currently unknown to you. You have faith in your *agility*. (The analogy isn't entirely apt because unexpected change is even more prevalent in business.)

If you are in business today, you probably have been swept up with management ideas such as lean and mean, business process reengineering, and certainly in accounting methods, activity-based costing. All of these assume that you can and do know essentially everything you need to know about your environment and processes. Management is presented as a matter of analyzing these facts so that your actions can be effective and focused. We will look at all of these techniques in depth later on, but for now, let's just consider lean manufacturing.

Being lean generally means getting rid of the unnecessary. To be lean, you understand and cozy up to your customers and also narrow your focus to a small set of suppliers. You understand what you want to accomplish and what your processes and assets are, so you can evaluate what doesn't add value and eliminate it. Also, since you understand your processes so well, you can constantly evolve them to be better, faster, and cheaper. This makes you more competitive, right? What could be wrong with that?

Well, the world is not so well-behaved. Nothing is constant; customers are increasingly fickle and unpredictable; innovation makes processes and products obsolete overnight (and the pace is increasing). Much of what you do—even when you do it right—isn't fully understood by anyone in your organization. No one is safe from being blindsided.

Consider Toyota. The idea of *lean manufacturing* was concocted by American management consultants to describe a collection of practices that Toyota developed. This management technique leveraged Japanese-peculiar strengths: extremely stable supplier linkages enabled by interrelated banking interests; a homogenous workforce willing to be tightly coordinated by cultural dictates; and a clear, constant vision of the target market.

But Toyota went far beyond the useful bounds of lean. The Japanese banking system collapsed under the weight of stagnant capital; about half of their U.S. cars are no longer made in Japan, and they have found their workers in the U.S. plants to be not so pliable. But the biggest change is the unexpected shift caused by the U.S. market's irrational love affair with the sports utility vehicle. Toyota is now in trouble—and backing off of what we call lean to become more *agile*.

This book will help you understand agility in a practical way and will provide you with some new tools; later chapters provide detailed background on how we came to understand agility. It is based on research sponsored by the U.S. Department of Defense to find new techniques to address three problems which cumulatively make weapons cost twice what they should:

1. Weapon systems take 15 years or so to develop, but key technologies in them change sometimes every three years. The product therefore becomes a moving target.

2. In order to manage subcontractors, they need to be selected and brought into the process early in the game. This means that key product and process decisions get frozen early in the game, making things inflexible.

3. The only way we have of managing complexity is to turn it over to very large prime, coordinating firms, who soak up scads of money using outdated methods (like lean) of tying it all together.

The cutting edge results are collected here under the strategy of the Agile Virtual Enterprise, which apply to businesses everywhere. This book will give you some real examples, some basic theory, and some practical tools that you cannot get elsewhere.

AGILITY IS DIFFERENT

A major challenge in life is discriminating what is changing from what is not. What is new in today's environment is that not only is the rate of change increasing but the things that change are changing. It's no longer sufficient to be fast, nor enough to be able to respond nimbly when change is recognized. Tomorrow, the benchmark firms will be those that engineer the ability to respond to specific types of change into their organizations.

When Wang Laboratories invented the word processor—an innovation that quickly created a billion-dollar company—shock waves hit the world's largest typewriter producer, IBM. IBM had dominated that market with the most preferred (better, cheaper, better supported) products, but they were initially unable to respond to Wang's innovation. Wang successfully redefined and dominated this market precisely because they took advantage of change.

Yet, Wang's market started eroding with the appearance of word processing software on personal computers. At that time, a Wang official confidently declared, "We're a billion-dollar company and billion-dollar companies don't disappear overnight." But when IBM faced and responded to the new realities by creating the word-processing capable personal computer, Wang was unable to change, and they were soon bankrupt.

At one time, vacuum tube giants GE, RCA, Raytheon, and Sylvania absolutely controlled the electronics industry. But they do not today; others seized many of the new opportunities. Are the current leaders equally temporary? There are so many examples of companies not able to change—to keep up—that one has only to go back a few decades to see a 50% turnover in the Fortune 100.

What did the losers do wrong? Most of these firms were paragons of good management; they delighted their customers with excellent sales personnel; they had, relatively speaking, flat, knowledge-driven organizations and empowered, educated workforces. But they could not anticipate change. Who can? Their actual problem was that they couldn't respond to the unanticipated change even when they knew it was happening. What they lacked was *agility*, which we define simply as the ability to respond to unexpected change. The research which we discuss here provides help toward a better understanding of agility as well as specific steps on how to engineer the correct amount and type of agility into an enterprise.

One thing is clear: agility is largely independent of other best management approaches that a business can practice. Your ability to make things better, faster, and cheaper today says nothing (or very little) about your ability to change (in a fast and cheap way) to make something else better, faster, and cheaper (or to respond in other respects to unanticipated changes).

If you have a flat organization, according to best-in-class standards, will you be more agile? Maybe not. In fact, what put Wang out of business was IBM roaring back by entering (some would say creating) the PC business. IBM was able to respond successfully because of the previously underutilized skills of their many-layered, redundant, and expensive technical management pool.

But IBM continued to be remarkably successful in responding to change in the PC business only as long as they could handle it in the same fashion as their typewriter business (when the PCs were still used as personal letter-writers and adding machines). When PCs started looking more like other computers, and competed with their other business (mainframe computers, which, inside IBM, used another management paradigm), they developed troubles. But that's another story.

If you have a lean organization, as conventionally understood, will you automatically have agility? Consider the following example. Toyota, as we've mentioned, and other Japanese auto manufacturers gained a foothold in the U.S. originally because they made small, efficient cars at a time when the oil price shocks made those cars attractive to United States buyers. Originally, the attraction to the consumer was simply the size of the car as well as a low price resulting from an artificially strong dollar. Quality wasn't part of the equation at first. U.S. automakers were stuck, having invested so heavily in plants and pro-cesses for larger, gas-guzzling cars that it was hard to adapt to the new kind of product.

Later, both quality and lean production techniques became competitive issues. Ford and GM rushed to become lean. The first targets were reductions in their supplier base, with the remaining small pool of suppliers being more qualified, which meant that the suppliers had to become lean themselves, sloughing off excess capability. Most initial success was in drivetrain suppliers. Both GM and Ford went from a very large pool of suppliers to a highly inte-grated, much smaller set. Savings were not immediate, but the financial mar-kets thought it was a great idea.

Meanwhile, Chrysler (now Daimler Chrysler) was not becoming lean as fast as Ford and GM, and it was not doing well in the market either. Consumers just weren't buying many of their dowdy cars. Chrysler decided that a good selling point would be to offer driver's seat airbags, and they did so. Ads, laid on thick and featuring their CEO, touted this advantage.

There are two versions of this story: one makes Chrysler appear wiser than the other. (In other words, did they create this opportunity or luck into it?) What happened was that Chrysler was far behind on becoming lean, insofar as reducing suppliers; and they had a large pool of steering wheel suppliers with all sorts of creative ideas and excess capabilities. Since installing airbags in steering wheels stretched existing processes considerably, it was helpful to have this large, competitive pool to help figure out a radical new idea in steer-ing wheels.

Ford and GM took years to adjust, hampered by their lean supply chains, which were efficiently targeted on old-style steering wheels. They had been forced to get rid of their idea people, and slough off their underutilized, seem-ingly unnecessary processes. Meanwhile, Chrysler attracted a substantial num-ber of crossover buyers, which gave them a whole new life, saving the company. One version of the story has Chrysler targeting their competitors' weakness accidentally. Another, less likely, version credits Chrysler with inten-tionally hitting their competition where they were weak—lean but not agile.

We assert that agility is something separate from being better, faster, cheaper, or merely being profitable *today*. Rather, it is the ability to be profitable *tomorrow*, presumably by being better, faster, and cheaper in different ways. Agility is a concept that investment firms implicitly understand and use. Everyone can see how profitable you are today; that's not the most important question. A savvy investor is more concerned with how likely you are to grow and be profitable tomorrow.

In a sense, agility is free. You can get a limited amount of agility by employing good management practices that you may adopt independently of agility concerns. For instance, good customer monitoring has to be helpful all-around. If you invest in better, more robust insight into customer needs in order to be profitable, that's also likely to help you be agile. But most agility will cost money. You'll invest in agility as a hedge to manage risk, much as you already do with insurance coverage. Some would say the least useful kind of agility would be an excessive capability for change and especially for change that is in the wrong areas—in other words, agility that you never use, but that you spent your stockholder's money on and didn't need. But even more crucial in many cases is the agility that you do need but just don't have, which hurts your position. This can be crippling. So consider agility to be just like insurance.

This book describes research on metrics for engineering agility. The metrics are intended to provide a first step toward a management science of agility and to be immediately useful to managers wishing to make informed decisions about agility. One application is in a three-step agility assessment. Many millions of dollars have gone into today's management tools, so it would be foolish to consider replacing those. Step 2 provides a new tool that integrates with the processes used in steps 1 and 3.

Step 1 in the assessment evaluates the threat; identifying the areas in which, and the extent to which, agility would be required. This step allows you to make an educated guess on how unstable the sand is under your feet and in which direction it is likely to shift. Our new metrics will not help with this particular evaluation, other than generally to illuminate the dimensions of the problem. Conventional actuarial analyses can cover this problem, fitting right in with other strategic evaluations of change within the environment.

Step 2 evaluates your ability to address the threat. It is here that we will be able to help you predict the time and cost of change, given specific configurations within your enterprise.

Step 3 directs you to specific tools and techniques, ideally through case studies, to address and correct your specific agility weaknesses. Several groups are working on this problem; the most notable are the Agility Forum at Lehigh University, and the three National Science Foundation-sponsored Agile Manufacturing Research centers. As with step one, our metrics only generally inform this step, except through some rules of thumb we'll provide.

The targeted initial use of our metrics is as a tactical tool: you presumably already have a corporate or enterprise strategy, which has as a component where and how much you want agility. You may be faced with a given number of alternatives; for example, whether to build in-house or outsource among competing members within your supply chain. Naturally, you have ways of evaluating the time, cost, and quality of these suppliers in a static situation. This book will help you additionally determine the time and cost of change in the manner and extent that your strategy requires, so that the actual, real overall cost of doing business with them as conditions change can be evaluated by combining the cost of change from our metrics with existing measures of better-faster-cheaper.

Indications about the use of the metrics for the more technically challenging situation of strategic planning are also provided. Here, you would need to incorporate the metrics with your own (or your consultant's) strategic analysis tools; you would ideally have the ability to perform quick evaluations as well as high confidence simulations; and you would have the ability to evaluate many options with many alternatives, taking into account numerous factors in your organization and those of your partners, competitors, and customers. The technique presented will help with all this. Perhaps the best use of this type of strategic agility is as an active competitive weapon, not merely a response, as in one interpretation of the Chrysler experience. An example of agility as a weapon is available in the famous Burger King assault as described in the next section.

Finally, we expect that one result of adopting this approach to metrics will be the appearance of certain rules-of-thumb for particular situations in agility which can be applied even without the specific analysis by our metrics. These rules do not appear without the formal underpinning that are presented here. In addition to the targeted use of metrics by strategic managers and middle-level decisionmakers, we also expect, based on our work with them, that these metrics will be used by the investment community to evaluate companies' future prospects.

Burger Wars

Sirius-Beta conducted a large number of agility case studies for the Department of Defense and National Science Foundation. For those studies we interviewed a number of companies from a completely different perspective than the then-prevailing trends and discovered some surprises. (The insights included here come from a senior vice president/strategist at a fast food parent company who spoke from experience.)

Most of us will remember the early days of the burger wars. McDonald's was the Toyota of the restaurant business; it emphasized lean processes based on burgers, shakes, and fries, and it took the nation by storm, offering the advantages of low cost and convenience. My informant described wonderful examples, well known in the literature, he said, of detailed studies of such concerns as: the optimum combined grill/spatula size to flip so many burgers at once; a multi-nozzled squirter so that all condiments could be splorted on all burgers at once; a shake handling process which knocked a second off preparation time, and so on. The entire kitchen was based on the most efficient processes geared to an extremely limited menu. A tremendous investment went into understanding those processes, designing the best equipment and training to support them.

McDonald's ended up with a huge physical investment in equipment that was optimized for a small, standardized menu set. Enter Burger King. They put themselves on the map by pursuing a brilliant strategy: they figured that people would tire of prefab burgers alone, if they were reminded of the monotony. So they began via advertising to sow dissatisfaction with the standardized condiments on pre-made burgers.

Burger King also designed assembly line equipment and processes which cost more, but were more agile in a way that their competition couldn't match. You might remember the system: a two-tiered moving grill conveyor, the top for toasting the buns, the bottom for the meat. Burgers were custom made one at a time, the process beginning with the customer's order.

The tactic was to emphasize that the customer could have it *their way*, with a tailored set of dressings. And they advertised the dickens out of it, educating the customer to expect more, and thus severely undercut McDonald's. During this period Burger King's growth far exceeded McDonald's. This provides an example of agility employed as a tactic specifically targeted to the weaknesses of a lean competitor. But the initial agility was focused on the physical infrastructure, exactly as in flexible manufacturing. In Chapter 8 the difference between agility and flexible manufacturing (and its cousin, mass customization) is described.

The longer term strategy was even more interesting. Burger King figured that they could use the equipment and kitchen layout for a larger, more dynamic menu. It was specifically designed for agility in this way. Burger King impinged on McDonald's business by offering a steady stream of specialized sandwiches, emphasizing their variety (including different shapes, a feature very hard for McDonald's to imitate). They knew that by changing consumer expectations they would force McDonald's to completely reinvent their processes and to replace all of their equipment.

It worked. McDonald's had to toss out the lean approach, as well as all their special equipment, and replace it with a more flexible physical plant. The resulting cash demands on McDonald's allowed Burger King to grow unchecked to be a nearly-equal competitor, since they could use their money for marketing and expansion. Incidentally, McDonald's learned a lot about using the physical plant as a competitive weapon through this experience. In the process of remodeling, they invested in playgrounds in the restaurant, creating a niche and providing an attraction that Burger King could not boast.

The burger wars are an example of agile adjustments in physical and legal/ explicit (in this case, the process plans) infrastructures. As it turns out, the processes and equipment used today have been revolutionized by changes in the information infrastructure. Burger King, McDonald's, and others are now pretty much the same insofar as processes and equipment are concerned. Meanwhile, Rally's and others have made a thriving business by entering the niche that McDonald's left: a very limited menu produced by an optimized, cheap kitchen.

The dynamics are similar to the Chrysler steering wheel example. In both cases, agility was a strategic weapon against a superior competitor. But Chrysler's advantage was in leveraging the agility it found. Burger King's genius was in understanding and creating agility.

The burger war historian told us that significant competitive differences among the big players now focus on a variety of human, social, and intangible elements. Some of these shed light on our soft agility studies which we will explore later. For now, we can at least notice these four categories of infra-structure—physical, legal, social, and informational—all of which provide opportunities for agility.

Competitive Games

Examples of agile organizations are distributed through the book. Con-sumer electronics is one of the most dynamic sectors and the game console industry is one of the most interesting.

The story begins with Nintendo introducing their NES to great success to capture a market orphaned after the Mattel/Atari collapse. Their approach was much like Microsoft's in the personal computer business: Capitalize on the large user base to quickly build a massive cadre of good and not-so-good devel-opers to deluge the market with, creating a proprietary product stream which completely dominates the market.

Along comes Sega with a superior platform, the 16-bit Genesis. Originally, it only had a few games, but each was the best in its class. In a new business model, Sega worked only with a select group of developers. Newer games were few, but excellent. It was a formula that was successful. Nintendo, completely stymied, was sunk. The release of their Super NES was much too late. Nintendo had lost, because Sega changed the rules.

Nintendo held on to niches (the Japanese market, Gameboy), while Sega moved to consolidate power with the release of Saturn. But the rules were to change again: Sony, a master of advertising, recognized a malleable market. In a blizzard of advertising, they swept in with their PlayStation and completely beat the pants off of everyone through marketing rather than product excel-lence. The older players had wearied themselves in a features war, and Sony trumped them with promoting image.

But it's not over. Recently Nintendo moved to redefine the industry back to excellence of product. They introduced their Nintendo64 (with Mario64) and sold out in stores everywhere in hours. The consultants who worked on this project revealed the hidden strategy: In an industry with huge leadership swings (Mattel to Nintendo to Sega to Sony and back to Nintendo), the winners are the ones who can both completely redefine themselves in response to threats as well as strategically redefine the rules to be most uncomfortable for the competition.

The trick is to become *agile*, and to use agility as a weapon. Ironically, McDonnell Douglas, the group that designed the space station and redesigned and redesigned and redesigned it in response to a fickle customer (the micro-managing Congress) until learning how to change the rules so as to manipulate the situation, was Nintendo's model.

There are lots of concepts in this book, and to set the stage we have many stories. The ideas are built around stories and case studies that exhibit key con-cepts. At times you may wonder how a story relates, but we will bring you back to tools and methods. Definitions and related discussions follow. Finally, we give you the new tools for engineering the Agile Virtual Enterprise.

Chapter 2

An Historical Example

Much of Sirius-Beta's work has been devoted to helping shape U.S. Department of Defense investments for the domestic industrial fabric. At the start of this project, we were befuddled by contrasting speculations on best strategies to reinvent the relatively broken manufacturing infrastructure, so we searched for some hard data derived from similar prior situations. What we found was surprising in terms both of the successes and the failures—and convinced us that historical cases can be helpful for understanding the virtual enterprise and, incidentally, the government's role in providing supporting technology.

MILITARY RESEARCH "CAN" DO'S AND DON'T'S

Military research has influenced daily life to a much greater extent than most of us realize. For example, the British military sponsored the development of the now-ubiquitous tin can in 1810. This innovation brought to critical mass forces that revolutionized agriculture, since canned food could be distributed like a manufactured good. The military's concern was the long range projection of supportable military power, and this one advance played a consequential role in the expansion of the British Empire. Keeping troops supplied at a distance is a real factor in projecting force.

What is surprising is that the can opener was not invented for nearly another half-century. It ultimately appeared as the result of a small U.S. Army research project, and the new can openers played a role in the early days of the U.S. Civil War, since the South lacked them. In the intervening years, cans were opened by whatever was handy: Knives, chisels, or even shovels and bayonets.

It has been reasonably speculated that during this 50 years time more military casualties resulted from opening cans than from combat.

Why did it take so long to invent what we now consider such an obvious device? It was not the lack of a well-funded military research effort. In fact, substantial amounts were spent by the military on can research. But the requirements for the cans came from the planners, not the users—so the efforts focused mostly on the optimum size and shape of cans for the variety of logistical packing situations encountered (ships, trains, carriages, knapsacks, donkeypacks, etc.).

There were many cases where even the most (retrospectively) obvious innovations eluded the research establishment, both military and civilian. Several lessons here helped us immensely; one of these was the value of historical study.

A REVIEW OF BEST AGILE PRACTICES

In 1994, we were tasked by the NSF to review best agile practices in businesses today. The study was intended to move the vision and practice of agility a giant step forward. Sirius-Beta was tapped to lead the virtual enterprise effort. The Agile Virtual Enterprise Focus Group directed the research, both in the agenda and in some of the enterprises to survey.

In terms of the agenda, the Focus Group was faced with a conundrum: The only enterprises we could survey were existing ones working on current problems, but the only way to test them for agility would be to look back a few years to see if they had responded well to change. Some of these case studies are reviewed in Chapter 10. Indeed, we were right to be concerned since several of those we found agile in one way failed the ultimate test of being agile in ways that turned out to be important. Some group members felt that we should have looked at historic examples instead.

The first major industry we were directed to look at was the movie production business. It is an enterprise that manifests itself in very high value, short-lived partnerships, varying greatly from situation to situation. It is also for some a highly successful industry, providing a significant source of foreign trade (in fact only bested by commercial airliners and subsidized grain). And its role in technology development is significant and growing.

We consulted a knowledgeable movie insider and were exposed to a remarkable collection of virtual enterprise practices in movie production. Unfortunately, in several interesting cases, we were unable to overcome proprietary wraps on competitive techniques, so we were not able to openly discuss the case at the time. The good news was that our contact possessed some rare knowledge; he knew how one of the movie industry's best practices evolved, and we were able to work out a deal which revealed a lot without mentioning names.

The movie business relies on a contract tradition that keeps legal instruments very lean, relying on a near-Talmudically comprehensive, but implicit set of ethical principles. Underlying that is a large body of case law governing the virtual enterprise. Together, they provide a sufficiently robust adjudication mechanism that allows partnerships to be made quickly and cheaply. Sometimes they are very close to insubstantial. Remember when Kim Basinger was bankrupted for reneging on a simple, verbal statement that she would do a picture?

This case law and partnering tradition can easily be traced to the early oil exploration business, according to our informant. Los Angeles in its pre-movie days was an oil boom town, and the movie people adopted the existing local legal infrastructure. These legal practices originated in the home of oil exploration, Pennsylvania, which it in turn inherited from the previous oil industry, namely, the whaling business.

With this historical case, we could test agility in a longer time frame and simultaneously satisfy our interest in solid examples outside of the common buzzword analyses. What we found greatly expanded our understanding of how an agile virtual enterprise could work.

The Whale of Fortune

Among the many facts we discovered was that the use of whale oil had profound effects on our culture. The candles made from it were much brighter and relatively smokeless compared to the tallow candles which had been the standard. This superior lighting afforded people a much wider range of nocturnal activity; government and business were better able to function at night; and public performances of all sorts could now be held after dark.

Whale oil also altered our society's relationship with time. The fine lubricating oil found in the head of the sperm whale allowed for the advancement of mass-produced precision machining. The pocket watch became the first technology product for the masses. It is hard to overestimate the impact a scheduled day has had on the way we structure our lives and businesses.

The advances of timekeeping and artificial lighting allowed the first corporate bureaucracies to appear in the 1850s. These initially supported the railroads, and soon after, the retailers they supplied and the manufacturers that fed the whole business. As one would expect, there was a great demand for such revolutionary products, which translated into an enormous amount of wealth for those who could meet it. With an economic multiplier effect comparable to that of the semiconductor industry today, whale oil enabled the production of goods that could be sold for a thousand times the cost of collecting the oil used to make them.

For several decades, first from Nantucket Island off Massachusetts and then primarily from the nearby New England town of New Bedford, expeditions were launched and received which supplied 90% of the whale oil used in the world. This tight grip on such a lucrative market meant that whale oil played a more important role in maintaining a favorable balance of trade for the United States than any other product, even tobacco or cotton.

The whales from which the oil was extracted were hunted mainly in the Pacific and Indian Oceans. How was it that such a crucial industry stayed almost exclusively centered in two small towns located so far from the point of extraction?

Virtual Whaler Dealers

Geographical and professional isolation allowed for the evolution of a unique and very effective system which for many years put a brand new, fairly high risk/high payoff, virtual enterprise in the water at the rate of one every two weeks. The return of each whaling expedition triggered the formation of another. It was considered an invitation to bad luck to reuse the same combination of partners, so during the six to nine months it took to recondition the ship for another voyage, the owner of the boat assembled a new group of key players who would join him in setting up the basic physical and social conditions needed for a successful venture.

The primary partners required to launch a voyage consisted of a ship owner, an insurer (of the ship and cargo), a provisioning financier to supply the expedition with food and other consumables, a captain, and often a manufacturer who agreed to buy the oil at a set price. This component of the partnership was formed in the first couple of months, the partners being determined partially by availability.

A month or less before the ship was ready to sail, a secondary group of partners, the crew, was formed. They shared a distinct *cultural* background; almost none of them had, or would ever, serve in the navy or the merchant marine. This professional distinctiveness, coupled with an intense *geographical* concentration, fostered the development of a unique culture based on the virtual enterprise.

Every voyage included a team of skilled craftsmen—carpenter, blacksmith, cooper (barrelmaker), and a sailmaker (often a boatwright, a rigger, and even a cook were also in this class)—whose combined expertise allowed the enterprise to respond effectively to a broad range of situations. Each of these professionals, along with the tools, supplies, and sometimes apprentices they brought aboard, formed an essentially self-contained business which was integrated into the enterprise as a whole. In these cases, it was not just the person who signed up for the voyage, but their business.

From the shipowner to the cook, everyone was paid with a pre-arranged percentage of the take. The size of the shares varied widely, depending on what value one was expected to add to the venture, and was negotiated at signing. (Ishmael, the narrator in *Moby Dick*, signed up as a deck hand for 1/300th of the profit. Ishmael's companion, Queequeg, who was almost turned away by the shipowner as a pagan, was ultimately offered a substantially larger sum than his friend after he demonstrated remarkable skill with a harpoon.)

As in the current movie industry, the contracts which formalized these partnerships were very lightweight (usually, for the whaling crew, just a small chit, often marked with the illiterate's *X*, containing the person's name, occupation, voyage, and share), but were supported by a well-developed, culturally based code of interpretive ethics. This code of ethics, originally Quaker, was also reflected in a large body of case law (managed by the court in Boston) as the whalers sought interpretations for the wide variety of unexpected situations they encountered.

Shaped by precedent, this case law grew sufficiently robust to support the lightweight legal agreements of the virtual enterprises which together comprised an immense industry. This very same case law governs the virtual enterprise today—the same kind of infrastructure used by our contact in the movie business to support speedy but robust lightweight contracts.

The constant reconfiguration of the same people, from the same place, into different small groups created a situation where everybody knew everybody. Word quickly passed that one particular blacksmith was an incompetent loafer, or that another could do the work of two men in half the time. An organizing entity had access to a potential partner's reputation, which had been established by the observations of hundreds of peers who had worked closely with him. This capability—a service that might be provided by tomorrow's reinvented unions—had the effect of keeping the quality of the teams high. The rapid turnover (each voyage took about two to four years) also hastened the evolution and universal adoption of best whaling practices.

The Guild

The tradition of learning from combined experience was especially apparent in the relationship among captains. They were the *process planners*; they knew what had to be done and in what order. Their combined body of knowledge was continuously expanded and refined through rigorous professional collaboration, which was institutionalized by each in the form of the captain's log.

It was a primary part of every captain's job to take detailed notes each time a whale was sighted and to record when and where they were absent. A specialized shorthand evolved; for instance, they marked, with specialized stamps, the type and approximate size of the whale. They wrote down the direction in which the whale was going, at what longitude and latitude it was seen, at what time of day, the weather, any notable antecedents, and even the disposition the whale. In this way, they provided documentation for significant process innovations afforded by a combined analysis of all such logs during the six to nine month period of virtual enterprise formation—the period of strategic planning.

The U.S. government, aware that these efforts were essential for maintaining an American lead in the whaling industry (and hence dominance of the sea), authorized the navy to sponsor research into *knowledge representation* to help improve the quality of the captains' logs and of the subsequent analysis. This was likely the first military-industrial joint research in process modeling and planning. In related research, the navy also invested in navigation, sea flow, animal migration, and weather prediction aids, transferring the resulting technology to the captains.

The resulting jargon, tailored for describing the pertinent details of the profession, acted as a form of security protection, as only an insider would have been able to extract the full meaning from a captain's log. The process plans were shared freely among the captains of Nantucket and New Bedford, but not with outsiders. Collectively, they contained data taken from thousands of expeditions and were used to discern the migratory patterns of the desirable whales. With this information, the American captains could find the whales at any time of the year—an ability their competitors lacked.

Realizing that the captains and their collected knowledge were the reason for the United States' advantage in the whaling industry, one entrepreneurial British nobleman visited Nantucket, expecting that, having seen their preferred setting, he could then build an even more favorable one in England and lure them there. This plan failed, even though he constructed a very nice town, only one of many unsuccessful attempts by the international competition.

The Gilded

Agility is often displayed as an ability to recognize and capitalize on a changing situation as an opportunity. One whaler, Captain Starbuck (not of coffee fame), hearing of the Gold Rush in California, correctly assumed that success depended not on metallurgical, but on organizational skills, the same skills that the virtual enterprise routinely exercised in whaling. He led an expedition which was typical of many others. With the ability to form and transport well equipped, versatile teams to the area quickly (some ships on their way to the whales heard the news of the gold and diverted en route) the whalers made very effective miners.

At first, while they were still able to find buyers, they sold their ships for scrap in San Francisco; later they simply abandoned them in the bay. Testifying to the sound design of these virtual enterprise partnerships, the same basic team was used for mining—except that there wasn't much use for the sailmaker. (Levi Strauss, one such sailmaker but not a whaler himself, built a significant business making durable pants for the miners out of the abandoned canvas, rivets, and sailmaking processes. This is its own lesson in agility.)

Complementing the suitability of the whalers as a unit, the partners possessed a constitution well matched to the challenges of mining. These men were used to living the hard life; family separation, poor food, and long hours were the norm on a voyage. They were accustomed to delaying financial gratification and following orders, even while handling material of great value. Apparently, they could also limit their consumption of alcohol well enough to stay alive for the duration of the mining process, a skill lacked by many of the other miners, some of whom were successful in other regards.

For those interested in a case of agile response to *economic disaster*, the first oil well was drilled in Titusville, Pennsylvania, in 1859, right at the height of the whaling industry's golden age. Petroleum, now available in great quantities, quickly became cheaper to produce than whale oil, and could be used to manufacture similar things. Each new rig in effect represented a broadside to the whaling industry. During the worst period, demand for whale oil fell about 15% a year for 7 years.

The whalers responded by drawing up new process plans and retooling—with the help of the navy—in order to shift away from hunting sperm whales in the Tropics; they moved to the Arctic to hunt baleen whales, whose long flexible teeth (baleen) could be sold to manufacturers of corsets, buggy coaches, and umbrellas. The industry stayed strong for another 30 years, the whalers having effectively doubled the life-span of the most prosperous years of their trade.

A notable feature of this agile response is that they didn't find this market; they created it by advertising to influence fashion. Many notions of the exaggeratedly reshaped female body, which continue today, were created to extend whaling! Another example of the strange universe of unlikely consequences.

SOME LESSONS LEARNED

The whole experience just described taught some lessons about the agile virtual enterprise. Our project assumed that it was possible to create some management techniques to engineer the agile virtual enterprise. What we discovered in this historical research is an agile virtual enterprise-enabling environment, or several of them. So it is reasonable to conclude that some features that were important in this example would also be desirable to engineer into an enterprise.

Initially, the whaling industry depended on a unique, homogenous culture, isolated geographically (on an island, Nantucket, before it included the deeper port of New Bedford), religiously (Quaker), and professionally (not mixing with other marine cultures). But over the life of the example, many decades, this culture, without adaptations, likely would have stagnated. One historian speculates that several challenges to the culture were instrumental in keeping it strong.

When the center of the oil industry moved to the mainland, it became separated from its Quaker heritage, which was then rather intolerant. Quite interesting is the subsequent assimilation of people from different national and ethnic cultures. Over time, the community became diverse, as other nationalities and natives from primitive locations, many from the South Pacific, and some from Africa, were assimilated. This seemed to prompt a reinforcing evolution of the culture. Was it an accident that it was the custom to change crews each voyage? Perhaps it was an instinctual move?

Much has been made of trust in agility discussions. The whaling example used a very lightweight contractual infrastructure. Clearly this was based on trust, but much of that trust seems to have been based on a confidence that the law would apply just principles to arbitrate in unknown situations. It appears that this by itself constituted a significant barrier to entry into the business by countries whose law was based on code.

The comparative cases of privateers (sanctioned pirates) among French, Spanish, and English opportunists clearly shows the value of common law (or case law) as a foundation for trust in the ships. In both the English privateer and the U.S. whaling situations, a simple system of shares was made possible. Systems based on code law were fragile, since the conditions of such adventures were so unpredictable. Cheating and mistrust, and a subsequent lack of robust recourse in the justice system, were more prevalent among the privateers from countries with code law.

This common (or case) law basis of trust carries over today in the film industry, where agents inside the culture form share-based virtual enterprises predicated on ethics that are attuned to a (still developing) case law. It appears to be no accident that the centers of film activity in terms of quantity and diversity are all former British colonies—India, Hong Kong, and, of course, the United States. French film industry executives often complain of a structural difference that stifles them, a stifling that is actually exacerbated by government subsidy (and, in this case, the greater the subsidy, the more stifling). A closer look at the implications of case or common law versus code is found in Chapter 4.

It is notable that, despite substantial wealth and energy, the whaling industry never became vertically integrated up the food chain to include the manufacture of products. This lack of a tight linkage allowed agility in changing the food chain from oil to baleen. It also provided agility in allowing those manufacturers to switch to petroleum as soon as the opportunity appeared.

The linkage to the precision machining chain was also very loose. The United States during this period was never able to catch the Germans and Swiss, whose innovation was highly dependent on sperm whale oil lubrication. (Incidentally, that oil continued to be used until the 1970s for applications of the most demanding precision, like gyroscopes on the Apollo mission, and similar military missiles, until being replaced by the oil from the Jojoba bean.) So it seems that a loose supply chain coupling is often more agile, which is contrary to current lean thinking.

Finally, we looked closely at the government (mostly navy) support of the industry. Evidently what was most useful was infrastructure research on navigation, recordkeeping, map making, and on specific high-tech tools like telescope optics. Government research apparently failed in all the direct tools, like improved ship, boat, harpoon, and storage container designs. In each case, the market responded faster and better with new solutions. These bubbled up from the users, and the then-growing patent system provided meaningful incentives. It is worth noting that the deliberate exclusion of patent coverage for infrastructure elements contributed to the concurrent lack of market incentive.

Following the evolution of whaling to petroleum to movies across the country could lead one to all sorts of unsupportable speculations. A smart observer of social issues has suggested a limit which she thinks has been shown in the stability of whaling's social/cultural system. She believes, as we probably all do, that there is a limit to the amount of change a social system can accommodate. But she goes further in characterizing the limit as not one of breakdown, but one where power tends to be collected in a few entities.

The effect is that social coherence is maintained by the concentration of power over the interactions in the enterprise. It is as if the system surrounding the enterprise is able to evolve in ways apparently harmful to society in order to survive. This view of organizational evolution provides another paradigm.

The adaptation of the whaling industry was a result of what actually happened when the system was stressed in transitioning to petroleum. When he first encountered the oil business, J. D. Rockefeller was a clerk, a man with no recognized direct business value to add. What he apparently did add was a simple, strong autocratic control paradigm that acted, ultimately, as an attractor for immense wealth. The system needed this to survive, since the various social balances that had evolved over time were inadequate for the magnitude of change being experienced. So the system in effect chose Rockefeller's autocracy as a survival strategy. (A similar analysis, the analyst suggests, could apply to the personal computer software industry and Bill Gates.)

We will return to many of these issues when we address what we call soft modeling, the ability to reason about social/cultural issues in the agile virtual enterprise such that one can make decisions.

Chapter 3

The Social Factor

Social and cultural dynamics in the context of business collaboration make it tough to understand what is going on. Management decisions, at least the kind we want to support, are based on analyses of facts. But you have to be able to represent those facts and dynamics in some rational way in order to even have the problem on the table.

Modelers usually gloss over the fact that we just cannot represent social and cultural dynamics, because, well, there just are no laws of cooperation like we have of physics. That is why we have so-called soft sciences. Whenever the problem truly comes up, it gets put in the "too hard" column. And indeed, we originally decided to focus on the well-behaved space of business rules and such. But we found this impossible. Consider the examples that follow.

WATERWORLD

In Chapter 2, we learned a lot about agile virtual enterprise dynamics and possibilities from the movie business. The movie *Waterworld* presents an interesting cultural example. *Waterworld* was filmed for the most part on floating sets. Two of these sets were to be constructed from scratch, as is typical of most movie sets. However, there was a longer development period for this film than for most, which would have allowed more time for set planning and construction.

The production company was faced with two choices in assembling its virtual enterprise to supply these sets. The default choice involved using the existing pool of craftsmen who were already a normal part of the industry. These people understood the foibles and peculiarities of the business. The other choice was to hire technically proficient workers from outside of the industry.

Sets are designed to convey an artistically inspired feel in sympatico with the other creative collaborators. But it also must accommodate the mechanics of camera placement and movement. In both cases, frequent changes to the sets are communicated verbally through the day in an artistic language which would be mostly unintelligible to outsiders, and many of the changes would be effected overnight to ready for the next day's shooting. This way of working among designers, engineers, and craftspeople, and certainly the language and the nuances which underlie it, is unique to the industry.

The existing community available to the *Waterworld* producers lacked the engineering and safety skills necessary to deal with floating sets. To provide those skills would have required sending nonemployees to school—an option for which there was ample time. The alternative was to go outside of the traditional movie set community (which shared the culture) to a company which understood the engineering and safety issues involved, but which did not share the culture.

The producers had a firm estimate of costs to use the existing craftsmen. To this, they added about $3 million for engineers' schooling, safety training, and additional insurance. The Japanese conglomerate which had recently acquired the studio vetoed this route as too expensive and directed instead that an outside group of marine experts be used.

Thus, a contract went out to a well-known shipbuilding/aerospace concern to engineer and construct the sets. This company followed a model, conventional in their industry, where all the requirements are first set, then the design and engineering performed, and only then are the items finally manufactured and supported. Needless to say, there was a substantial distance between the cultures of the engineer/shipbuilder and the rest of the movie production's agile virtual enterprise. Artistic effects are alien to the shipbuilder, and all communication is explicitly engineering-based; it is modeled (meaning explicitly represented) in some way.

This cultural distance became an important factor. The virtual enterprise presumed ad hoc flexible responses, based on an implicit group vision of artistic intent. The partner worked on a very rigid, sequential set of non-artistic processes, each one of which needed explicit documentation. But directors were used to verbal descriptions using language which puzzles outsiders.

Production costs skyrocketed as many small events slowed down the process and compromised the artistic value of the end result—one such event was the accidental sinking of one of the sets! The estimated additional cost, over the original cost of construction, was about $80 million. As it happens, that is the amount that the Japanese management was forced to eat when unloading the production company back to North American owners.

It is clear that a metric that measures the cost of social differences certainly would have been of paramount utility in this case. Even if based on the roughest of approximations, it could have warned of the high order of magnitude in cost difference.

ROLE OF CULTURE AS AN AGENT

Indian Software Collectives

Here is an application with which many of us contend: software development. We have been talking to a large company that develops software as a product. Often, firms such as this have to choose between make-or-buy (with regard to software), and one of their buy options has become quite interesting. In researching the options, we encountered the relatively new phenomenon of Indian software collectives, in which a professor, usually in what we would call a junior college, trains a significant number of students in the rudiments of computer programming. These trainees are then set up in their homes with modest PCs and are marketed to the West by the professor or a colleague.

The main value of these collectives is not that the hourly wage is cheap compared to the West, though that is the case. What matters most is that these collectives can produce relatively bug-free software in half or a third of the time as their U.S. counterparts. The reason is strength through selective ignorance.

In the West, a typical software development team is composed of creative individuals who have been exposed to many philosophies and controversies. It is very hard to decompose a problem and get everyone working on exactly the same script and to use the same procedures to resolve interface and common service issues. The most desired software coders are the brightest, but each of these has their own ideas that slightly color their implementations. These slight differences and philosophies are the cause of both the most numerous and the most vexing bugs.

In rural India, on the other hand, each of the programmers has been exposed only to the professor's limited views. He or she decomposes the problem, and that's that. No controversies are raised because no one knows any other way, and because questioning the professor is culturally unacceptable. The resulting software therefore does not represent the most sophisticated approach, and the product may not be so capable, but it has the desirable quality of working seamlessly and being delivered much faster to market. That's what matters with software.

Software buyers in the United States are tempted in their evaluations of the potential use of these teams. On the surface, they appear to win hands down. But there are subtle questions of mapping the cultural needs of the customer to the cultural approach taken by the programmers. Not the least of these is the ability to anticipate future improvements and maintenance. That is most often the reason for the U. S. programmers' small differences with each other. Subtle user-philosophy issues come into play as well, and sometimes they make the difference in customer satisfaction. There's an art to this, and a reading of customer desires, that often is lost in crossing cultures.

Our goal was to discover if future agile virtual enterprise metrics which cover cultural and social issues would be able to measure cultural distances among the customers, the software publishers, and the gaggle of coders. We think they might; they must.

The Role of Culture

We believe that introducing the idea of social factors as an agent can be helpful for characterizing social effects on agility. For example, one of the best places in the world today for agile virtual enterprises is Russia. Many, many small businesses are starting as the economy converts to free market capitalism. A large number of them are aggregating into opportunity-driven agile virtual enterprises, and some of the component companies are being created in order to fill a role in a virtual enterprise. The organizer in many of these cases is the Russian mafia. (In chapter 7, we define these as Type 1 agile virtual enterprises. For now, in a Type 1 you have identified a niche, product, or opportunity and aggregate a virtual enterprise to meet that need. The dynamics are different in a Type 2, where you've identified some capabilities and you seek a market or product.)

In this situation, a decidedly cultural agent plays a real role, that of virtual enterprise organizer. But many of the forces involved are conventionally cultural. The mafia certifies partners and enforces an ethical law, and the mechanism for this enforcement is less a result of violence (though that happens), than it is how people assume the process will unfold.

The Russian Mafia

When the Suppliers' Working Group that we led studied the 100 most successful virtual enterprises, worldwide, it was struck by the efficiency of some large, then-Soviet, enterprises, particularly in the aerospace sector. For example, the Energia Very Heavy Launch Vehicle accomplished its goals in less than a third of the time and at half the cost of an equivalent NASA project. This was without a profit motive, a national emergency, or advanced information infrastructure. It appears that something very much like the mafia effect was the mitigating factor. Analyses by Russian social scientists trace this effect to the early days of the nuclear arms race. The Soviet nuclear scientists were in fact under a real threat of death upon failure, and often outperformed their U. S. counterparts, even adjusting for espionage.

Clearly, not all the lessons come in terms of direct transferability of a particular culture, because we cannot introduce the threat of death into the risk/reward structure of the agile virtual enterprise. But there is a lesson here in the potential utility of a culture-based agent. Our case law-based movie example shows the utility of an agent. Virtually everyone has an agent in the movie business, including caterers and drivers. The primary benefit of having an agent is not to handle logistics, as might be supposed. The agent is trusted with negotiating and forming the lightweight no-contract contracts we cite: the agent is trusted to certify the performer for that function. The penalty for betraying trust is ostracism. Both trust and ostracism are social mechanisms.

The same dynamic is seen in a midwest-based agile virtual enterprise, a bidding collective (what we'll later define as a Type 4, or watered down Type 2). There are essentially no external agents involved: The CEOs of these small companies speak for themselves. But the same trust/ostracism social mechanism is involved. Here, the companies are geographically proximate. But more important is a long agrarian tradition of community by shared trust. Being expelled is not just a business action, but one that affects standing in the community. That same community establishes the fabric of ethics that governs the agile virtual enterprise. The agent is the rural community itself, which shares many features with the Russian mafia.

Finally, the community as agent can even be seen in the Indian software collective. Here, there is the play of a strong class/caste system, and the membership in a higher rung of the middle class for coders. The price is in reinforcing the importance of the academic culture (and the role of the professor) as the organizing agent.

Social historians believe this same artificial elevation of the professor as an organizing agent for industry was a key factor in Germany's early industrial progress. Incidentally, the absurdly high regard demanded by professors in Germany has been cited as the reason that no German university can match an MIT or Stanford for vitality and institutional agility in high tech. This may be a case where agility in one dimension (the ability to quickly organize around a common vision) may compromise agility in another dimension (the ability to adjust one's vision based on the advance of technology).

An Automotive VE

An example of the consequences of a cultural agent can be seen closer to home. Several years ago, we participated in planning for a massive virtual enterprise in the automotive industry. The idea was to take advantage of all the manufacturing processes for cars.

The first idea was to continue to remanufacture cars after they were sold. This idea extends the virtual enterprise well into the customer base and past the initial sale. In one mode, the conventional car company would sell a car with an additional warranty: new technology and engineering changes would be inserted for a specific number of years, in addition to both functional and cosmetic repairs. This would greatly increase the value of the car to the buyer and incidentally provide a robust, continuing after-sale market to the car manufacturer.

A Japanese manufacturer recognized that great gains in conventional market share were unlikely and that they had already moved up the value scale to luxury cars as much as they could. But this firm—typical of several—continued to engineer autos after the first manufacture, so that later models differed from earlier ones to a much greater extent than U.S. and German models. In the latter companies, the engineering peaks right before manufacture, and then stops, unless some safety issue is uncovered.

So why not continue to re-engineer the model for years after the sale? After all, quite a few benefits result, one of them being the extended leverage that could be obtained from the engineering data and designs for the model.

The second operating mode for the potential virtual enterprise was to remanufacture autos originally manufactured and sold by others, but which had a major engineering flaw. The numbers on this are impressive. It turns out that most cars are taken off the road not for systemic, auto-wide failure—everything wearing out at once—but because of point failure in a single system. In other words, if the transmission was poorly designed and fails again and again, the car is junked. Or a car is damaged in an accident and not repaired because the transmission has had chronic problems. The virtual enterprise would focus on such bad actors—and models were drawn up for many such cases—cars with good systems overall, but which had one point failure, a poorly engineered subsystem or component.

The virtual enterprise's job would be to design a newly-engineered replacement component, and either upgrade a car retail (with the owner bringing it in) or wholesale (with the purchase of large numbers of the cars from junkyards or used car dealers).

The virtual enterprise would link small engineering, manufacturing, and installation shops to perform the task in a highly distributed way, along with central agents—the broker, the original engineering base, a telecommunications infrastructure supplier, and a financial agent who provided insurance to the virtual enterprise and insurance and funding to the small partners. Anyone could engineer the new part, whether working alone or taking advantage of the manufacturers' database. Such a part could be manufactured by the original designer, or the design could be advertised for licensed manufacture by others. Yet a third party might be involved for the actual installation.

We represented the government in this instance; among the reasons for doing so was the massive recovery of value in previously junked cars to the U.S. citizen. The potential was for hundreds of millions of dollars a year being returned to society, the best kind of virtual tax cut. The infrastructure used for this virtual enterprise could be reused, and expanded into other sectors.

Obviously, this did not proceed, even though the partners were available, and the money, numbers, and technology were all right. What killed it was the intimidating social role that the organizing agent would have had to play. Cars play a large cultural role in American society, helping people define their identity. This dynamic is less pervasive than it was before the invasion of foreign manufacturers, but many Americans still seem to want a big company to which they can give their allegiance, and get back a sense of self. A distributed entity is harder to identify with. We did have examples of national and ethnic identity, which are distributed, amorphous and somewhat artificial, but it was felt that placing such responsibility with Japanese car managers was untenable.

Moreover, a critical mass of the small innovators would have been drawn from a pool of shade-tree mechanics (the millions of mechanically inclined, perhaps entrepreneurial, but untrained mechanics not associated with a big firm). The cultural issues associated with bringing these people together were considered formidable, especially so considering the location of the test case, a very rural state. The Japanese decided that there was no way to manage the cultural issues; in other words, appropriate cultural metrics (including those for agility) and the management tools they would inspire, were again lacking.

The impetus for distributed auto manufacturing shifted to China. The idea of reuse had been shelved, but the idea of manufacturing cars without a conventional prime was retained. This virtual enterprise, as now planned, will consist of a large number of small shops in China, feeding distributed, small, decentralized parallel assembly of autos for export.

The coordinating agent in this case is the Chinese People's Army, which in fact is the largest commercial entity in the country, perhaps the world. They provide significantly more value than the Russian mafia, but the idea of a culturally-based agent is still there.

The Japanese are to provide infrastructure and virtual enterprise management techniques. The cultural situation is addressed in two ways. The previous heterogeneity problem of the U. S. study is erased by going to China, and by selecting locations there with deep homogeneity. The arbitration and arranging agent's cultural skills are greatly simplified since the techniques used will include the same as those of the Soviet Mafia, namely coercion.

Defining the Culture

The ideal agent will not only understand the cultural issues, being able to make informed decisions through metrics, but may be able to determine certain cultural characteristics. Whether particular instances of such action are desirable is another issue. For instance, it may be desirable to have the Russian mafia in order to ease the formation of agile virtual enterprises, but they are undesirable socially for other reasons.

It has long been the case that non-virtual enterprises have engineered their culture. For instance, General Electric has for decades spent large sums on understanding itself, designing where it wants to be culturally, and "normalizing" all its employees to the culture's practices, values, and policies.

This normalization often extends to the customer base. We already mentioned automobile manufacturer loyalty. The car companies spend substantial amounts on auto racing, with the intent of attracting the kind of blind (or at least largely independent of product issues) loyalty that is given to sports teams. The idea is to determine by design some of the cultural behavior of the consumer.

Probably none have explored this territory as thoroughly as the cigarette companies. Some companies have aggressive programs to adjust the culture of the consumer, for example with *Virginia Slims*, marketed to young women, or "repurposed" *Kool* cigarettes to African Americans. The Suppliers' Working Group concluded that these companies had the most developed models of cultural influence we could find, and used them as the leading case for proven principles in this regard.

Chapter 4

Cultural Memes

THE ENGLISH AND FRENCH ENGINEERING PARADIGMS

Our mandate included looking at potential differences between the civil and defense manufacturing communities. We did so, and concluded that the differences were solely in the contractual and regulatory infrastructure. But what causes this are deep-seated cultural differences—we can see it in engineering approaches.

This is of interest outside the defense community, because, since World War II, manufacturers of complex products like airplanes and cars operate in a defense-industry manner. These are people who worry about managing a supply chain rather than supporting a more profitable virtual enterprise with the same players.

It happens again and again that engineers from a commercial perspective look at a problem and produce differing results from those of engineers associated with defense or government. Variations on large water projects, nuclear power installations, and the Strategic Defense Initiative are a few of the generally recognized high-difference areas. Certain of the less public ones involve environmental and transportation engineering risks, and some argue that the effect is also seen in health and criminal risk analysis.

Of the differences which one encounters, those which are most interesting are not the ones arising from varying priorities or politics, but differences that run so deep in world views that they seem to underlie the actual mathematics. We count ourselves among those who believe that the differences can be traced to a well-recognized difference in engineering traditions between eighteenth-century France and England.

In England, engineering grew out of a strong guild tradition, which stressed commercial practicality. Engineers and civil servants rarely mixed. Even in the military, where the use of engineering skills was heavy, the tradition was to keep a distinction between warriors and engineers and to utilize contractors where possible for engineering tasks. Having engineering skills provided scant introduction to either military or political society.

In contrast, French engineering touted its origins in the mathematical elite, many of whom in the eighteenth century were French. Military officers were expected to be competent engineers, and civil and engineering life were strongly intermingled. For example, the French established the world's first engineering university in 1794, the École Polytechnique, on Rue Descartes (see Devlin, 1997).

Championed by Napoleon, the school and the graduates were hailed as the hen with the golden eggs for France. That literally has been their symbol since. This was in fact a military school; aspiring engineers wore uniforms, carried swords, and drilled. The lower tier students studied at the École Centrale des Arts and Manufactures and were destined for mere commerce. The upper tier went on to graduate study at the École Ponts et Chaussees (bridges and embankments) and became known as ingéniers de l'état. These men had a profound influence on the bureaucracy, and hence over all of French society.

The French model of engineering, therefore, evolved with large, often extremely expensive, ambitious, and visible projects. These were designed to serve the society as a whole, and the benefit to the engineers was in advancing society. It would have been considered crass to have applied values of personal profit to any project, which, of course, was the English default.

The French invented the engineered organization—the bureaucracy—but only later in far richer and larger countries (the U.S. and USSR) would their ideas on both engineering and civil management become supercharged as the prime technique for conducting the cold war.

Of course, being an English colony, America, especially New England, followed English tradition as its industries grew into the nineteenth century. But the French tradition was inoculated with amazing effectiveness in both American and Russian militaries. Russian czars were eager to europeanize their nation and so entered into a long exchange program with France, then the prototype of European culture. That exchange continues to this day. Soviet engineers and bureaucrats were sent to France for study at the Polytechnique and imported the paradigm back into their country. Surviving the revolution, the paradigm was well suited to the Soviet totalitarian direction events took and especially came into play after World War II as the entire country had to be re-engineered.

Communism, social engineering in a very basic sense, can be linked to this paradigm, and many believe that it wasn't war, boneheaded and cruel dictatorship, or socialism that killed the Soviet Union. Instead, it was their blind following of massive, centrally managed engineering projects for the common good, without the feedback loop for immediate, finegrained satisfaction that market forces provide. Perhaps most disastrously, even agriculture was centrally engineered.

At any rate, the British model dominates American commercial life, essentially all of our economy, and has been quite successful because innovation has been linked to personal reward. But the French model gained a toehold. How and where (in the military) is instructive.

The colonies were losing the war of independence. The English nearly had the rebels beat, but the intervention of the French at Yorktown proved decisive. The primary asset the French sent: Military engineers and sophisticated materiel. The lesson was not lost on General Washington, and among the first acts of the new nation, which he ramrodded, was the decision in 1778 to establish a national engineering school. Because of difficulties in getting the nation's institutions going, this was not established until 1802, at West Point, New York.

Modeled directly after the École Polytechnique, the school was dominated by imported French professors. Its mission: To produce engineers for the nation, incidentally through the army, which was seen as necessarily synonymous with technological progress, much as today's Peoples Army is regarded in China. Of course, over the next few decades, more and more non-engineering and scientific subjects were introduced until we have the military academy in its current state.

Meanwhile, the English-inspired idea of practical science caught on in the U.S. commercial sector. The two traditions competed, each dominating in different regions of the country. The French model was adopted in the north, with the establishment of an engineering school at Rensselaer Institute in 1835. By midcentury, Rensselaer was the leading engineering school in the country. The reason this French approach flourished was the same as for the school's founding and success—the railroad. Railroad monopolies (for our purposes, the same as government agencies) needed engineering skills to build a vast network, including many challenging bridges. The idea of large, centralized projects serving the institution was very French.

In the south, the English model started to grow from grassroots need. The centers of schooling in the south were the universities of Virginia and Alabama. Their model of commercially-driven engineering directly contrasted to that of West Point and Rensselaer and was so noted at the time in competitive recruiting pamphlets.

Alabama's initiative was destroyed by the civil war and never recovered, and it is known more widely today as an athletic franchise. But what happened in Virginia is interesting. The head of their practical science program, in fact the only full-time professor in it, was a young fellow named William Barton Rogers. He was trained at William and Mary (together with Harvard, they were the only two advanced schools in colonial times). His father, a chemistry professor at William and Mary, knew Thomas Jefferson, who considered the founding of the University of Virginia to be his finest achievement, instructing that only that fact appear on his tombstone, nothing about his role as a founding father of the U.S. (Those instructions were not followed—an earlier statement about also being proud of the Declaration of Independence and the Virginia Statute for Religious Freedom were included.)

Jefferson believed that the country was making a mistake going with the French model at West Point, which was finally established during his presidency. He had spent several years in France as the U.S.'s first ambassador and had made a careful study of their model. He considered it insidiously undemocratic. He very much wanted his university to grow as a school based on the English model and often promoted that idea at William and Mary to the senior Rogers until Jefferson died in 1826.

So Barton Rogers lead the charge at the University of Virginia, but he left in 1846. The university had hired a Jewish professor that year to teach Hebrew and Greek for Biblical study. The student body was so intolerant that they pistol-whipped the new professor. When the dean passed a rule outlawing guns in class, unruly students shot him. This thuggishness, coupled with the institution of slavery was too much. Rogers decided to take his mission to a more enlightened locale.

He spent a few years proselytizing the idea of a school for democratic/commercial engineering and practical science, and served as president of the young American Association for the Advancement of Science. Finally he established MIT, then called Boston Tech, on the British model which quickly became very strong, and provided a model for linking innovation and science. This permeated through civil society and commerce. The program in Virginia died.

Supporting this development were strong Emersonian ideas, local to Boston, of the importance of individual principle and intellect, as opposed to those of an institution. Around 1880, more international students were drawn to MIT than to the Polytechnique, signaling a change of values in Europe, and the emergence of the English model of innovative commerce.

While the Russians became thoroughly French, the U.S. developed a bicameral paradigm, with French dominance in various governmental and military affairs. The French tradition can be seen through the large centrally-run projects of the Army Corps of Engineers, which began in the early nineteenth century with a national system of canals and lighthouses, and was revived with the production miracle in Dayton concerning World War I aircraft (described in Chapter 6). It was further sustained between the wars by large hydroelectric programs and continued through the nuclear bomb and energy projects on through to the Apollo missions. The tradition also can be traced worldwide, with the French themselves often leading the way, as with the Suez and Panama canals.

Such influence is clear today in every U.S. weapons system and throughout the defense industrial base. It also affects all our large manufacturing businesses to some extent. A recognition that a completely different engineering paradigm is involved becomes a prerequisite before any enlightened comparison can be made between business processes and the underlying culture in the defense industrial base. We think any attempt to bring commercial practice to the defense domain should acknowledge the 200-year battle between these memes. (A *meme* is a self-promoting idea, sort a mental gene. We explore the idea of engineering memes in Chapter 6.)

Military electronics and software, for example, differ from their commercial counterparts in profound ways. The conventional thinking is that their requirements are different, so a different culture has emerged in response to each. We propose the opposite—that the cultures came first. Notably, whenever agility is required in the defense base, an English-type organization is introduced into the system. Thus the nuclear weapons complex has its Sandia Labs and the defense aircraft industry has (or had) the Lockheed Skunkworks.

An Example of Conflicting Memes

The U.S. Air Force has a missile gap, and this one is real; it could cost lives. Our fighter airplanes (and those of many U.S. allies) rely on a specific air-to-air missile as their primary weapon in dogfights. (Dogfights are still considered the primary threat for air superiority on which essentially all current strategy is based.) This mainline missile, once known as the Sidewinder, in its current advanced version is called the AIM-9M (air interdiction missile).

In 1985, U.S. intelligence was shocked when a new, then-Soviet, air-to-air missile was observed in Finland. This missile, which we call the AA-12 (using the NATO designation of air-to-air), is superior to our missile in a couple of key areas. If our F-14, -15, -16 and -18 (and future F-22) pilots meet in combat with a well-trained MiG-29/Su-27 pilot with this missile, we would likely lose. We could have met this missile over Iraq (which had them) with disastrous consequences, and the chances of encountering it soon in another conflict are substantial.

As soon as Israel received word on the missile threat, they were able to design and field a missile with equal or superior capabilities. This process took six years, and the missile is now flying. Subsequent analysis shows that the original Soviet development took five years. (The French now also have a fielded response.)

The U.S. started at the same time as the Israelis, and we are now in the midst of a planned 17-year path to fielding our answer, the Raytheon/Hughes AIM-9X. But all weapon systems—every one in the U.S.—experiences delays and cost overruns. Surprisingly, the time and cost penalties are amazingly constant, and these have been studied and described by Norm Augustine, retired CEO of the largest defense contractor in the world, in *Augustine's Laws* (Augustine, 1983). Adding in this constant delay, we could be looking at a 24-year response cycle.

Why does it take the U.S., the world's richest military power, holder of the most advanced military technology anywhere, an estimated 17 to 24 years, under severe threat, to do what others can do in 5 or 6 years? All the reasons will be debated for some time to come. But at least one reason is already clear: Our defense industrial base, particularly our missile supplier base, is broken from using a mixed French/English paradigm.

A recent study concluded that for a long time, starting shortly after the beginning of the Reagan buildup, we have been losing our supplier base at an alarming rate. It's not because defense contracts are not profitable; they can be. It is because the difficulty of performing for the government, even as a second or third tier supplier, forces a company to commit fully to being either a defense or commercial supplier because of the way that processes are constrained.

Two efforts at improving the defense industrial base, lean practices, and CALS (a standards program explained in Chapter 8), may have actually made some elements of the situation worse. A problem with lean practices results from prime contractors moving to reduce and prequalify their supplier base. This lowers the cost to the contractor in the short run, because it is easier to control the suppliers, forcing them to conform (or preselecting them because they do conform) to a wide variety of VE-related practices (in fact all of the ones that the metrics cover).

This means that Westinghouse (now Northrop Grumman), for example, will do business only with smaller clones of itself—clones in regard to practices—and only with companies that answer a need that is in the current profile. This lowers their cost of doing business within the relatively small scope for which the Westinghouse VE was engineered. But this limits a primary reason for creating interesting VEs: The ability to team with exceptionally different types of organizations compared to your own in order to create a new competitive advantage.

In the defense case, the result of these practices is that what had been a large, flexible, and innovative pool of businesses has evolved into a set of small, stable communities that are associated by sector and often by prime contractor. The result is both costly and unagile. In situations where capabilities need to be stretched quickly, as in the AIM-9X, the ways of bringing new skills and technologies into this pool are expensive both in time and dollars.

LESSONS FOR MANAGEMENT METRICS

In the dominant defense (or French) model the product, the processes, and the skills used to support the processes, as well as the work breakdown of the processes, are all specified by the prime contractor on behalf of the customer in a centrally-managed, top-down fashion. In the commercial (or English) model, a fine-grained, bottom-up collection of functions is empowered by market forces. These functions are empowered to change all the items (products, processes, skills, work breakdown) in a way that manifestly results in better, faster, and cheaper products.

So it would seem that a lesson emerges here for agility metrics in the defense sector and similar enterprises (automotive, aerospace, electronics, computer hardware, and software giants). The transactions that are supported must include those that deal with this idea of market forces (the linkage of value added for recompense) adjusting the processes. For example, a transaction boundary between a prime contractor and a subcontractor is less agile if the primary contractor insists on controlling the details of the processes that the subcontractor uses.

Consider the example of the Sidewinder. The Soviet AA-12 virtual enterprise ran under a French paradigm throughout and was effective; the Israeli virtual enterprise was thoroughly English and was equally effective. It's when you combine the top half (customer to prime contractor, French) with one and the bottom (prime contractor to subcontractors, English) with another as in the U.S. that the system becomes crippled.

LAW FOLLOWS ENGINEERING

Around the world, we find two primary models of how law is built, and these differing law systems correspond closely to the two engineering trends just discussed.

The type of law many people immediately think of is *code*. This originated, as far as we know, from such early examples as the Babylonian Code of Hammurabi, and became incorporated in many later hierarchical societies, their governments, and religions (including Judaism, and thence to Christianity and Islam).

The basis of code is that some wise person or body is in authority to make law. These (usually) men proscribed conditions relating to certain situations. If a new situation—one not originally anticipated—arose, the authorized body would expand the code. Code was the model for Greek and Roman law, which has been inherited by much of the western world.

Opposed to code is an idea that originated with Darius (about 500 B.C.). Darius organized the Persian empire based on the idea of federating many states (satrapies) while preserving the local cultural diversity. The idea was that no one could make comprehensive law from the top down; there are just too many special conditions and local exceptions. So the idea of common (or case) law was developed. It was used by segments of European societies which were on the outside fringes of the Roman empire, notably the Celts (in the British Isles). Beginning with the famed Magna Carta, and evolving into its present form by the seventeenth century, common law made a comeback in Britain and the British Empire.

The key idea is that a jury of common people could evaluate a situation and extend the meaning of prior law as made by a legislature. That judgment then became a *case*. Subsequent juries were to consider both the original law and the subsequent case with equal weight. Over time, of course, the cases would often grow to eclipse the original law, resulting in a bottom-up, dynamically redefined basis of laws that were self-adjusting.

Several advantages resulted, but the one that interests us here is the simplicity of contracts that this allowed (which we noted in the movie industry example). Instead of having to write a contract that covered all possible contingencies, one only had to record what was really intended by the agreement. The large body of cases that was presumed to exist and to be based on common sense justice, instead of bureaucratic foibles, could be called upon to adjudicate differences if things went wrong. This increased the burden of the trial system, but greatly decreased the burden on the contract law system.

The U.S. inherited this system of common law when it transformed from an English colony, one of only a few countries to do so (concerning legal systems). Actually, each of the fifty states individually inherited this system, and have evolved fifty similar threads. Federal law issued by the central government now, however, tends to be code-oriented. For example, the Uniform Commercial Code was needed nationally to expedite interstate commerce, and it deliberately concentrated all facets of making the law in a few, powerful bodies.

Today, there is a mixture of code and common law in the U.S. Most provisions of most contracts in the commercial arena rely on case-based state laws. Some commercial sectors (like movies) can be very agile in their contracting practices because this situation still obtains. The bad news: Americans go to civil court more than anyone else. The good news: In some sectors, the decrease in the cost and time of devising domestic contracts is vastly less than in, say, Germany and Japan, our current international competitors.

This is a system in which any lack of trust among the parties is handled by a presumption of trust in the case law, rather than in the corporate lawyers. We believe this to be a structural advantage for the U.S., and especially so in the agile virtual enterprise context.

Defense contracts not only are code-based, but more centrally mandated than any other sector of the economy. The contracts are based on code, the Federal Acquisition Regulations (FAR). Worse, the combination with the French engineering paradigm results in every detail of the product and process being detailed in code, through specifications. Engineering decisions about processes, skills, and work breakdown which elsewhere are fluid, are captured explicitly in the contract and supporting code. The result is a brittle, unagile system that cannot respond, for example, to a severe missile threat in a timely way.

We believe that these competing influences cannot be wished into harmony. Indeed, many benefits result from the institutions that exist. The challenge is instead to create greater agility within the existing situation.

Chapter 5

Empirical Principles of AVEs

HIGH CONCEPT IN THE VIRTUAL ENTERPRISE

Consider this as a continuation of the whaling/movie example. In that story, we suggested that the U.S. film industry was both relatively agile and a good example of continually formed virtual enterprises. Very good money is made by a few savvy people (though never the ordinary investor). We originally thought that though successful, this was somewhat accidental—that the lightweight, code-based virtual enterprise association contracts just happened by luck. Still, it seemed that there were some elements in this natural evolution that could be engineered into other industry sectors.

Since then, we've burrowed deeper into the situation, developing and exercising insider contacts. This has been a difficult process because the agility *evolved* rather than being engineered. Few movie managers—even successful ones—know what's going on at the level that we find useful. Much of what follows was jointly discovered by working together with them in a discovery process.

In this chapter, we'll find out about the dynamics and importance of the movie VE. Then we'll tease out some principles. Much of the discussion is concerned with how an agile virtual enterprise is formed. In revisiting the movie business, we particularly wanted to touch on what we can take away in deliberately, consciously *engineering* an agile virtual enterprise (or an agile supply chain) and also contribute to the discussion on trust and change concerning agents.

The Movie Industry as a Prototype

Not so long ago, in the 1930s, the movie industry was configured like today's automobile and aerospace industries. The market was dominated by a very few large, stable companies. The big five were: Loew's/MGM, Paramount, RKO, Twentieth Century-Fox, and Warner Brothers. They were deeply vertically integrated, including control of the distribution by ownership of theaters.

Competition among them drove them to what today we call lean manufacturing practices: flat organizations, prequalified suppliers (in which they often had an interest), a version of just-in-time practices. They were leaders in novel accounting practices, using what clearly today can be seen as activity-based costing (but without the glitz). Also, they were innovators in intellectual property law.

The height of this trend continued through World War II. After the war, Japan had the opportunity to engineer an industrial policy. We were told by a key man in devising that policy that they studied and refined techniques from three sources:

- *The British system of civil service and empire governance.* This system, which the British based on Persian models, had been internalized to facilitate their imperial ambitions. But because of the way they mix government and industry, it also became entrenched in business. Key discriminators here are flat organizations and decentralized power.
- *The U. S. food distribution system.* The just-in-time movement of perishables from California, where most of the produce was, to the East Coast, where most of the people were, was heralded worldwide as a miracle. (Incidentally, current attention is focused on the Iranian food distribution system. In the U. S., everyone along the literal food chain can get paid when their product or service is delivered, because money can be borrowed. In Iran, Islamic law forbids usury. There is an advanced experiment underway that makes each member of the supply chain a partner in shares, who gets reimbursed when the product is sold. The value of the product, including how much survives the pipeline, isn't resolved until the point of final sale. This makes the supply chain more attuned to the strengths of balancing market forces. But it requires a complex accounting system. In fact, both accounting and arithmetic were invented for just this purpose.)
- *The U. S. movie industry.* This sector had several attractive features. It was more profitable (as an industry) than other sectors, it mixed culture and business in an apparently leveragable way, and its vertical integration extended to the customer. Japan knew that it had to establish a new model, selling to customers abroad, and was interested in how the engagement of customers could be engineered.

Only the first two were publicly discussed with the occupiers. General MacArthur, as the military governor, facilitated building an infrastructure based on these principles. Before the war, Japan was controlled by a few powerful families in feudal organizations, *zaibatsu*. MacArthur outlawed these, to be later convinced that they should be reinvented as *keiretsu*, vertical corporations modeled after the zaibatsu, but with what he thought was the democratizing, western ingredient of market pull. Deliberate emulation of the movie business was the model that convinced him, applied first to the shipbuilding and then the automotive sectors.

The principles extracted from food distribution and movie production benefited greatly by being abstracted from their originating domains; the process formed the basis of a set of engineering principles for enterprises. Later, when the much refined principles were abstracted back by the U.S. from Toyota and other Japanese automakers, theorists in the states dubbed the collected diverse principles lean.

The point we are making here is that the movie sector in the past successfully served as a model for agile virtual enterprise engineering principles. The movie industry has changed since then. While the U.S. has lost its steel, machine tool, consumer electronics, and shipbuilding industries, and taken big hits in the automotive and semiconductor sectors, Hollywood continues to dominate its now greatly expanded worldwide domain.

Let us sketch just one more example in the Japanese thread. Akio Morita, the founder of Sony, was knowledgeable of, and extremely interested in this history. He followed Hollywood closely and was convinced that Americans were not aware of (what we now call) the agility principles that had evolved right under their noses. He felt that Japanese restraint and circumspection could turn these into a new generation of enterprise engineering principles. In *The Japan that Can Say No* (Morita and Ishihara, 1988), he suggested that a new handle for world dominance could be contrived.

Sony purchased a major Hollywood studio in the late 1980s, Columbia, for twice its book worth, because it was the one most closely associated with the agile, high concept ideas we will explore next. To run it, they hired executives whose only qualification was their association with the technique. In announcing the acquisition, Morita briefed the *kisha club* (the exclusive Japanese insider pool), citing the MacArthur legacy and pointing out a new model beyond lean. He presumably did the same within *keidanran*, the business association widely considered the true power in Japan. This led to his election as chairman of *keidanran*.

Matshusita immediately followed suit, buying MCA/Paramount. Instead of a slow osmosis of concepts and philosophy, they pushed harder, selling out at a loss soon after. Being less sophisticated, they were the unhappy players in our *Waterworld* example.

Hollywood Evolves

Meanwhile, back to the Hollywood of the late thirties. The U.S. broke up the movie enterprises, based on antitrust concerns. (This seems anachronistic today, comparing the then five equal competitors to, say, Microsoft.) Distribution and production functions were severed, breaking the link to the customer which was well understood. Other factors intervened; the result was the evolution of the packet-unit system. This is one example of what we've been calling the virtual enterprise: the prime contractor (the production company) identifies the market need, and provides the plan or intellectual property that addresses that need. It also arranges financing, which includes providing the highest capital items.

Production assets (cameras, props, etc.), formerly owned by the companies, were distributed among many small companies which could be quickly assembled to produce a film, the virtual enterprise dissolving immediately thereafter. It took a little while to optimize this system to the point that it exists today—hugely successful (see Chapter 6 for how it evolved).

Novel ways of sharing risk (distributing financing), managing liability, and exploring new ideas have been developed to support the packet-unit system. But what concerns us here is the method that evolved to understand and deal with the customer after the prior connection was broken—the much studied technique called *High Concept*.

High Concept

High Concept appeared in the mid-1970s and utterly dominated the U.S. film industry for a while, and is still prevalent. A High Concept film is one that is based on a succinct and detailed description of the product, including all features of the product that would be valued by a customer. Movie products are complex, involving several exhibition modes of the film (theater, TV, video tape, U.S. and foreign distribution), as well as associated music, book, toys, theme rides, etcetera. High Concept is so named because it ties all elements across these media and all elements within the product (story, stars, and such) into one clear statement of philosophy and style.

The underlying assumption is that the customer's need can be tersely, understandably, and logically characterized; that is, *modeled*. That understanding, however broad and involved, has a simple core, which by itself covers all the important element of the project. To quote Steven Spielberg: "I like ideas, especially movie ideas, that you can hold in your hand. If a person can tell me the idea in twenty-five words or less, it's going to make a pretty good movie."

The conventional wisdom is that a High Concept film is a stupid film, catering to a feeble, low-brow common denominator. But this isn't necessarily so. *Jurassic Park* is no more a high concept film than *Schindler's List*. The notion of High Concept is thoroughly studied in film schools, and consistently practiced by producers, who are organizers of the virtual enterprise. It's also considered difficult to master.

In all these considerations, the primary purpose of the High Concept description is to guarantee that the movie (and associated products) has each stage of its production targeted to how it can be successfully sold to the public, meaning it has a coherent tapestry of hooks for marketing. Naturally, just being High Concept doesn't guarantee that the film will be good, or successful, just that it has a shot (at financial success at least).

To repeat: Everyone in the industry understands High Concept as a way of modeling the customer's need/desires; managing constraints, and coordinating a coherent, understandable response. It's considered a device for marketing, with the emphasis on the link between the prime contractor (meaning the producer) and the customer. It also helps a prime contractor understand its core competencies and special strengths; the kinds of films a studio plans are often described in High Concept terms. In other words, it is a description of a strategy to reach customers *in terms understandable to the customers*, which the producers use to form a profitable link with the customers.

A High Concept description is succinct; for instance, *Flashdance* was a *Rocky* for Women. Almost always the description builds on prior experience, and familiarity with the precedents is culturally necessary for membership in the community. However, masters of High Concept develop the description to an arbitrarily deep level, with specific tailoring for each of the major disciplines involved.

Recently, in analyzing how a few studio heads consistently ripped off conglomerate investors buying the studios (including Sony), High Concept has been implicated in a different link, as if the image product was an image one passed up the ownership food chain. It's an interesting theory—the value of the production house was artificially inflated by mastery of High Concept techniques. Managers who know how to use High Concept to successfully make a product valuable also use the technique to make the company itself appear valuable from the investor perspective.

One can clearly see a simple reflection of High Concept in the current fad for mission statements, which firms use to describe themselves to their investors and stockholders. It's small potatoes compared to how well developed and fluid High Concept is in films, but the same idea. However, that use of High Concept is not cogent to agility because it is static, more superficial and focused within the firm. High Concept is for market-driven products; mission statements are for institutions.

Working with the movie people, we think we have helped uncover an unacknowledged but perhaps critical role of High Concept in another link: the culturally-based relationship among the prime contractor and its subcontractors in forming the virtual enterprise.

HIGH CONCEPT IN ORGANIZING THE VIRTUAL ENTERPRISE

How It Works

All studios currently use the packet-unit system of production which essentially means that for every picture, a new virtual enterprise is created. We found that the formation and operation of the virtual enterprise was more agile when a good High Concept for the product existed.

When the Agile Virtual Enterprise Focus Group created the Agile Virtual Enterprise Reference Model (described in Chapter 10), we paid particular attention to the need for a clear definition of the opportunity, the strategy anticipated to address the opportunity, and the ersatz corporate culture of the virtual enterprise. Given this, we felt that the scope and role of each partner could be teased out; when the opportunity changed, the change in its description can direct changes in roles and responsibilities of each partner.

For example, if the direction of the movie changes in midproduction to be more comic, many partners must change the way they do things. How do they know what to do if it differs from what they planned? In the industrial context, if a feature of the product changes (perhaps as a refinement of the market definition, or perhaps as a technological breakthrough), how does a partner know what processes to change?

High Concept fills that role nicely as a tool in building an agile virtual enterprise. The techniques and institutional support that have evolved around the High Concept idea in a very large industry might be instructive, and applicable to, our initial target domain of the defense aerospace industry.

In a movie virtual enterprise, High Concept is composed by agents. Some are agents in the showbiz sense, individuals who professionally think and negotiate for writers, actors, directors, and sometimes other major participants like cinematographers. Labor unions are key agents, since they provide and certify the appropriateness of a majority of the participants to the various companies involved. Some of the agencies are not human, but are gathering mechanisms where High Concept search and exposure can be accommodated. Success on a film, including keeping costs low, depends heavily on everyone having the same idea of the style and purpose of the product. Partners are evaluated based on their experience with and understanding of elements in the High Concept. To an astonishing extent, the High Concept fully serves as a script of sorts that the agents can use to quickly and competently stitch together scores of virtual enterprises per year.

We see the High Concept statement as a tool for binding the enterprise to the customer. In the movie example, it was forced by losing the monopoly of moviehouses that allowed Hollywood to remain aloof. Similarly, the High Concept is a tool for binding to temporary production assets in lieu of the in-house production assets of times gone by. It can be seen as a way of binding the various small partners to the customers in the context of the whole system.

Connection to Lightweight Contracts

The central feature of High Concept is a description of *style*; High Concept films themselves are dominated by style. In the High Concept definition there are all the cogent elements of the soft stuff both in and behind the product. That is to say that High Concept captures the *feel* of the picture as part of its product description.

We've already talked about a structural advantage the U.S. has in building virtual enterprises on its case-based contract law, and how Hollywood utilizes that advantage. High Concept provides a scaffold around which these lightweight contracts can be built. A good contract is an agreement of what the parties will do, what they intend to accomplish. The contract's primary value is in recording the agreement, but the agreement is eminent. The deeper the agreement, the better the virtual enterprise. The High Concept is both a collection of concepts around which two parties can agree, and also a text representation of what those concepts are.

Movie concepts are lightweight because they rely on the High Concept for all the hard to capture soft parts (meaning intangibles, goals), add some quantitative stuff (number of carpenters, working hours), and leave the exceptions largely to pre-existing culturally based case law or its equivalent boilerplate.

Agents in the Strategy

A discussion of contracts is a discussion of trust. In building the VE, you need to identify the agents required to build and maintain the virtual enterprise and determine what it means to trust them. The way that High Concept definitions are put together depends on a notion of who does what, so the identification of agents (at least types of agents) follows directly. For instance, if a detailed High Concept for a science fiction film required flying monkeys you would approach one or more special effects agents to approach which among differing processes best achieves the effect. It would have to be consonant with the desired overall philosophy (and their constraints: time/cost) and you'd have to know who could do it.

Those types of agents have evolved in the system. They *speak* High Concept as a cultural attribute. They tend to be trusted in several ways:

- There's trust in their integrity, in the sense of conforming to ethics, morals and values. The penalty for breaking this trust is ostracism. This type of trust is independent of the High Concept idea the way we're using it. But in interviews, members of the community spoke of these ethics, morals and values in High Concept terms. There is a widespread belief that Jewish religious and social traditions provide a historical ethical basis for this.
- There's trust in the ability of the agent to understand and internalize the High Concept, translating it from the technical needs of the agent's area of expertise into the vocabulary of their suppliers.
- There's trust that the right supplier, artist, or whoever has been selected by the agent. A poor experience with a partner translates directly into a negative for the agent. This is inductive trust, while the others are deductive.

Agents can be completely independent persons or companies, they can be representatives of one or many potential performers (as in the Creative Artist's Agency), or they can be part of a diverse organization, such as the development director of Industrial Light and Magic. The point is that trust is relative, and High Concept gives a calibrating foreground against which trusted agents can be evaluated.

Three AVE Principles

All this is leads up to a succinct statement of the three key principles that you must master in order to have an AVE generally:

•You must have a robust system of agents that autonomously act to configure and optimize their system, not because you so direct them, but because they are acting in their own best interests.

•You must have a way of providing a common goal to the diverse agents so that their efforts optimally converge on what you want, and what the customer needs. So far, we've been calling that High Concept, but a better term is *feature-based modeling*, which we will discuss in the next section.

•You must have a way for all the components of the enterprise to be rewarded and punished by contracts, but you cannot rely on predefined, static business boundaries, nor expensive, static, old-style contracts. You need to be able to have fuzzy business boundaries, even perhaps having the original corporate identities essentially vanish for the project.

FEATURE-BASED MANUFACTURING

You can probably see how a system of agents and contracts can be implemented in your industry. But if you are like the rest of us, you are having some trouble mapping the idea of high concept to the world of manufacturing. In response to this concern, a special workshop was conducted to create a roadmap for manufacturing technology fifteen years out, sponsored by the Departments of Defense, Commerce, Energy and the National Science Foundation. The result is called *Feature-Based Manufacturing*.

Some of its key features are excerpted here. We use them to build a framework for Feature-Based Manufacturing, which is simply the High Concept idea made to function in the more complex manufacturing enterprise arena, and to provide a context for the tools presented later in the book.

Needs for a Feature-Based High Concept

Building on research by others (Agility Forum, 1997) to define an agenda for next generation manufacturing, we built a reference framework of research needs with the following categories broken down according to discipline.

Enterprise Resource Management: Included in this category are all problems associated with understanding, engineering and managing/optimizing enterprise assets including through the actual operation.

•*Human Resource "Engineering" and Management:* This means more than people and skills; it represents a broader view which includes enterprise and community cultures, the mechanics of collaboration (including trust), and management of soft issues such as tacit and strategic knowledge. The key problem here is that social and cultural sciences are soft. Tools and techniques are based on models and metrics that are similarly soft. They do not form a foundation for a rigorous engineering-like discipline. Therefore, human and knowledge assets are managed by intuition or often not at all. This is a key need.

•*Asset Engineering and Management:* The group extended this definition from an equipment focus to include all assets: capital, intellectual property, and goodwill, as well as tools and facilities. (Human assets and the knowledge they carry are sufficiently unique to deserve their own subelement above.) Tools currently exist to manage assets within stable, monolithic situations. Where we are weak is in highly dynamic (reconfigurable, rescaleable, reassignable) environments where the value of assets change in an agile environment. This is especially so in a context of evaluating customer value and also in understanding the value of knowledge. New business models cannot emerge until this barrier is eliminated. A new generation of quality tools is required, which evaluate the value-added quality of assets (and activities).

•*Supply Chain Engineering and Management:* Current models of supply chain emphasize the primecontractor-subcontractor relationship. This was extended to encompass fluid, opportunistic virtual enterprise models of partnering. We currently have rudimentary asset management tools; these depend on a solid business model and static assets. No tools exist to support agile virtual enterprise asset management.

Financial Management: Current practice breaks this into two parts, forecasting/estimating and cost collection/reporting. These were combined by the group because a large part of the problem is that they are separate.

We should be able to perform virtual manufacturing (by simulation) for cost planning by exercising the activity control models of the enterprise in different contexts. We should be able to do the reverse as well, use cost values in evaluating assets and capabilities (among many partner scenarios) and *compile* product/market opportunities. We currently lack all but the most rudimentary valuation systems, and no cost/value simulation tools.

Stakeholder Responsiveness: The group's opinion was that if this were supported well with information-enabling tools and infrastructure, the category would envelope the entire original functional model, the thing that defines and drives the whole enterprise. The definitions of this element were also expanded from the standard view to make them more complete.

•*Enterprise Stakeholder Responsiveness:* This was expanded to include stockholders, employees (including potential and retired employees), the local communities, and the enterprise's suppliers (and their stockholders, employees, and communities). Today, we do a good job of abstracting financial data as metrics for near-term stockholder value. But we lack more sophisticated abstractions for longer-term value: market share/strength, asset/skills enhancement, goodwill, defensive posture, and such. Yet the stockholder demographic is increasingly interested in profit tomorrow, not so much profit today. Similar value abstractions need to be created for other stakeholders.

•*Customer Responsiveness:* This was enhanced so that a more direct vision of relating what the customer wants (satisfaction features) can be considered in engineering the product and enterprise. We know how to design products given product requirements, but we do not know how to formally represent a customer's needs in terms of real customer values and how to extract from that product requirements. This lack, currently filled by intuition, prevents us from having value-based enterprise engineering that truly includes the customer.

•*Society Responsiveness:* Often this means just environmental regulation, perhaps an obligation not to leave a community. It was expanded by us to include all the stakes that society has in increasing the well-being of its citizens in more robust enterprises. The problem of course is that we have poor methods to understand the dynamics of society and how those are benefited by market forces and emerging trends in industry. Worse, the science by which we design and measure research to enhance such dynamics is essentially nonexistent. The refinement of a roadmap and the direct management of the research needs research to better understand itself.

Instead of these tools, conventional research focuses on product data and process management functions. We strongly feel that those are mere tactics used to deliver value to the customer in an engineered environment and at least are encompassed in the expanded redefinition of the model. At most, in some of the future visions described in the next section, those problems become moot, solved by new paradigms rather than brute force.

THREE VISIONS OF THE FUTURE

In order to meet these objectives, we defined three visions of the future enterprise which are achievable in the near term with realistic research investments. (We also created detailed research and product roadmaps for each.) The research presented here is a giant first step. In fleshing out these visions, the meaning of *manufacturing* is not limited to discrete, product-driven sectors (aerospace, automotive, electronics). The third vision is the Feature-Based Enterprise that utilizes high concept-like ideas. The two that precede it are interim steps that enterprises can take today, using more or less existing methods.

Vision 1: Open Agent Enterprises

An open agent enterprise leverages the idea of each unit (in the simple case, each division or partner), large and small, simultaneously working for diverse goals, but the environment is engineered in such a way that optimal enterprise behavior emerges. A benefit of this approach is that it does away with the impossible complexity associated with deterministically understanding and modeling every facet of every partner for every contingency.

What characterizes this vision is that the selfish actions of each member changes the overall enterprise so that it optimally converges on a state that best serves the strategy and the customers. The cost of this vision is the widespread sharing among all partners of strategic information which generally tends to be closely held.

In such a vision, we would expect to see value added activity improvements identified, evaluated and implemented at much lower cost than currently. Today, the overhead of rationalizing small improvements in a top-down system model prevents most incremental improvements by "intrapreneurs" because they are too small to bear the overhead. Such improvements might be identified (and implemented?) by agents external to the enterprise (extraprenuers?).

The benefit is that managers avoid the complexity problems and associated huge costs and risks of current methods. This way, every player can be presumed to be moving the enterprise forward. There are two key problems: every agent needs to see essentially all information (there can be few secrets); and the non-deterministic behavior of the agents has to be *seen* in some way by engineers/managers in a deterministic-like way so that business can be planned.

Vision 1 Requirements

Framework/Infrastructure Design. The difficult part of well-designed agent systems is not the agents, but the information soup in which they interact. Substantial information must be available to all agents, including financial and process information that is currently considered confidential. What this means is that we need a way for formatting the information that is used for tasking a component. Today, it is a matter of specifying what the product, cost, delivery time, and quality must be. In the future that information must be richer, so that the partner has access to what is actually trying to be accomplished by the enterprise (and, incidentally, the temporary definition of the product, cost delivery time, and quality).

Agent/Feature Conflict Resolution. Agents need to be made aware of what behavior is beneficial to the enterprise, so there needs to be an identification of what those value features are and how they decompose to agent granularity. This task is the minimal solution to allow some behavior as a simple version of Vision 3. In other words, a partner, even a small partner, needs to be able to evaluate the value of each change made in one of its processes. The value of that change may not look so good locally to the partner's manager, but be of major significance to the enterprise. The way this can be supported is by a set of metrics, similar to the ones we talk about later, that support this evaluation. That way, you don't have to have a big clock designer in the sky, each part of the clock can in a way design itself.

Object/Feature Conflict Resolution. The standard model for programming is now object oriented. But objects are not the best normal form for activity features because they hides details as a strategy for managing complexity, which is the opposite of what we need. Some bridging technology must be developed. This is a tough one. The programming world is rushing to object-oriented techniques in order to solve some problems in effectively making applications. This philosophy works well in its own area, that of application development. But it is pretty bad for the kind of transparent modeling we need. Fortunately, the modeling community is coming up with some good alternatives. In Chapter 11, we will indicate some of those alternatives.

Open Agent Systems Environment. This task produces the functional environment that generates benefit. No big challenge here. This is just a plumbing job that connects everyone to the models noted above. Those models will contain the information coming from the strategy to the enterprise, and the information from the enterprise on process configurations on how to support the strategy. Presumably, in the near term, this will be something internet-based.

Integration of Mixed Paradigms. Business paradigms are not going to completely change, and top-down deterministic management systems will still be useful. This is a problem: We know how to operate deterministic enterprises, and (except for the needs noted above) we know how to operate emergent enterprises. But how do we manage enterprises that contain both paradigms? How do we make emergent behavior look deterministic for certain functions and vice versa? Some strategic decisions and legal/financial views need to know what is actually going on. This is less a problem for technologists than for financial analysts. The problem is that enterprises are understandably run on numbers. Behind each number is a presumed auditability so that someone can find out details at whatever level she wishes. This assumes that the people at the top know (or can know) what is going on in detail (this is often fiction, but never mind). What this vision must include is that some details cannot be known, only that you have trust in partners to "do the best thing." So instead of auditing a partner's processes like drilling and painting, one audits the partners processes to support the enterprise's strategy. These are the *trust metrics* which we will introduce.

Vision 2: "Regular" Agile Virtual Enterprises

The second vision addresses similar problems to the first. How to create opportunistic, short-lived partnerships that are strategy and market-driven. But it takes a less specific technical approach. Both assume that radical change will be pushed by technology breakthroughs, this vision is less dependent on a single approach (that of agent-based technology).

What is envisioned here is practical support for novel partnering models, beyond supply chains to *dynamic value webs,* where assets are obtained, mixed into the temporary web, and sloughed off when unneeded. Processes and skills will be fostered, and grow in a reusable, probably modular, way so that plug and play asset composition can occur. Near-instant contract mechanisms will be supported.

This vision accommodates and harmonizes two anticipated customer trends: The move toward true, customer-driven mass customization and the move toward mixed product/service delivery. In the latter, one may not buy a simple product (for instance, a car), but a service that provides, maintains, and upgrades the product at specific value levels.

Vision 2 Requirements

Create a Defined Language for Interoperability. The classic enterprise integration problem is redefined from one that relies on anticipating and freezing interfaces and attacking by standards, to one that has introduction and arbitration mechanisms for components to allow what the group calls *self-annealing* systems.

One approach to sharing information is by simple standards; you just force everyone to represent the information in a common way. But in the VE, that is overly constraining. What we need is standard way to define the way the information is structured, so the receiving system can sort it out easily. This is the much-desired *information federation*, and the key is the defined language.

Relationship/Value Web Management Tool Suite. The first task deals with planning and operations generally. This task deals specifically with the more difficult issues of business metrics. The old method was charging for product or service. This method charges for value. This task is a minimal version of Vision 3. The metrics we cite here are those which measure a partner's contribution, the value they bring to the enterprise. Today, the value is supposed to be related to the partner via less rich product-related specifications.

Complexity Management Tool Suite. A significant problem is the complexity of management systems. This is conventionally managed by reducing the scope or overlaying business process restrictions and simplifications. This task greatly expands that envelope to allow managers more freedom to do what is right, especially in two complexity-producing ways: Highly opportunistic virtual enterprises with promiscuous partnering, and nimble niche fulfillment. This is perhaps the technical barrier to Agile Virtual Enterprises. All this information flowing around will be very expensive to keep both vital and protected. Fortunately, in the last chapter we can point you to a breakthrough that's in the works for the complexity problem in general.

Assurance (Fear Removal) Mechanisms. In spite of all the aforementioned tools, virtual enterprises will still have a trust barrier to overcome among its partners. This collection of tools mitigates (but does not eliminate) the problem by providing loosely collected tools that leverage the interoperability language. (These tools support all partners concerns.) Trust metrics are the key here.

Vision 3: Feature Driven Enterprises

In some ways, the feature driven enterprise, or advanced agile virtual enterprise, is a more radical vision than the other two. But it was evaluated as a more near-term possibility because the technology push requires less radical change in existing management doctrine and financial tools. This book supports all three visions.

In current practice, a customer need is identified and turned into product requirements (with problematic product data exchange requirements); then, in a similarly difficult transition, the product data gets transformed into process plans (with their own sharing problems). Over all this are different primitive representations of activities, costing, and quality. Substantial, costly, and risky difficulties arise from trying to integrate all this and incidentally still keep the customer in mind. It is impossible to integrate reasonably.

The research group suggested raising the level of representation which integrates the enterprise to a notion of features. *Features* would be defined as any product or enterprise attribute or activity that adds value to targeted customers. This same notion of value-defined features would have views for different versions of product data, various aspects of processes, and a new paradigm of value-driven quality. Such value features would be the integrating representation across the enterprise, so many of today's product data exchange and financial and enterprise integration problems would vanish.

These features bind the enterprise to a common purpose, and serves as a sort of High Concept language.

Vision 3 Requirements

Defined Feature Language. As with most federating enterprise integration solutions, the solution depends on an overarching language. But this is a metalanguage of sorts by which the different models in the enterprise can be described. The lexicons of later tasks are the bindings from the feature language to each model type (the language can seen as a value ontology). An *ontology* for something is a collection of definitions and principles that describes the world in which that something exists. This is important because we don't want the situation of partner A translating what they are doing in terms that partner B can not understand. This is expensive with many partners and there is never any assurance that you can get it right. Nor do we want everyone to use a lowest common denominator language for their activity, because that dumbs down everyone. Instead, we want partner A to be able to look at partner B and have access to all the information (the ontology) that will help understand what is going on.

Translational Toolset (Mapping between Domain Lexicons; from Legacy Applications to Feature Applications). The lexicons of the previous task provide the formal basis for this task. Here, tools, models and metrics that support conventional functions are mapped. Concerning ontologies, one doesn't want to wade through the whole definition of the world just to understand one fact. The solution to this is to have targeted collections of terms (lexicons) that pertain to specific process areas. A planner uses a different language than a sheet metal former and (usually) has different needs. These lexicons just make the process of looking at information and getting what you need cheaper.

Distributed/Associative Databases. The mappings of the previous task provide a dynamic fabric of associations whereby the enterprise can be easily integrated and managed. A suite of databases and associated tools that use that capability will greatly enhance whatever function they address. An old-fashioned database requires that all the data to be formatted one way and collected (or essentially so) in one central location. But we want all the "data" to just drift along with the many partners who own and use it, and for it to appear as if it is unified somehow. We already have come a long way with this. Given the ontologies and lexicons, this type of database is within reach.

THE BOTTOM LINE

What we have here are three approaches to implementing High Concept. The first vision does it by sharing strategic goals among the partners, so that each can map its strategy to the enterprise's and anyone in the enterprise can see a mismatch between a partner's goals and the enterprise's. This is a solution by business process, more or less just sharing.

The second vision implements High Concept through a technological solution that simply maps process information through some magic bullets of federation technology. The third vision is a synthesis of the two—one describes what the enterprise wants to accomplish in terms of value features, and everything flows from that: who is involved; what they do, and how they get compensated. This makes many vexing existing problems associated with the information infrastructure simply go away. These three visions merely extend the three ways that we've found High Concept to be implemented successfully today.

Chapter 6

Agility and the Defense Industry

MANTECH, MOVIES AND THE SPRUCE GOOSE

The movie industry is an exemplar of one type of AVE. In the first installment of the case study, we found that Jeffersonian ideas about federation and Quaker beliefs of trust/consensus supported an AVE-based whaling industry. The meme gets established in case law and is carried via oil wildcatters to the movie industry, merging with Jewish ethics.[1] Along the way, military investment plays a supporting, but not pivotal role. This example was also published by the Agility Forum as a report and on its web site and captured widespread attention, though the meme idea appeared to be largely overlooked.

In the second installment, the insight went further by revealing the influence of the lightweight, case-law based system of trusted agents and agreements. Two pieces of information came to light. The first was that the movie business provided a primary template for Japanese ideas of enterprise engineering we now call lean, and that template was empowered through military guidance. The second piece of information is that the movie business has evolved since then to be more of a virtual enterprise, using what they call a packet-unit system of assembling frangible supply chains. To provide a nexus around which these supply chains can integrate, High Concept, a highly evolved mission statement is often used. Also of note is the recognition of the importance of these new ideas of agility and VEs by some Japanese business visionaries.

This case study may have an extraordinary final chapter, which we recount here. Although we were not able to verify it as thoroughly as the other facets, if true, it can add substantial value to the task that has been done. The theory is that the original idea of forming opportunistic, agile supply chains was developed by the Department of War's Manufacturing Practices Group at Dayton, Ohio (precursor to the Air Force Manufacturing Technology Directorate which managed our research). It was formed for the shipbuilding industry during World War II, in an attempt to create an instant additional capability.

This was during a period when the head of General Motors, acting as an army general, had gathered the Allies' best industrial thinkers at (what is now) Wright-Patterson Air Force Base, which was the management center for war production. Some of these thinkers from the maverick Howard Hughes' company developed the idea of making tens of thousands of *Spruce Goose* aircraft, monster wooden airplanes designed to replace submarine-vulnerable steel and concrete freighters. For uninteresting reasons, the war department fought the idea of the product, while supporting the techniques which would have created a massive nationwide VE of small companies for producing the airplanes.

Discouraged concerning the *Spruce Goose*, Hughes turned again to making movies after the war, transplanting these same AVE process innovators and their ideas into that business. Though Hughes' films were usually second rate artistically, his packet-unit production system kept them profitable, providing a mature alternative to vertical integration which everyone in the industry had adopted by the 1970s. This AVE infrastructure was what later attracted Sony's Morita in search of a revitalizing paradigm.

We got the story from retired Hughes executives, but were unable to see documentation because of the extraordinary internal security requirements set up by Howard Hughes. But the story is believable because of the known legacy of defense sponsorship for novel business and manufacturing practices, including soft issues. This we briefly survey in the following paragraphs and Figure 6.1.

Our research was sponsored in part by the U.S. Department of Defense. When they got into sponsoring agility, many people already recognized agility as a good idea, though not an entirely new one—after all, businesses have been responding to change for centuries. So, why would it be necessary to sup-

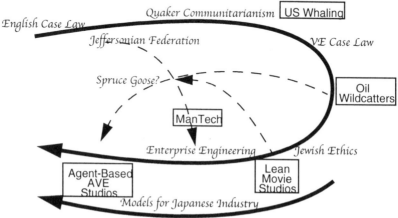

Figure 6.1   A Sweeping Case Study

plement market forces with government sponsorship? Wouldn't underlying tools for agility appear as a matter of course? At the time, the answer was no.

THE NEED FOR AGILITY

Why Now?

The examples we've given are from the past. What has changed now to make agility of more imminent concern to managers? The dynamic of interest is the ratio of the rate of change that gracefully, spontaneously occurs in the business organization, compared to the rate of change of the environment. As the latter grows, the need for agility increases.

The ability of organizations to change, generally, is not remarkably better than in the past. And for the kinds of products that are increasingly of interest—high value-added technology-based products—it could be argued that change becomes much more difficult. Many of today's organizations are larger; new products require more communication among different disciplines and functions; and each discipline's tools and methods are becoming more mature, and often less amenable to change.

But the rate of change in the environment is growing at an ever-increasing speed. The technology that goes into products, and that which goes into the processes to make them, is changing to an increasing extent. Competition has increased as we have become more of a world market. The customer is becoming more demanding, more educated, and more fickle. And, finally, the rate at which the investment community re-evaluates its position has increased.

All of a sudden, the need for agility is no longer a matter of a few situations. The majority of enterprises in many business sectors need to increase their ability to change, simply as a matter of survival. Soft issues are central to the problem domain.

Why Government Support?

The situation has changed from one in which agility was only occasionally important, to one where it is critical. This has happened fast, much faster than the support market (tools and technologies) has been able to respond. The support market, consisting of academic theorists, tool suppliers, and consultant practitioners, is what businesses depend on to develop and support new business practices and underlying technology. This support infrastructure is itself un-agile and has not been able to respond with adequate agility tools without the aid of outside stimulus.

The situation was a natural for government research attention that traditionally works in areas which market forces do not address. Especially appropriate is investment in the underlying scientific and engineering principles upon which tools and techniques can be created. And this is precisely the area in which we, and others, are working. This government investment was intended to help accelerate the development of market-funded tools.

What would happen if the government investment in agility was not made? We believe that various large companies would have developed some agility tools anyway, as a matter of survival. But because those tools would comprise a competitive advantage, we suspect that they would keep them for themselves. And, if the resources of such companies are committed to internal tools, it would starve the open market of the majority investment and customer base needed to reach critical mass. Agile virtual enterprise infrastructure tools and techniques would not appear in the market; therefore, small companies would not be able to participate in AVEs unless they were under the sponsorship of bigger firms, a most undesirable situation. The result might be better supply chains for some of the major firms, but we would never realize the idea of many of these large firms being made obsolete by alliances of more nimble smaller ones.

NECESSITY OF GOVERNMENT INVESTMENT

There are copious examples of closed solutions without government intervention in both business practices and technology, in pension funding, in telephone infrastructure, and in railroad technology. In all cases, the trend was toward closed solutions, and the government gently intervened. Today, we can hardly imagine the business world without openness in these areas.

One example of a good case for government investment is the original plan for SEMATECH (Semiconductor Manufacturing Technology) Consortium. The U.S. had gone from being the major supplier of semiconductors in the world, to about a 25% share and falling. Japanese firms were taking much of the business. The *keidanran* (formerly the elite inner circle, now more of a chowder and marching society) was the main Japanese strategist.

The reasons were due in large part to the high cost of forming a sizeable integrated enterprise from a diverse supplier base. The primary business of semiconductor firms is not the manufacture of silicon chips, as one would suppose, but the manufacture of semiconductor manufacturing facilities, or fabs. These fabs currently cost over one billion dollars, with the cost escalating drastically. The useful life of a fab is alarmingly short, less than a decade, at which point essentially everything original is obsolete. Everything in the fab is provided by other parties, thousands of them, and every fab is different, markedly so, from its predecessor. The business game here is to integrate these thousands of partners quickly and efficiently into a high-yield integrated whole. Profitability is wholly a product of timeliness and elimination of waste.

Japanese manufacturers were able to excel because their monolithic, vertically-integrated *keiretsus* were able to gather and lock in the majority of suppliers and dictate integration standards to the remainder. It is a crude way to integrate an enterprise; it trades agility for integration, which results in less innovation, but greater speed in the sense of quickly and cheaply creating a new fab.

In the U.S. the best suppliers innovated constantly, and they sold to all comers. But since each customer had different integration strategies, over time substantial energy was spent both on the supplier and prime contractor side in integrating instead of innovating. It was an un-agile system, resulting in fabs that were not effective learning organizations. This is at root a soft problem, depending on human, cultural, and knowledge management factors.

To complicate the problem, Japanese concerns, working with government subsidies, were buying equipment and technology suppliers from the U.S. industry and then just closing them down. The idea was an offensive move to make integration harder, even impossible, for the remaining suppliers who spent sometimes 60% of their budget figuring out how to integrate into fab architectures instead of improving their product.

The SEMATECH consortium was formed to address this problem. Industry and the Department of Defense each kicked in what so far is a billion dollars to address the problem of creating an enterprise integration strategy that increased agility, thus allowing for federation of processes and equipment from an increasingly innovative, competitive supplier base.

The U.S. response was one which leveraged the traditional way of doing business, relying on agility through market forces (though the formation of the consortium was before the term became used in this context). Industrial partners included IBM, AT&T, Intel, and Digital as well as other high tech giants, and the idea was to address collectively what these giants individually could not, even with massive and otherwise effective research efforts.

The Defense Department involvement was keyed toward protecting the domestic supply of a key component of weapon systems; this threat was underscored by the publication in Japan of *The Japan that Can Say No* (Morita 1998)—coauthored by Morita, the fellow that studied movies after the war and then later bought his own agile studio. That book described a Japan which controlled the source of technology for U.S. weapons in such a way that U.S. access could be denied, and world events controlled.

The case for Defense investment and collective focus on agile infrastructure was clear and uniquely American. The early progress toward that agenda at SEMATECH formed the basis of agility research. As it happened, for a variety of reasons SEMATECH has changed its focus from the agile enterprise integration problem to more mundane and simpler efforts in standards and preserving the supplier base through subsidy. The idea of an innovative, agile domestic supplier base driven by, and fed by, free market forces has been abandoned. The semiconductor firms (to whom national defense is not a business concern), have been forced into the Japanese camp. Today, each major U.S. company has tight, multiple relationships with formerly threatening Japanese competitors. The idea of a domestically-based strategic industry has been lost. Agility at the basic level is no longer on the agenda, yet the taxpayer investment has doubled.

This is why the group of suppliers of information infrastructure to the world (IBM/Digital/H-P/NCR/AT&T), who incidentally were also members of SEMATECH, rebelled and formed the Suppliers' Working Group, which we led. This group utilized some of the antitrust protection of SEMATECH, but none of its bureaucracy.

THE ADVANCED RESEARCH PROJECTS AGENCY

This agency, over 35 years old, alternates between being called the DARPA (Defense Advanced Research Projects Agency) and the ARPA, depending on somewhat fickle congressional guidance. It is an agency of the Department of Defense, chartered with being the premier center for high risk, high payoff projects for defense needs. DARPA is well known for its many innovations in the area of basic information science, with a focus on precompetitive infrastructure.

DARPA has also dabbled in dual-use and manufacturing technologies, with mixed results (DARPA sponsors SEMATECH). We believe that the problems of agility, at least the ones described here, are matters of precompetitive infrastructure, instead of being manufacturing issues per se. As long as we adhere to the former, we are rooted in DARPA's traditional charter and proven strengths (DARPA partly sponsored the effort in agility which is reported here). In this area, they are arguably the premier agency worldwide in understanding and addressing fundamental issues.

Air Force ManTech

The Manufacturing Technology Directorate (ManTech) in Dayton, Ohio, is less well known to the general public, but they have in many ways an even more interesting history. ManTech is chartered with insuring that the domestic aerospace defense industrial base has the most modern underlying technologies.

ManTech's legacy is truly impressive. Its predecessor organization was created in 1917, shortly after the entry of the U.S. into World War I. Although the U.S. manufacturers had developed the first practical airplanes, the domestic defense establishment had ignored them. The U.S. had only 23 aircraft at the outbreak of World War I, while the adversaries had over 500.

The organization was set up to manage the production of all Allied aircraft together with the required infrastructure. This has to be the mother of all virtual enterprises, involving the coordination of international plants to build a capability which for practical purposes did not exist at all. Within 18 months, nearly 30,000 aircraft were produced! What makes this feat so much more amazing is that the landing fields, logistics, repair, and training were created from a dead stop. Often, these tasks included massive projects in physical infrastructure for host cities—sewage, roads, and the like.

One thing that made this possible was the collaborative transfer of information among partners. The most popular plane, the DH-4, was of British design, but the engine was designed in France and the armaments in the U.S. The coordination of information on design, manufacturing, and support from diverse sources under mostly local control required a new science of management. They termed this new management science, *systems engineering*. Our agile virtual enterprise requirements for new insights in management continue very much in this tradition.

After the war, Europe's military kept their defense plants under government control. The U.S. did not. Even then, Congress, without having an industrial policy per se, believed that defense strength was linked to a free-market based industrial base. The Dayton center, renamed Manufacturing Methods, was chartered to assure that the best underlying technologies, especially in enterprise practices, were employed in this industrial base.

Even at that time, there was a recognition that in order to have a strong defense industrial base, complementary commercial industries needed to be robust. Since there was no real market for aircraft, Dayton helped create one. by engaging in three pilot projects. First, they heavily promoted airmail, creating customer demand for this service. Second, they developed the idea of regularly scheduled passenger service, as was already customary with rail service. But investors weren't biting. So they operated, as a demonstration, the world's first regular air passenger service: From Dayton to Washington, to Langley, Virginia, and back. (Langley was the nation's aerodynamic research center, later birthplace of NASA as it migrated out of DARPA.) The success of this venture convinced investors and spawned today's airlines. Finally, they created an annual showcase so aircraft manufacturers could competitively display their latest innovations. This, in combination with a secure customer base, ensured technical progress for decades and served to create an industry culture. The event, much reinvented, still continues today as the Dayton Air Show, and its popular successors continue in other cities.

So, although our Army Air Corp's defense posture was poor at the beginning of World War II, Dayton was once again able to spin up a VE-based global manufacturing enterprise. The numbers here are equally impressive in scale (about 100,000 aircraft domestically, about twice that worldwide), but in this case there was a pre-existing base. Notably, the enterprise was less hierarchically centralized than one would imagine and depended heavily on peer-to-peer agile collaboration.

To maintain a strong base in postwar precompetitive infrastructure, Dayton played a leadership role in developing the underlying technologies for numerical control of machine tools, computer integrated manufacturing (CIM), enterprise integration, and, currently, the Lean Aircraft Initiative. All of the predecessor research was conducted under either their or DARPA's sponsorship, usually both. Seeing a new, important opportunity, ManTech managed (for DARPA) the effort reported herein, the Agile Virtual Enterprise Metrics project.

WHY WE WERE SPONSORED

The Suppliers' Working Group (the $40 million proprietary study we facilitated out of SEMATECH) came to a number of findings concerning advantages and benefits to the U.S. economy as a whole.

U. S. Benefits Relative to International Competitors

We studied the costs of integrating and managing processes in the U.S. compared to the international competition. The results were startling. The study focused on high-value manufactured components, because this is where the major competition exists. (A high proportion of foreign low-value manufacturing and assembly directly benefits U.S. business anyway.)

In every case examined (automobiles, commercial aircraft, consumer electronics, small appliances, semiconductors), the major determining factor in the competition's relative success was not low labor cost, access to cheap capital, or the benefit of government-sponsored research. Rather, it was the low cost (relative to the U.S.) of integrating their enterprises. (A parallel study was performed, with similar results, on the Soviet—now multinational—military aircraft enterprise.)

The reasons for this are related to how we and our competitors traditionally do business. When Sony designs a product, they do so knowing who is going to build its components, so they can predict or dictate what processes are going to be used. The typical Japanese enterprise is a very stable, vertically integrated enterprise. The typical European enterprise is similarly, though less, integrated and stable, but without the shared ownership which characterizes the Japanese.

A typical U.S. enterprise is dynamic; the rules of composition are dominated by the forces of competition. The major benefit of this system comes from the innovativeness of small, agile businesses. In this area, the United States is unparalleled. However, the cost of quickly integrating processes of a small business (or a component of a large corporation) into the supplier chain is excessively expensive in terms of effort, time, and cost. This amounts to a critical disadvantage for U.S. enterprises.

In a growing number of U.S. industries, a quantity of small business innovators are being driven out of the supply chain by the increasingly high cost of doing business. Pressure comes both from within the small businesses, who would rather put resources on their core competencies, and from large prime contractors who prefer to reduce the number firms under them, to reduce the cost of integration overhead. An otherwise classified study has reported a disastrous decline in the number of small, and presumably innovative, businesses involved in the current generation of aerospace weapon systems. This phenomenon was directly linked to higher costs.

The studies indicated that if the cost of assembling an integrated U.S. enterprise were lowered, then the relatively stronger engines of innovation and competition would put every high-value U.S. manufacturing enterprise at a structural advantage. The international competition would lack the agility to keep up, as their staid, long-lived structures would be slow to evolve. Their reliance on vertical integration and stability is intrinsically unagile.

Additionally, it was found that improved capabilities in nonmanufacturing information infrastructure in many cases resulted from improvements originally funded by the manufacturing sector. When VE suppliers were polled under nondisclosure protection, it was found that 62% of all improvements underway were driven by market forces originating with manufacturing customers. (All numbers in this section are from 1993.) Thus, other business enterprises (financial and retail services, or petrochemical/pharmaceutical industries) and nonbusiness enterprises (government and nonprofit activities) will benefit directly from attention to the industrial VE.

A surprising competitive advantage was discovered: The use of common (or case) law in the U.S., as we've already discussed. Most of our international competitors (the European Union, Japan, other Pacific Rim countries, and China) use law based on code. The movie/whaling example showed one direct advantage from the U.S. system. It would be desirable if the infrastructure, and specifically the metrics, were engineered to leverage this advantage. So we can consider this both as a present structural advantage and as a potentially greater advantage.

The idea of suppliers of VE infrastructure is a new one, so we had to conduct some market surveys to understand the dynamics and characteristics of the VE marketplace. The studies used the Suppliers' Working Group (Goranson, 1992i) definition. VE infrastructure technology suppliers were found to be different from VE service/application suppliers. The latter are characterized by large users (Boeing, GE, GM, the manufacturing side of IBM, for example), who supply services to themselves, and system integrators who supply services to others. The service suppliers can add value only within the range of the capability envelope provided by the technology suppliers. Therefore, the chief pressure-points for VE capabilities are the technology suppliers.

This group of companies is surprisingly small in number, consisting of IBM, Digital, and a loose federation of companies (including those mentioned) which add value to UNIX (Hewlett-Packard, Sun, and then NCR). (Microsoft, Apple, and Unisys were not critical players in the manufacturing enterprise as of 1992, the time of the study. Since then, Netscape and NeXT/Apple have also emerged as potential players.) That these companies are in the process of redefining their infrastructure products is good news for the VE program. Also important is the fact that all of the major suppliers are U.S.-based firms.

In fact, if the larger companies are decomposed by national geography and VE-related infrastructure products are assigned to the decomposed elements, some interesting insights are gained. If one counts a non-U.S.-based component of, say, IBM as a foreign company, and the U.S.-based component of a non-U.S.-based company also as a foreign company, 73% of all VE technology still comes from a U.S.-owned component based in the U.S.

The U.S., therefore, currently has most of the jobs, the technology, and the market of a potential VE infrastructure economy. As the VE market grows, the U.S. will experience growth in this market sector as a first order economic benefit. It is notable that these VE technologies fit the traditional definition of strategic technologies: They are the beginning of the food chain for most of the world's industrial economy. It is possible that, as routine integration becomes simpler, the systems integration middleman business will shrink. As a result, U.S.-dominated VE technology suppliers will become more strategically important to world business.

U. S. Benefits as Suppliers of VE Infrastructure Processes

By most measures, the U.S. is the most active developer of process-related intellectual property in the world. In separate study, we sought to understand the potential for new trade based on the licensing of process-based intellectual property from one firm to another. It is considered unlikely that an enterprise would wish to transfer processes which it uses to competitive advantage to a competitor. So attention was given to processes that could be traded across business sectors.

This was a difficult analysis; while businesses know how much they spend on hardware, and try to know how much they spend on software, there is presently less incentive for knowing how much is invested in process development. Proprietary information supplemented new floor surveys (under our initiative) in statistically representative manufacturing companies. The category of process-related investment was called enterprise characterization (Goranson, 1992d). In general, this category consisted of all explicitly captured process information that is recognized in some way by the information infrastructure.

A staggering $160 billion per year worldwide is spent on enterprise characterization. Within specific sectors, such as semiconductor manufacturing, 90% (plus or minus 5%) of a huge amount of money (tens of billions) was spent on characterizations which are common (i.e., shared and potentially transportable). Seventy per cent of the money was spent on characterizations found to be common across the electronics and the automotive manufacturing sectors. Transportability of processes in the case of service sectors was not easily determined. Of these expenses, 70 to 90% was deemed actually feasible for commerce (i.e., for selling processes), depending on the industry. The enterprise characterization components had a surprisingly long life, a half-life of 7.6 years. This indicates that a several hundred billion dollar economy in process technology is theoretically possible, though in practice it is somewhat further limited by other legal and market forces.[2]

U.S. firms would benefit by being able to avoid reinventing processes by acquiring those not in their core competency, including processes developed overseas. Some U.S. firms would benefit from selling processes to non-U.S. companies in other sectors, allowing increased investment in new processes.

User Firms Can Leverage the AVE

Often, industrial users consider the primary advantage from VE to be in its empowering of some technical strategy which they deem important to their competitive posture. These strategies are diverse, and none of them apply to all sectors. But in each case, the VE can provide an underlying infrastructure which empowers agile/flexible/rapid-response/lean manufacturing, total quality management, concurrent engineering, soft/virtual prototyping, or electronic commerce. Occasionally, the user will eschew these concepts to focus on a single metric, such as improved quality, reduced costs, reduced cycle time, enhanced markets, or flattening of the organization.

For many of these cases, limited tools already exist. But the market for any one of these applications is too small to effect a major change in the basic infrastructure. Yet if one envisions the components of the AVE as including elements within an enterprise, then the technical requirements of the AVE cover many of the harder issues of these applications of enterprise integration. The VE provides an overarching concept that unifies some technical issues among the components and opens the market sufficiently to warrant addressing the tough problems.

Champions of all the approaches have presented business cases. Some of these are more developed than others. But it is clear that if the AVE contributes to the success of any of them, major benefits to industry will accrue.

Currently, many of the major VE technology suppliers are hardware suppliers or allies. This is a legacy of how the market developed: first as operating environments, then as layered middle-ware components in (a) larger system architecture(s). Often the operating environment is the competitive discriminator among suppliers, and the barriers to entry are substantial. As proposed, the AVE will *open* the market so innovative firms could enter all or part of the market. This could help revitalize the software industry by itself, and most of the likely entrants are U.S. firms.

What is the Defense Advantage?

The case here is straightforward and follows the long-lived ManTech tradition. The Defense Industrial Base is less than 5% of the manufacturing domestic product. It is simply too small to support any particular type of VE infrastructure, especially one that promotes a radical idea like agility. The only way to get improved VE infrastructure into the defense base is to see it widely accepted and supported in the domestic commercial base.

Elsewhere, we make the case that there are few barriers to cross in tailoring the AVE tools, specifically the metrics, in cutting across defense and commercial users. Fortunately, the defense users of interest, teams which design and manufacture complex weapons systems, represent essentially the same type of constituency for agility as in the commercial base. In the latter case, the users will be teams making high value-added consumer products.

A second order benefit concerns the two meanings of dual-use technology. The conventional use of the term applies to a team's ability to adapt existing processes from commercial use to military in times of crisis. But there is a much more promising vision which agility empowers. If there is a high degree of agility in practice, then defense AVEs should be able to readily form in non-crisis situations, drawing from the civil supplier/subcontractor base. This larger pool would provide for more competition and thus lower prices and increase innovation.

In fact, the need for this latter vision is already upon us. The U.S. defense strategy depends on an ever-increasing ability to field more and more sophisticated weapons while at the same time reducing support for a dedicated infrastructure to do so. Only a commercial base capable of AVEs can support this need.

THE STORY SO FAR

Let's review. So far, we have provided some background and some case studies that should give you a good idea of what we are about and why. By example, we have intuitively defined agility in a narrow way, and virtual enterprises in a rather broader way. While the problem is old, it is now more important and for the first time we can engineer agility into the system.

There are three principles apparent from the examples for what enables an AVE: agents to certify and indemnify; lightweight agreements; and a High Concept-like coordinating mechanism which can be implemented in a few different ways. Trust underlies all.

Many books might stop there conceptually. But what we intend to do is to bring some rigor to the process so that an enterprise engineering discipline can be created to support managers. We hope that you have an inkling that this can be pretty radical stuff that you can use to outwit your competitors and make you rich and famous.

We proceed in the next chapter by more carefully defining the AVE. Then, we define what it is not, by contrasting the AVE with other trends and strategies that you may be familiar with. Finally, we'll discuss some issues and problems. Having laid the groundwork, we introduce you to the new tools that managers are using to plan, optimize, and manage AVEs.

Onward!

NOTES

1. There is a story about a rabbi, a single, highly trusted Los Angeles resident, who acted as an honesty broker in early Hollywood. Though he seldom arbitrated directly, he was consulted often in the 1930-40s about "what was right." Many of those interviewed in Hollywood thought the film sector as a whole had more trust in its agreements than business elsewhere and credit it to "Jewish ethics" which at that point can be seen as taking the place of the similar Quaker ethics of the whaling instance.

2. A much more detailed Suppliers' Working Group document on these issues is available for internal government use from the Air Force Wright Laboratories Manufacturing Technology Directorate. This combined proprietary information from many sources to obtain results and is not available to the public.

Chapter 7

Definitions

Let's take some time for definitions before we burrow into methods, because many of the words we employ are used differently by others, even some common words. For example, in our international meetings, we no longer use the word *collaboration,* even though it cleanly hits the core of what we are about. Our French and German colleagues have attached a different, and very unhappy, meaning to that word.

So what is an Agile Virtual Enterprise, and what is it all about?

VIRTUAL ENTERPRISE

Believe it or not, we actually have a great deal of trouble with the term, but we just cannot seem to come up with something better. The first problem is with the word *virtual.* Many people use this term to mean "not real," as in virtual reality. Virtual manufacturing is the technique of simulating a factory wholly in a machine, usually to evaluate a set of processes. Virtual prototyping is the method of creating a product in three dimensions on the screen in virtual reality to ensure, for instance, that mating surfaces fit and that the thing can be assembled. The term is further complicated by folks who have Virtual organizations, where workers telecommute rather than spending the day in central locations. We mean none of these things.

Our virtual enterprises are opportunistic aggregations of smaller units that come together and act as though they were a larger, long-lived enterprise. The *virtual* here is meant to convey that many of the advantages of a large enterprise are synthesized by its members. In the most interesting case, this synthesis is temporary, built around a specific opportunity. When the opportunity fades, the virtual enterprise vanishes into constituent parts to reassemble into other configurations.

Many in our early research used the term Virtual corporation as well. But we chose to move away from that because the point of coming together is to create a product or service, not to create an organization or corporation. By putting the enterprise in the driver's seat, we emphasize that everything is motivated by a specific need, ideally a customer need. How that is met may be by new, perhaps unfamiliar, models of corporation and organization.

We have chosen to use *enterprise* rather than *corporation,* because the latter presumes that there is a shared vision of a corporate identity. *Enterprise* conveys the meaning that the shared focus is the project at hand; corporation implies a conventional organization whose control is centralized, which is not what we mean. The VE is unified by its mission and distributed goals, not its control system.

Our concise definition of a VE is a *temporary aggregation of core competencies and associated resources collaborating to address a specific situation, presumed to be a business opportunity.*

Four Types of VEs

Even with this definition, we cover a lot of ground. The entities could be individual corporations, separate divisions in a corporation, or other entities, such as consumer groups or labor unions. So we've broken things down into smaller categories.

Several different types of aggregation have been identified which range from more interesting to less interesting. The more interesting engage in novel business relationships which involve risk and reward. An attempt has been made to incorporate all of the different views in a set of definitions that represent four types (see also Figure 7.1):

- Type 1: An aggregation formed in response to an opportunity. In its pure form, this is the prototypical (and most interesting) type where an entity identifies an opportunity (or recognizes a change) which takes advantage of a core competency. Then the entity (normally the one that recognizes the opportunity) acts as organizer to identify and creatively integrate partners with complementary, required core competencies.

  An example may be someone who, a few years back, identified a need for an online store, then found partners to design the site, and provide and ship the product after an order from their warehouses. It is not a pure type because it is not designed to dissolve.

- Type 2: A relatively permanent aggregation of core competencies that largely pre-exists, and which is seeking an opportunity. Generally, new members must be brought into the partnership in order to address the opportunity. Large corporations are often examples of this type when they have many perceived core competencies.

• Type 3: A supplier chain which, while using relatively conventional business relationships, exhibits agility in responding to market needs. Electronic commerce also fits into this group when it employs traditional (albeit automated) business transactions.

• Type 4: A bidding consortium. Such a group relies on relatively conventional business relationships in its interactions. But it employs agile practices in response to market needs, and it acts as a Virtual Enterprise in representing collective capabilities to a customer.

One perspective holds that Type 2 is a special case of Type 1, differing only in the emphasis on the search for the opportunity and possibly the granularity and importance of the central core competencies. Another view, not in contradiction, suggests that each type can be cast in terms of an agile supplier chain or, alternatively, electronic commerce. Considering AVE types in this light helps envision growth paths from a current, less virtual situation.

Each of the four types could result in Virtual Enterprises which are useful and profitable but not agile. The Agile Virtual Enterprise (AVE) is one that simply responds well (at low time and cost) to unexpected change. As a rough discriminator, however, a Virtual Enterprise is an AVE if it is formed with the intent of (or openness to) dissolving or quickly and cheaply reconfiguring in direct response to a change in the opportunity.

Of the four types, the latter two are less agile and virtual. The discriminator is the ability of each component to change the way it does business within the context of the AVE. For example, a supplier chain relies on well-established boundaries to guide the way it integrates into the system. If the supplier were capable of realigning by having shared employees and supervisors (if that were

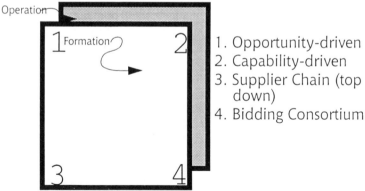

1. Opportunity-driven
2. Capability-driven
3. Supplier Chain (top down)
4. Bidding Consortium

Types 3 and 4 may aspire to be types 1 and 2
Few pure cases seem to exist
Best practices may be of different type

Figure 7.1 Four Types of Virtual Enterprises

beneficial), it would be more like a Type 1. There is a large class of actions that could be taken to integrate processes. For that reason, Type 3 AVEs tend to look more like Type 1s as they become more agile. Similarly, Type 4s "aspire" to be Type 2s. Supply chains can exist in any of the types.

In our surveys, we found that few real world cases cleanly fit these types. All were some combination, which is why we draw the square zone in Figure 7.1. Most of our cases were more in the middle than at the corners. Also, some cases were more one type in formation (always more agile in formation) and another in operation (this is shown by the two planes in the figure).

In yet other cases "best practice" was agile because they adopted, for that process, a temporary personality which was of a different type AVE. An common example was where a staid large organization created an internal AVE in order to launch a product into a narrow opportunity window. In fact, this instance was so common, the Focus Group believed it would be the normal case for AVEs in the near term.

AGILITY

A dominant definition of the agile enterprise is one that responds to (and ideally benefits from) unexpected change. Unexpected is the key word; the ability to build in response to expected change in the manufacturing domain has traditionally been termed *flexible* manufacturing, as distinct from agile manufacturing. But it would be possible to have a flexible enterprise without having an agile one. (The same is true of a lean enterprise.)

Many versions of the VE exist. A VE is agile only if it is formed with the intent of dissolving or reconfiguring, so it is possible to have a VE without having an AVE. Each of the four types of VE could be profitable and useful but not agile. The AVE is often thought of as one that exhibits a critical number of characteristics, developed by the Agility Forum, which describe agility. As a rough discriminator, however, a Virtual Enterprise is an AVE if it is formed with the intent of dissolving or quickly and cheaply reconfiguring in direct response to a change in the opportunity.

More particularly, there are a number of conditions that can change and affect an enterprise (more fully discussed later in the chapter). An agile response might be required concerning a negative change as well as to address a positive opportunity. For example, a positive opportunity would be a newly identified customer niche, or a leveragable technology. A negative change may be a new restrictive law, a raw material that disappears, or a customer who has been enticed away.

Agility as Creativity

Notwithstanding the previous definition, there are a number of other interlocking definitions of agility, each of which has utility to some community. The Agility Forum uses a concept of mass customization, a more general definition advocate. We add one more general concept, an intuitive definition creativity. The purpose is not to supplant any of the others, but instead to provide an natural equivalent to other characteristics intuitively applied (such as better, faster, cheaper).

An ideal enterprise, virtual or not, is a living, creative entity. It is both self-conscious and aware of its environment, and it is capable of creatively responding to changes either inside or outside. In this sense, the agility of an enterprise is the capability to be creative. As our research program developed, the nature of the agility paradigm became more clear. Few have recognized that agility is a radical new paradigm. It represents not an evolutionary new step of another, now well accepted paradigm like lean manufacturing; instead, it can be regarded as revolutionary.

Being cheaper, better, and faster today is not sufficient to be agile. In fact, it can happen that moves made to make one's enterprise cheaper, better, and faster may make it less agile.

Agility is the ability to change to be cheaper, better, and faster (more profitable) in a dynamic sea of change. This recognition of agility as a new paradigm is not without consequence. Metrics to deal with agility will be a new kind of metric; it just won't do to rely only on existing measures. (Notwithstanding this, the metrics need to map to profitability as defined by the enterprise's strategy.) It probably is also the case that at least in some situations, the new types of metrics for the new paradigm will require new technology and forms of non-technical infrastructure.

Types of Agility

The capability of a component in the VE can be analyzed as follows:

1. Characterization of what it does
   1.a. What it adds to the whole
   1.b. What it makes
2. Characterization of how good it is
   2.a. Internal agility
   2.b. Internal performance (quality, etc.)
3. Characterization of how well it partners
   3.a. In a static situation (to respond to initial change)
   3.b. In a dynamic situation (to respond to continual change)

If one were creating an information base on potential partners, it should gather these six types of information, each with a temporal modifier. The modifier may record how the baseline information is compromised. For instance, normally a partner may be capable of supplying 1000 widgets a month, but they've just booked a big job, so now only have the available capability to produce 500. Agility can be temporally modified. Say, for example, that the supplier has just entered into an agile situation with Ford. That means that sense-response mechanisms are attuned to the Ford/supplier context. So its ability to be agile in a partnership with GM could be temporally compromised, until the VE with Ford is dissolved.

Overall, there are these four contexts for agility:

1. The sum of internal agility of each of the components.
2. The (probably quite different) agility of the VE as a whole.
3. The ability of each component to quickly/cheaply aggregate.
4. The ability of each component to quickly/cheaply change the aggregation boundary.

There is a layering here; there are higher and lower types of agility. It is possible for a firm to be agile internally, but to not be able to agily form a VE, or contribute agility to the VE. If that is the case, the firm may have agility appropriate to its local plan, but it is of a low order.

Much better is the type of internal agility that contributes to external agility, agility with your partners. In the four contexts, the following nesting exists, each a dependent subset of the preceding:

•The ability of each component to quickly/cheaply change the aggregation boundary.
•The ability of each component to quickly/cheaply aggregate.
•The sum of internal agility of each of the components.

This is to say that the agility of the VE comes from the ability of each component to be added, or subtracted, and to fluidly change its relationship with the partners, plus the skill of the VE's organizer (some will prefer to see the organizer as the VE *engineer*). In order to measure agility, we should be looking at the boundaries among components and the internal processes that support them. That is our target for the metrics. The other contexts for agility are of a lower type. It would be possible to satisfy the simpler notions of agility without supporting the higher types.

Incidentally, this leads us to a controversy in the agility community. Some hold that agility is something that can mean a great deal, just within a single company context. Others suspect that to be true, but also believe that a much greater reward (more scope at less cost and time) from agility comes only from its VE context. We've sided with the latter perspective, and now believe that, in any case, agility in the VE context is substantially cheaper and much more effective than internal agility.

Other Agility Definitions

Whenever a rich idea finds a time that's right, it proliferates in poorly behaved ways. We've seen it in the software community as object orientation has caught on and essentially taken over. There are many definitions of what constitutes the approach and its philosophy and on first sight, they're all nearly identical. But the deeper one goes, the more different they seem.

In our studies, we've experienced the same thing with patterns and memes. In each case, there is not a central idea, but a collection of ideas living under one general buzzword. Often there are few real concepts that unite the collection.

Agility is such a rich, timely concept.

We initially had some trouble with the definition of agility because we were naively looking for a single common thread among all the researchers. Instead, we now believe there are three concepts of agility co-existing under the word (and associated sponsored research). All are useful, but to a large degree orthogonal.

The first definition's central concept is *mass customization* and supporting ideas like being close to the customer (providing solutions). In this sense, Levi's is agile because they can make custom fitted jeans; Mack is agile because a large part of their business is unique trucks. Let's call that Agility1.

The second definition, Agility2, covers companies that thrive in *change*. But change here is a constant in the environment. It could be seen as *changerate*, and often is driven by technology. Avionics businesses must be agile because technology development makes products obsolete at an increasing rate. Casio is agile because customers want mouse watches yesterday, waterproof watches today, and lighted watches tomorrow; in this case, the changerate is driven by the customer. We're using the term changerate, so as not to step on the similar MIT-developed term, *clockspeed,* and also to make an observation. Clockspeed can be interpreted as the rate of the instrument rather than of the phenomenon being measured. In our modest research we've found that both are important. The general case is the speed of the context.

Agility1 is a new way of doing business, and probably has the largest pool of enterprises to which it applies. It is revolutionary, if it is a real phenomenon, and there should be lots of opportunity for consulting, assessments, and training. Most everyone will want to explore it and many will want to pursue it. The Agility Forum has grown into Agility1.

Agility2 is a logical evolution of lean for businesses whose changerate is high. Lean was difficult to understand in a meaningful, applicable way; we should expect no less of its future. A large percentage of the agility community fit the Agility2 category, including the university-based centers and projects, in particular the Agile Manufacturing Research Institutes, Arizona State, and MIT. Agility2 agility is only of interest to high clock rate sectors of enterprises, probably a smaller group than that which can benefit from Agility1. But while the user community for Agility2 is smaller, agility is probably essential for their survival.

But wait. Is the future of an agile avionics or missile supplier as they come to terms with changerate in mass customization? Probably not. We think Agility1 and Agility2 have some overlap, but it is largely an almost accidental and uninteresting result of the fact that most businesses have similarities.

Agility2 agility deals with an expected and constant (or constantly accelerating) type of change. Laptop manufacturers have a high changerate, but the rate of change is predictable (although the details of new technologies are not). It would be possible for a firm to optimize its ability to deal with this expected change and actually lessen its ability to deal with unexpected change. Similarly, Agility1 doesn't help with unexpected change or opportunities. Mack Truck is often described as having Agility1, but can it make money supplying major sub-assemblies to Caterpillar when a construction boom hits? Can they easily leverage a core competency in truck cab sleepers to move into combat tank sleepers if an opportunity hits?

Levi Strauss Co. is also a common Agility1 example, because you can order a pair of jeans to your specific measurements; Agility1 is equivalent in some circles to mass customization. The money for Levi's may not be in jeans, it might be in custom measuring of shoes, or something else. Does furthering Agility1 or Agility2 increase their ability to change in these unexpected ways? We can easily invent examples where Agility1 and Agility2 act against this adaptability. There is a third kind of agility, Agility3, which concerns itself with adaptability—the ability to change when an unexpected opportunity appears, or if the earth shifts beneath your feet.

Agility3 has a much larger community for whom it is a major concern: most businesses never know the opportunities they miss and few believe in buying insurance against change until it is too late. This is the most revolutionary agility. Certainly it has the most challenging set of problems; measuring an ability to adapt, to learn, is no easy matter.

Agility3 is of concern in the defense sector. We know we need to counter a threat, but we know neither what the threat is nor what technology will be available. And we have found many in the civil sector who are looking for Agility3 agility without necessarily calling it agility.

In this book, we address Agility3; our tools are wholly in the Agility3 area, and it is only in that area that the metrics apply. It is our view that some of Rick Dove's early investigation (Dove, 1995), and Ken Preiss's theories on dynamically coupled systems (Preiss, Goldman & Nagel, 1996) is pure Agility3. These are two of the most prominent early writers on agility.

These are three relatively unrelated concepts each with their own, independent act under the agility bigtop. This realization has helped us a lot in interrelating the various research efforts, and we hope it helps you sort out what you encounter.

Role of the Organizer

The competence of the organizer is key to the general success as well as the agility of the VE. While the organizer is often a prime contractor, there is no requirement for this; it could be a minor player in the operation, or someone with no role in the operation, such as a broker or consultant.

As noted, agility in the VE is dependent on the contributions, of different types, from each of the members. But it also depends on the special ability of the organizer to engineer and manage that potential. The other players have one set of metrics for how agily they can be organized. The organizer may have another set pertaining to how well it can organize an AVE. This will be a partnering consideration for everyone involved, because surely an indicator of success is the strength of the VE integrator.

These organizer metrics are not difficult to understand and use: They'll be similar to, and in most cases identical to, metrics that are currently used to evaluate the ability to engineer or re-engineer an organization. Our metrics will not directly measure this organizer's ability; we measure the potential that is there, but not the manager's ability to maximize that potential.

It could be that there is no central entity that is the organizer. Perhaps the organizing entity is itself a virtual entity composed from several sources which may or may not be involved in the operating VE. Perhaps the entities are self-organizing, the organizer being diffused in rules. Some Silicon Valley VEs are of this type. The Whaling example has some elements of this type.

An interesting case is when the customer is the organizer. Naturally, the options just listed are available. Any of these cases can be ideal from a market responsiveness point of view, assuming that the customer is the best judge of what is needed. (But there is ample evidence that this is not always the case.) We've noted that the Defense AVE is unique in the role that the customer (meaning the DoD acquisition manager) plays in the AVE. This is the sole area in which the commercial and defense AVEs differ.

TYPES OF CHANGE

The metrics must have two parts: The context of the change and a measure of the effectiveness of the strategy to respond. Usually, change is categorized into the following five groups, often associated with a state diagram (see Figure 7.2).

- Resources
- Technology
- Processes (internal conditions and mechanisms)
- Environment (external conditions and mechanisms)
- Demand (customer conditions and mechanisms)

Often, agility is considered in the context of change in the customer base. but we've discovered a larger set of contexts of change. It's assumed that we need to measure agility in any of these five categories, and that there is no particular level of importance. We've changed the model in Figure 7.2 to consider

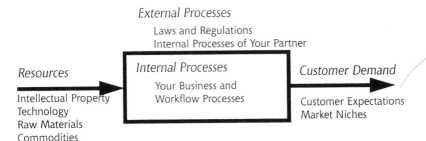

Figure 7.2 Unexpected Change (Positive or Negative) Can Come from Any of the Four Key Areas

technology as a resource. This is because, for our target customers, agility is not a response to technological innovation, but instead it is a business response which might be empowered by technology. The assumption doesn't ignore technology, but requires that it always be evaluated as a resource.

Some object to this view. It is easily demonstrable that technology is a major driver of change. We agree, but technology in this model refers only to technology that *supports* the enterprise. This use of technology has not traditionally been a driver of change except in the context of the other factors. For example, technology empowers certain types of customer demands.The boundaries among the last three groups (processes, environment, demand) may indicate a difference between agility in the virtual enterprise and in the non-virtual enterprise (single firm). In a single firm those boundaries are solid and well understood. In the VE those boundaries (and possibly those of resources) are blurred and movable. At the least, it's assumed that internal and external conditions and mechanisms have no real boundary and instead represent a spectrum.

So one set of metrics will address the ability to move boundaries beneficially in a VE for example:

•to make an external resource internal
•to harmonize an external disruption by incorporating it internally (to empower unions in the enterprise, for example), or
•to damp customer oscillations by bringing them into the enterprise in some way.
These would not apply to the non-VE case.

It is also evident that agility may be pursued for some strategic reason that is not prompted by an external or uncontrollable change. Perhaps some strategic reason appears; for example, one might want to develop the ability to partner with a company to trump their abilities from going to a competitor. While this would fit in the above view, it would not appear if the only driver were product-related cost and time.

Examples of types of change are shown in Table 7.1.

METRICS

In the previous sections, we've defined what constitutes a VE—what agility is and what it isn't. We now turn to the nature of the metrics required to address the engineering of AVEs. This section breaks down the various characteristics required of the metrics to support the engineering/management process.

What Are We Measuring?

The term *metrics* is applied to a number of situations. What do we mean?

To some, a metric is a measure of improvement. In this case, some technology and/or management technique is brought to bear to accelerate a change. Retrospectively, one can observe that some element of the VE is improved: for example, partner selection is speeded, or engineering change processes are reduced. The comparison of the improved situation with a similar, but unimproved one results in a measure of effectiveness. This is a *retrospective* measure. We do not address this situation.

At the shop floor level, the term is often applied to characterize the performance or envelope of a given equipment or cell. Thus there are a class of metrics that track improvements on processes which managers routinely use. Many quality-related metrics are of this type. Our metrics are not the same as these, but there are similarities to many of these metrics that are derived not from observation, but by exercising some model of the process and are parametric.

Another class of distinctly different metrics are metrics that measure the cost, time, and quality of processes not associated with change. An example is the metric that measures the time-to-market. Another class of metric deals with how cheaply, well, and fast an enterprise or VE can do things. Our metrics, which only measure the time and cost of *change,* will be combined with these base case better-faster-cheaper metrics to determine the total time and cost associated with the whole system under conditions of change.

If a company merely improves its existing processes, which it might consider as a change, our metrics would not apply, since we do not consider a refinement of a process an ability to respond to change. In fact, by our Agility3 definition, no agility measure applies.

In another case, if a company exhibited agility in the past in response to change, our metrics still might not apply, since past agility indicates nothing or very little about future agility. Concerning the future. our metrics address only the time and cost associated with the *potential* that a system has to accommodate future change.

Table 7.1   Examples of Types of Change

		A Positive Example	A Negative Example
Unexpected Downstream	Customer Behavior Change	New Niche Identified	Customer's Expectations Change
Unexpected Upstream	Material Change	New Raw Material	Disastrous Loss of Raw Material
Unexpected Internal	Process Change	New Process Developed	A Key Expert Retires or Dies
Unexpected External	Regulatory /Partner Change	New Competitive Tools	New Regulatory Requirement

Upstream Metrics

The kind of metrics the AVE needs are upstream metrics rather than down-stream metrics. A *downstream* metric is the conventional kind, related to benchmarking. It looks at a process and extracts some performance measure from it; for example, for monitoring the process. When the measures are compared to a large body of similar processes, one process can be benchmarked against the others, and management decisions made accordingly. But continuity in the context is essential. Downstream metrics don't convey knowledge about the internal workings of the process, so they cannot tell one how to improve the process, only that the process needs to change somehow to improve the number. Moreover, since there is an assumption that the future will be extrapolated from the past, they tell us little about adaptability in a new context.

Upstream metrics are based on the internal mechanics of the process. An understanding of the metric is based on the understanding of the process. Upstream metrics can answer questions that a manager/planner may have about how to improve the process. There is a precedence for these kinds of metrics in manufacturing based on an engineering analogy applied to physical processes. The project applied this method across all the elements in the VE associated with agility and identified by the Reference Model described in Chapter 10. This was done by understanding the causes and effects of agility, as if models of the system were simulated.

As with upstream and downstream metrics, there is a similar division with the models that support them.

Some models are used only to evaluate the enterprise, or some part of it. The analysis is performed and the model is discarded, unless of course the analysis is continuous and the model must be maintained. But there is a more robust class of models, that are used to actually *control* the enterprise, in which case there is a relationship between the control model and our upstream metrics.

This notion of upstream metrics at times has been confused with metrics of leading indicators, common in process industries. Yet upstream metrics is a much more powerful idea; leading indicators only give you a warning of impending change assuming that your experience base is robust and conditions are known, but they do not tell you why things will change.

Some agility metrics might be based on necessary conditions, but we intend to extract those conditions as a result of the principles involved and their metrics, rather than the other way around. For example, some contend that flat organizations are necessary for agility. (A flat organization is one that has relatively few layers of management from the top to the bottom.) Based on that assumption, they derive a measure of flatness and apply it to agility. This is the case of a class of metrics often used by the agility community, in our opinion mistakenly.

Instead, the metrics project came to a more basic understanding of what really causes agility. For example, one would expect that in many situations, the resulting metrics would advise flattening of the organization, but the exceptions to this rule of thumb are many. How would you know whether they apply to you if you didn't know how flattening produces agility in your type of organization? Insight into actual processes emerge by applying the metrics. More importantly, a chain of logic is established that helps justify high confidence decisions.

Dynamism of Metrics

Most metrics are static; they report on a factor in a snapshot sense. Agility is the potential to make change in response to change. Metrics can project current capabilities in today's context into a new set of capabilities in another context. Therefore, the agility metric is dynamic.

All such metrics are collections of interrelated numbers. One collection will convey the dynamic nature of the changing capability. Another will show how that collection can be accelerated or delayed at different costs and for different times. Because of this, there may be a concept of acceleration or inertia. In other words, the metric takes into account the running start an enterprise may have.

Agility metrics are different than many other metrics in the manufacturing enterprise. Flexible, lean, and quality paradigms, for example, presume that there is always a better level of flexibility, leanness, or quality which would help the enterprise. The optimum level is a trade-off between better quality (for example) and its marginal cost.

Agility follows this rule to a point. In ways that an enterprise needs agility, there is always a cost/benefit balance that metrics can inform. But there is another set of trade-off points, where further levels of agility are not good, and in fact might hurt an enterprise's strategy. Agility is insurance, and investment decisions need to be made accordingly. It is possible to have too much insurance (or the wrong kind). The ability to accommodate a change that is unimportant or unlikely to occur represents the wasting of resources. So where quality mavens can say that there is never too much quality, we cannot say the same for agility.

Difficulty of Benchmarking

Elsewhere, we have distinguished between upstream metrics and downstream metrics. Examples of downstream metrics were benchmarks. The intended meaning of *benchmark* there was an after-the-fact snapshot metric whose utility is in comparison with other snapshots. In making the distinction, it was assumed that upstream metrics are more difficult because they require insight into the actual processes involved, whereas downstream metrics do not.

There is a more fundamental difference, not captured earlier. Agility is defined as the potential to respond well to *unexpected* change. Any metric that is useful tracks that potential. A downstream metric can do no better than measure how well a process (or an enterprise as a collection of processes) responded to a specific change. So a downstream metric might have some utility for benchmarking a process against other instances of itself, but in order to be useful to another process in another organization, a thorough normalization must take place, making sure the process and the general context is similar between the two cases, including the specific unexpected change.

Here's where we run into difficulty. Benchmarking as commonly applied is the process of comparing many companies, identifying the best in class, and then presumably comparing your organization with the purpose of improvement. Some benchmarks indicate the process to change, but most don't give insight into the actual mechanics of the change.

Benchmarking assumes that there is a well understood set of characteristics that are being benchmarked and that there is a meaningful sample size. Unfortunately, many people are under the impression that various Agility1 lists from the Agility Forum constitute that set of characteristics. Instead, those lists contain either characteristics that people think are likely to coincide with agility, or that were results of agile action.

Examples of the first are modular processes, flat organizations, empowered individuals, and so on. It may be that implementing these characteristics may make most enterprises more agile, but it is also clear that these are not the primary engines of response. Examples of the latter are the ability to retool a particular piece of equipment. So we lack the prime starting point of conventional benchmarking. We've noted that more agility is not necessarily better. The conventional benchmarking paradigm would assume that the case with the most units of agility is best in class.

All these perspectives on agility suggest that agility is a paradigm that falls outside of the scope of those that can be addressed by conventional benchmarking. In particular, agility is the ability to *react*. Any measure of reaction must capture the context (ideally itself in measured units) of the situation to which the enterprise is reacting.

Instead of conventional benchmarking, agility must look for a better way of accomplishing quantitative assessment, one that understands both the context (which might be unique from case to case) and the effectiveness of the response.

It is an open issue of whether there is any such thing as a downstream metric for agility that differs substantially from the upstream metric. This is probably the same question as to whether the upstream metrics of this project are sufficient for a new paradigm of quantitative assessment. We think probably not, but in any case quantitative assessment to satisfy the benchmarking agenda is outside of the scope of our approach. All downstream metrics are probably going to measure the effectiveness of the tactic used to respond and not the strategy that drives it.

Two-Part Metrics

The metrics project was geared toward providing a single generic metric type, and guidelines (and examples) for tailoring them to specific processes via the Reference Model where information about agile decisions is desired. All these generic and specific metrics will be two-part.

The first part will characterize the *context* in which the agility is posed. The second, more simple part will characterize the *response* in cost and time. In other words, agility is the ability or capability to change well (in terms of cost and time) in a given set of conditions; which means that the project must provide a measure of the response in the context of a measure of the stimulus. This will not only measure the effect (ability to change), but also indicate the specific behavior that caused it.

The context issue raises many vexing problems, owing to the diversity involved. The project gets a handle on context by relying on a close understanding of what discrete infrastructure mechanics are involved. It may be that an alternative approach will allow the contexts to be characterized in terms of constraints.

Two of the underlying concepts of agility are scope and robustness. *Scope* refers to how large a domain is covered by the agile response system; in other words, how far from the expected set of events can one go and still have the system respond well. *Robustness* is a measure of how well the system responds, given a specific scope. These two go together naturally. They can be envisioned as a three-dimensional bump on a plane. The plane represents the universe in which the system operates. The height of the bump is the robustness of the system. The nature of the peak is not of interest here, but as one gets farther away from the peak, the system's designed focus, the robustness tails off and becomes flat.

Our project shares several characteristics of this hill. But in almost all cases, the width of what can be addressed within/by a single company is vastly less than can be addressed if VE-type partnering is agily available. Both figure's the height and area covered are very much (over an order of magnitude on some scale) greater if the VE is part of the agility solution. Therefore, we believe that the more interesting case for understanding and harnessing agility is the AVE context.

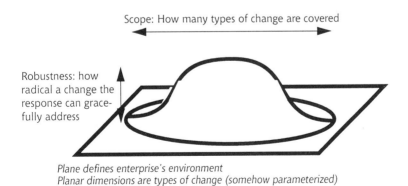

Scope: How many types of change are covered

Robustness: how radical a change the response can gracefully address

Plane defines enterprise's environment
Planar dimensions are types of change (somehow parameterized)

Figure 7.3 The Parameterized Agility of an Enterprise Can Be Seen as a Curve over a Plane

Quantitatively Scalable Metrics

Metrics are quantitative, that is, naturally based in numbers. This contrasts with subjective evaluations which currently characterize the study of agility. A subjective set of measures might be like those assessments that ask you, for example, to rate a factor on a five-point scale. Whether you pick a three or a four is subjective, based on your opinion. Once your choices are made, surveyors like to treat the answers as if they were formally derived numbers. But this is wrong.

Our metrics are formally based—there is a well-established link with the management and information sciences involved. Different persons evaluating the same process using the same methods will produce identical values. These values are denominated in standard units which are commonly used and carry intuitive value to the manager. An unsophisticated manager can understand the metric, while a sophisticated manager should be able to audit the underlying mechanics all the way to the enterprise's strategic measures of profitability and strength.

We can distinguish three concepts of scaling in the metrics. First, the metrics of interest are not process-dependent, nor linked to any specific granularity of processes. In other words, it should not matter whether the metric is applied at the level of an individual process (fine granularity) or at a coarser level, such as a cell or line. The square feet metric as an indicator of lean is a good example: It applies equally from the individual process to the factory; the fewer square feet a process has the more lean it is. An example of a metric that does not scale is quality. The sum of many quality processes does not necessarily result in a quality system.

Second, the metrics also scale horizontally across functions. It is useful that an enterprise component can be evaluated by the same metrics regardless of whether it is a shop-floor process or an administrative service. And third, the metric is internally linear, without discontinuous thresholds. In other words, the difference between a three and a four is the same as the difference between a four and a five. It should not be the case that at some threshold within an interval, the improvement is radical. Of these, the first is most important and the others are highly desirable.

In addition to the caveat just noted, there may be a barrier to the scaling when the process leaves the individual corporate boundary of the individual entity. For example, square feet as an indicator of lean may become relatively meaningless when applied collectively to several companies in VE partnership. This is to say that there might be different metrics or constraints used to measure the agility of a component than to measure the agility of the VE. In particular, the following types of measures may be used (see Figure 7.4):

•Metrics of the agility within a component (a partner)
•Metrics of the agility the component brings to the VE
•Metrics of the agility of the component within the VE
•Metrics of the agility of the VE seen as a whole

Because of the differences in focus, there may be a different set of metrics or a different context to metrics used by the organizing entity than by the partners being organized.

In particular, the scaling limit is probably traceable to when the representations of the features which characterize agility (transactions) are turned into numbers. In the tactical case, the numbers themselves are useful. But a simple combination of the numbers does not convey the same amount of information as a combination of the representations that underlie them. This is the traditional systems optimization problem: a simple sum of agile components may not result in an agile system.

This is why we use a scenario-based conversation breakdown (described in Chapter 11) to capture two elements of agility for a process in each Reference Model's cell: The intrinsic agility of the process and the agility contribution to the system.

Legacy Vs. Heritage

The nature of agility is anticipatory. Cheaper, faster, and better may deal with the situation today, but it is agility (and its little brother, flexibility) that will deal with the situation (ability to be profitable) tomorrow. Naturally, the focus on the ability to change can turn into profit today very quickly—how quickly being a part of the metric.

The relationship between profit today (as captured in lean manufacturing) and agility is an interesting and complex one. A similar relationship exists between legacy as opposed to heritage infrastructure.

Usually, the re-engineering process converts the as-is situation, often called a *legacy,* into a to-be system. Under this view, the legacy represents a barrier, or a collection of problems. Once the to-be situation becomes achieved, all will be well. But the world never rests, and your target usually changes by the time you expect to hit it. Agility deals with establishing the capability to change to a large and constantly changing set of as-is conditions.

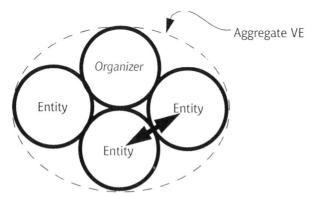

Figure 7.4   Agility within Entities, Among Entities, and of the System

It is useful therefore to define two classes of legacy: the legacy which exists before a re-engineering change is made (using the new term, *heritage*) and the legacy which exists afterwards. The *heritage* is what you inherit from others, for better or worse. Much of the game involves identifying strengths and weaknesses in this heritage and developing an appropriate strategy. A *legacy* is the heritage that you create for the future, with its own strengths and weaknesses. Ideally, the legacy you leave will be more self-aware and capable of leveraging itself than the heritage you are given. The point is that since conditions always change, your solution will never be "right." The answer is to not only make the shot, but to leave the cue ball in a good spot for the next guy.

The metrics of a project are targeted toward understanding the heritage in such a way as to improve the legacy in its ability to change itself beneficially.

Environmental Drivers

The metrics advise decisions. But one would expect that they would indicate generic strategies as well. For instance, it seems to be a tenet of VEs that (under normal circumstances) capital investment should be focused on core competencies and away from skills that can be obtained by partnering. The metrics should reinforce and clarify the limits of obvious principles such as these, but they should also indicate less intuitive general principles.

One secondary area where general principles would be useful is in the area of a VE-promoting environment. Clearly, some environmental factors can make it easier for the type of partnering that drives interesting VEs. Such environmental factors spontaneously appeared to support the whaling industry and may be in place today to some extent in Silicon Valley. It is not the purpose of this project to understand these dynamics; perhaps a follow-up on effort by others is indicated. But certainly, the behavior indicated by the metrics should shed light on the nature of this environment.

For example, much has been made of the legal difficulties associated with the VE. Some maintain that legal barriers are intransigent limiters, preventing interesting Type 1 AVEs from forming. These people maintain that a necessary condition for a VE-promoting environment is the legislative resolution of these and related issues (such as intellectual property rights and security).

We would expect the metrics to help indicate alternative approaches to these seemingly insurmountable barriers. Early thinking has already indicated some threads worth following in the legal infrastructure. The standard response to VE legal agreements is to try to generate generic, plug and play, instant contracts. But it is clear that such instruments either will be overly restrictive in the business relationships, or obese. The FAR (Federal Acquisition Regulations, which are used in the U.S. defense industry) were generated with just this lofty goal of an instant, generic contract in mind. Such thinking is dragging federal acquisition back to the middle ages.

Instead, suppose one focused on a set of ethical principles for arbitration. If these principles were simply based, they could form the foundation for resolving issues as they arose, instead of attempting to resolve all possible issues ahead of time. This tactic could allow for VE-empowering lightweight agreements. It is also a tactic that the U.S.'s significant international competitors cannot implement as easily because we use case law instead of their code-based laws. (Case law is based on this tradition of prearbitration, but the effect has been obscured. The whaling example reinforces this point).

Another, related problem deals with trust. Often, the primary purpose of a heavyweight contract is to mitigate distrust, and a large component of that deals with liability. In fact, the issue is who has to pay for liability insurance (either explicit or internal) to cover which conditions. The legal barrier here actually resolves to a technical requirement. What is needed are VE-sensitive actuarial tools to empower a VE liability insurance business. Probably, this would allow the insurance company to become a member of the VE. The point is, however, that the metrics measure agility, and they, or something like them, should be able to measure trust.

Strategic Links

All intelligent enterprises have a strategy, which represents a balance of profitability today and profitability tomorrow. The latter is a measure of strength and is a mix of customer goodwill, core competency development, intellectual property, market share, employee development, and stockholder value. Each of these has dependencies with the others.

In the future, agility will be added to this list. Until it is, every agility metric must have a direct chain of logic from the individual application of the metric to either immediate profitability or some mix of that and the six just listed.

Early in our project, it was thought that this chain of logic could be shortened. The reason being that the top level metrics (profitability and the six strength metrics) would have already been supported by a strategy. The strategy would have been supported by a set of strategic metrics, including the correct product, cost, quality, and cycle time.

Since the logic chain was presumed to exist between these four and the top level metrics, it seemed sufficient to make the new agility metrics relate only to the four. But it has subsequently been determined that agility is substantially different than the static strategies which support the four strategic metrics. (Correct product, cost, quality, and only then cycle time represents the historical sequence that has become accepted as a useful strategy. The metrics applied are listed in the same sequence elsewhere: cheaper, better, faster.)

The challenge is to provide a clear chain of logic from each of the new metrics, all the way to the top level profitability and strength metrics.

Rules of Thumb

We believe that many decisions that a manager encounters will be identical or similar to situations encountered by others. After a period of time and experience with the metrics, certain rules of thumb will emerge. We consider these rules to be among the best potential long-term products of our project. Managers can apply these rules without going through the effort of evaluation by the metrics.

The subject of agility has been discussed for some years now, and some intuitive results have emerged. For example, many people feel that the more flat an organization is, or the more empowered the work force is, the more agile the enterprise will be. This is probably true in many cases, but clearly not in all cases.

Application of the metrics is expected both to verify these intuitive suspicions and, more importantly, to indicate the scope within which they apply, and the limits of application.

We do not report such rules here. That is a project for future practitioners and consultants. There are a number of different levels from which the rules can be extracted, as shown in Figure 7.5. One can extract rules about strategies that are inherently agile for certain situations. Or one can develop specific processes that are always agile in certain contexts. Finally, one can develop more underlying principles within the enterprise that will be agile; one should find the communicative act breakdown of Chapter 11 useful for this.

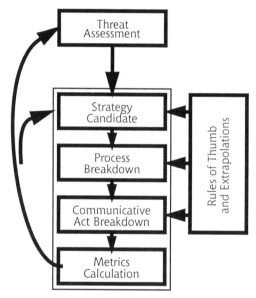

Figure 7.5   Rules of Thumb Can Be Extracted from Several Steps in the Process

Chapter 8

What Agility Is Not

Our experience has been that even after presenting the definitions we use, managers come to us and equate agility with some other practice that they are employing. This is such a common problem that we'll take some time to contrast agility with other trends that are out there.

Before we get specific, the biggest mistake we encounter is the assumption that agility is just being *fast*; if you are fast, it is thought that you must certainly be agile. But agility is something more subtle: You need to be able to recognize a threat, have the resources to address that threat, and then appropriately respond in a timely manner. You will be hampered if you are slow, for sure. But merely being fast doesn't make it. In fact, the key word is *appropriate;* the action must be one engineered to support your goals. Just responding quickly to your customers' desires can be negative, resulting in unproductive thrashing and burnout.

A second common mistake is the assumption that agility is an inherent good. There are lots of enterprises out there that thrive without being agile. And there are managers who think that agility is a single quality and more is better. But we've already discussed that agility is a strategy that is appropriate when faced with change. Not being agile in these situations is bad. But spending your resources on the wrong kind of agility, or an inappropriate level of agility, is almost as bad. The goal is to understand what you need, and engineer accordingly.

LEAN MANUFACTURING AND AGILITY

As we've already mentioned, some agility researchers have proposed that lean manufacturing and agile manufacturing are cut from the same cloth. But that does not appear to be the case. The Chrysler steering wheel case is just one example, and we've found extensive confirmation in industry.

Lean focuses on profitability *today*. Therefore, it works to lower costs, and possibly to reduce time of current product portfolios. Improving quality does not appear to be an intrinsic result of lean, but a result of concurrent adoption of complementary quality initiatives.

Agile focuses on profitability *tomorrow,* with the realization that tomorrow becomes today all too soon. So it focuses on the ability to change in order to improve cost, time, and quality.

Lean is *static,* agility *dynamic.* Our Best Agile Practice Study discovered many cases where lean and agile decisions were contradictory. However, let's look at this more closely; a high value area might be the overlap between the two. For example, many observers believe that flat organizational structures serve both philosophies, and it does appear to be true that flatness is an agile strategy in many contexts. This is interesting because there appear to be some agile moves an organization will make that will cost money (or involve some other kind of compromise), and some that will be free, a by-product of invoking some more near-term oriented best management practice.

The real value of the agility metrics is in understanding the costs and benefits of agile decisions that are not freebies. This may in many instances involve making a business case for deviating from lean decisions in the direction of agile decisions. In making this analysis, we've used the following understanding of lean:

- In the physical and workflow area (Physical Infrastructure), lean means *JIT* (just-in-time).
- In the business practices area (Legal/Explicit Infrastructure), lean means *flat* organizations.
- In the cultural area (Cultural/Social Infrastructure), lean means *empowered, motivated workforce.*
- In the information area (Information Infrastructure), lean means *client-server models* and *standard representations.*

(These infrastructures are a key part of how we define the business enterprise. They are defined in Chapter 10.)

One difference between lean and agile is how they originated. Lean resulted from a focused survey of what was the apparent discriminator for extraordinarily successful enterprises (in the automobile sector). The term lean intuitively fits some of the practices (just-in-time workflows, flat organizations, and a decreased supplier base) and came to be applied to others as well (Total Quality Management, empowered workforce, and a focus on customer needs).

As a result of this origin, lean practices do not derive from any underlying philosophy and they involve known methods and support technologies. Agility is quite different. It originated from an intensive, several-month workshop of business executives who were concerned with a specific need that they knew to be of immense importance to survival, for which they lacked existing methods and underlying technology. So, by definition, agility is an ideal that goes beyond current knowledge. And unlike lean, all agile methods result from a common underlying vision—namely, the ability to thrive when faced with change.

Each community has claimed the other as a subset, but we believe that agility has the stronger claim as being more evolved. Certainly, a complex relationship exists between the two. A compelling argument can be made—and has been—that agile is a logical evolution of lean. Contrarily, it can be argued that, in many dimensions, lean and agile are contradictory; several clear examples are available. Yet a third proposal is that each is equally apt and modern, but they address quite different needs. This is probably the best approach. Lean optimizes processes; agility optimizes the ability to adapt processes to new conditions. This view emphasizes the reinforcing similarities between the two.

Ultimately, this debate has no effect on the methods of this book. We believe all three views have some merit. Often, the difference boils down to philosophical differences so deep they are called religious preferences, or, more reasonably, the strategic goals of the enterprise. Equally often, the views depend upon the communities of interest.

We've come to believe that some sectors are understandably less concerned with agility than others. This makes sense and is proper, because some sectors are currently more stable than others. The tobacco, commercial aircraft, and automotive sectors, for instance, have a very large dependent constituency (for the latter two: airlines, auto repair, and, in both cases, travelers). Their product models take a long time to develop and, once ready, are replicated many times. New models are always evolutionary in almost every respect.

Sectors more likely to recognize agility as important include the defense missile community, entertainment, certain vertical markets for computers, all software, and a huge class of consumer products. So while lean is of interest to many sectors, agility is the dominant concern to a smaller but quickly growing set of businesses.

THE AGILE VIRTUAL ENTERPRISE AND ELECTRONIC COMMERCE

Here's a real problem: The focus of our whole effort is how business units can collaborate. Isn't that just commerce? And since we want to be faster (the mistake made above) and cheaper, doesn't that get handled by electronic, web-based commerce?

We get faced with this question so much; it is a real problem because some of our government and large firm research managers are not the most insightful people around. Slogans sell well with this crowd, and much of the research money goes to electronic commerce projects. What we are talking about with the AVE is a different beast altogether than electronic commerce.

Retail commerce is based on rigid business boundaries. Businesses are entities that are well-defined legally; they make a product (or service) and get paid. Electronic commerce doesn't look at redefining what it means to be a business and what business boundaries make the most sense for investors, managers, and customers. The AVE doesn't shy away from this. The fact is that most business definitions, and the commercial boundaries that support them, are a result of nineteenth-century notions. You make a product and sell it. The identification of customer is *local*, meaning that each business defines its customer needs only in terms of who it sees higher up on the food chain.

For example in the old way of thinking, Dow Corning simply makes silicone and they spend significant resources making sure that potential buyers are aware of their offerings and prices. Electronic commerce is an aid to this, by supplying an on-line catalog which is presumably more up-to-date and cheaper to maintain. Electronic commerce will also lower the cost and speed of placing an order from that catalog, though unless the product is software, it won't speed delivery.

In the new model, Dow Corning is a collection of core competencies and resources, whose primary product is silicone. They function with many potential partners to develop whole new classes of products that employ silicone, or some other component that is in Dow's scope. This does not involve catalog sales; it involves a merging of interests, so that Dow might well be in the business of market research and product chemistry for a new type of shampoo. Electronic commerce doesn't support this. In fact, some participants in the Focus Group considered a focus on Electronic commerce a bad strategy except for their cash cows. The feeling was that a reliance on the nineteenth-century corporate culture of "we are a business, here is a product from our shelves" fights the new, much more profitable model of "we are part of your business, let's create new products." It does so by reinforcing rather than dismantling traditional business boundaries. (A nice example of that is presented in Chapter 10.)

The Focus Group decided that Electronic commerce is a factor primarily in the realm of retail commerce—from the enterprise to the consumer—and it may change retailing forever. But a more AVE-based infrastructure needs to be created in the commercial space of the value chain. This company-to-company collaboration involves a shared effort to reach the consumer, accompanied by product component exchange and supply of services. In terms of dollars, this is a much bigger commercial market than retail sales. Also, our financial services partners believe that they are part of this value chain. If that is counted, there are two orders of magnitude (a hundred to one) between the business-to-business value chain and retail sales.

CALS

The confusion between these two sectors also has some legacy in U.S. Defense sponsorship. The CALS effort began in the mid-1980s as a response to the high costs of supporting weapons systems resulting from poor technical data. Originally named Automated Technical Information, it was renamed Computer Aided Logistics system (CAL), to fit the acronym convention of CAD/CAM. It has evolved through Computer Aided Logistics Support (CALS), in recognition that what was needed was a set of technologies and policies for many systems instead of a single new system, and then Computer-aided Acquisition and Logistics Support, in response to the insight that processes early in the cycle are involved and improved.

Today CALS stands for Continuous Acquisition and Lifecycle Support and lately for Commerce At Light Speed, the latter as a result of reaching out to the commercial sector by including data exchange associated with simple purchasing. In all these incarnations, CALS emphasizes standards as the way to improve the exchange of technical (and associated) data among organizations, in a version of electronic commerce. The primary discriminator between CALS and other standards efforts is the deliberate attempt to accelerate useful standards by imposing them through mandates on new weapons systems.

CALS was originally designed to lower the customer's (the military's) cost by working with primary contractors, essentially the "retail" barrier between the value-chain enterprise and the consumer. It was not designed to lower the cost to subcontractors of doing business, nor to make it faster and cheaper to associate with primary contractors, except for stable commodities. We expected, though, that this would occur as a secondary effect, once the standards involved become widely used and cheaply implemented.

But the opposite has in fact been the case. The requirement to use CALS standards and conventions is just one of a collection of DoD-specific mandates that collectively have forced suppliers either to focus on narrowly satisfying DoD requirements or to give up and abandon the Defense supplier base. So agility in the VE, early in the cycle, is compromised in order to effect savings to the customer's view of the product.

Moreover, since the standards don't look at re-engineering the processes, they have an additional effect of technologically freezing existing, possibly obsolete business processes. Naturally, this further counters the ability to change.

Part of the problem is that CALS takes a fairly unsophisticated view of process integration, viewing it only as lowering the cost of exchanging product data across an existing business or functional boundary. Agility adds the more advanced dimension of looking at process integration in novel business arrangements. Also, agility values the adoption of enlightened management techniques which drive technology, instead of the relatively crude instruments of mandates and official standards.

The bottom line is that the interesting AVE, type 1 or 2, works to break down solid corporate boundaries and collectively create value. Most Electronic commerce efforts reinforce those boundaries (by making them faster and cheaper). In reinforcing the static, they act against agility.

If all EC does is lower the cost or time of conducting business in conventional ways, for example advertising and ordering via the internet, then the order of agility that can be accommodated is low. In order to be interesting, party A should be open to, for instance, having party B's supervisors, equipment, workers, equipment, or processes intertwingled[1] with their own in some creative way so that the VE, in that area, resembles a non-virtual enterprise, a single corporation.

In other words, most other activity in the manufacturing enterprise considers the token being passed between entities in the enterprise is based on product information. The metrics project takes a different view. Since the focus is primarily on the *formation* of the VE, the product is the VE *infrastructure* itself. The focus is on how *processes* integrate, the dynamics of which are somewhat independent of the product data flow. What is sought are similar tokens in the form of process metrics.

There is a similar difference in paradigms between Electronic commerce and AVEs. Commerce's token of exchange is the monetary unit (dollars), and Electronic commerce continues that paradigm. The VE explicitly includes the customer, but it is assumed that the partnership is more intimate (potentially) than a conventional buyer/seller one. As a working definition, the VE deals with integration of processes, even across buyer/seller boundaries (and supplier-chain boundaries). Most Electronic commerce efforts reinforce walls at those boundaries by making them operate faster and cheaper.

FLEXIBLE MANUFACTURING

The difference between agile manufacturing and flexible manufacturing is more straightforward. Flexible is a subset of agile. In particular, flexibility is agility limited to the physical infrastructure, where we measure modularity, scalability, reconfigurability, relocatability; and storability. When we're talking about flexible cells, processes, warehouses; and even relationships, we generally mean to focus on the capital investment. Unfortunately, many of the examples of agility which have appeared are of physical agility, so cannot be differentiated from flexibility, which is not very revolutionary or even new.

Those examples do not constitute interesting situations so far as agility metrics are concerned. The Focus Group developed a working differentiation between flexible and agile: Flexible involves optimizing resources *within* your enterprise to be able to respond to an *anticipated* spectrum of product needs; agile involves the ability to optimize resources within, and to *get external resources integrated into,* your enterprise to be able to respond to an *unanticipated* spectrum of product needs.

The Focus Group developed this differentiation as a defense against uninteresting agility. We were often given as examples the cases of Mack Truck and Levi's. Mack offers many options among the many components of its trucks. The possible combinations are in the millions, so a customer has a very large collection of choices. Levis offers a service where they measure your body and on demand will manufacture jeans especially for you. These are good companies, we suppose, and the examples are good practices, but not interesting agility. What Mack has is a static vocabulary of offerings. If Mack had been agile, they would have been able to leverage their brand name (it is the Harley-Davidson of trucks) to take advantage of the sudden American shift into sport utility trucks, one of the largest optional consumer switches in history. Levi's will make pants custom pants, but they are all pants of a mature design. If they let consumers design their own pants (different cuts, different fabrics), that would be something interesting.

STATIC BUSINESS PRACTICES

If you are a manager, there are a collection of business practices that are so profligate they have passed beyond the buzzword stage into fodder for Dilbert: *activity-based costing, total quality management, business process re-engineering,* and *enterprise resource planning.* All of these share the properties of being applicable if two conditions are met.

1. Your world is stable; whatever you are doing now is what needs to be improved, and then will be quite fine.

2. You understand at a pretty thorough level what that world is all about; what your market is all about, and what you actually do (or need to do) to satisfy that market.

If you meet these two conditions, then all you have to do is refine your processes, by evolutionary re-engineering, to a "to-be" state, by weeding out those that aren't cost-effective, by improving the quality of those that are left, and by automating the process of controlling those processes. We believe that there are few cases where these two conditions are actually met, but we note that most of the world tromps to those drummers. It just makes it easier for agility to be used as a weapon against them. Suppose you've just turned your company upside down tuning it to the nth degree. You're going to want to stick with the status quo, right?

But a little more about the controversy concerning activity-based costing (ABC) and agility. Some believe that ABC is especially well suited to support agility, and there have been DARPA Agile Research contracts that support this view. But from the perspective that emerged through the Focus Group, it appears that ABC, as conventionally understood, is not well suited to aid decisions concerning Agility3.

Traditionally, ABC has been used to take an existing, stable enterprise which is well understood (or understandable) and decompose the costs in a more meaningful way than common accounting methods allow. The result can then be used as a *costing* method to derive the costs of existing products and minor variations on them. More advanced use of the technique can allocate time, risk, opportunity and other measures under the more general rubric of activity-based management (ABM). It is an accounting tool, nothing more. And you know the joke about accountants—they are the ones on the back of the ship who point out the icebergs you just missed.

ABM shares at least one major philosophical point with agility: The emphasis on the activity (or process) rather than on a functional breakdown of the enterprise (as in marketing, engineering, payroll). The latter is an artifact of a paradigm quickly becoming obsolete. You'll see how we build this idea into the reference model presented later. The commonality of this perspective may be what has erroneously brought the ABM and agility communities together. Some ABM-related practitioners use a transaction analysis paradigm that is very close to what is used in the AVE project. But there are problems.

ABM depends on the ability to extrapolate information about change from existing accounting-like data. At the simplest level this fails in the case of situations which benefit the most from agility, those that experience radical change. And there is a fundamental reason for this: ABM (and all accounting) extracts its numbers before the analyses are performed. The original causes and relationships that the numbers represent must stay still in a sense.

Let's put it a different way. It is a game of representations. Some are rich, some not. Simple numbers are not. For example, you can model your business in terms of activities. It makes sense to do your analysis on the models themselves, which is your richest representation. Then abstract the numbers so it makes the results easy to understand (such-and-such will cost so many dollars). Or, you can abstract the numbers out of the models, taking away much necessary context, and then do your analysis on the numbers. Everyone has a story about some dumb decision that was made this way. Don't you?

Even worse, there is no dynamism in ABC numbers; ABC metrics are static, *downstream* in the sense that was discussed in Chapter 7. Moreover, they are *retrospective*. Both of these mean the same thing in the agile context. ABC measures can be used to help understand what has happened, but cannot be used to predict the results of the activities in new circumstances. An upstream agility metric must allow the analysis to be performed on the cogent relationships themselves to produce numbers which are of the cost and time type.

We found other problems as well, though these are secondary in a sense, since the previously noted inadequacy is fatal. ABM depends on accounting-like measures as its atomic unit. It derives costs from costs. But it is very difficult atomically to derive costs from implicit, intangible, tacit activities in the cultural and social infrastructures. Likewise, it is difficult to accommodate non-deterministic phenomenon in the arithmetic functions that form the basis of ABM.

Also, the cultural/social infrastructure is one of the essential components in making agility and the VE function well. The ability to characterize it in an upstream way (understanding the processes) is essential, but is, for structural reasons, outside of the capability of ABM.

Because atomic transactions are captured as numbers, losing functional content, ABM methods are particularly ill-suited for understanding agility in the information infrastructure. The net result is that ABM is one of those methods that appear to be useful for helping one's enterprise to be faster and cheaper, and probably better, but it cannot help with making it more agile.

ABC could support agility. Notwithstanding the structural differences, it appears that ABC could end up being a rule-of-thumb tactic in supporting certain scopes of agility. For example, one of the features that we measure is the difference between how transaction process boundaries are handled. If the VE type is 3 (Supplier Chain) and the infrastructure issue under consideration is business processes, then how reward (meaning costs in this context) is measured means a great deal.

If two processes, one in the prime and one in the supplier, both figure their reward structure the same way, and if the granularity is higher, then the agility will be higher. *Granularity* means how detailed the breakdown of a value-adding process is; the higher the granularity, the smaller the processes. At a low enough level this means that rewards can be allocated at the level of the individual employee. This is not a result of ABC per se; at least, it is not the need for which it was created. Instead, it is a result of ABC being the same on both sides of the business boundary (as well as being consistent and being true).

Concerning enterprise resource planning (ERP), it is hard to imagine a situation where ERP is agile, at least in light of the ERP solutions that are currently being fielded. ERP pours concrete over your business processes.

TECHIE SOLUTIONS

Static business practices can be thought of as consultant solutions. But there is another class of techniques which get conflated with agility. Let's call these the "techie solutions" because they come from the pull of the information technology community. We are not saying that any of these are not useful, or are bad business. Only that they miss the point of agility. In this class we put *concurrent engineering, enterprise integration, product data management,* and *object-oriented modeling.*

Concurrent Engineering

Let's start with concurrent engineering (CE), because that's where we, and the defense research establishment, started a decade ago. The idea was to solve two problems, and, actually, we confused ourselves by mixing up the two:

- •It takes a long time to design a product the old way. That way is a long series of sequential events beginning with the definition of the product. We were working in the jet engine sector, and there are many engineers who have their hands on the design in turn. But it always makes sense for each engineer to "give a little" on their own optimization in order to make it possible for another engineer to do better on their end. For instance, the best design for the thermal guy may make life hell for the structural engineer, so it is best for them to come to a middle ground. And there are dozens of such teams. We wanted to create a sort of virtual lunch table, where everyone could collaborate a little, all more or less at the same time, and come to an optimized design. The goal here was to shorten design time and to get a better design because more options could be tried in the group.
- •The second problem was that regardless of the merit of the design to the engineers, we were seeing many products that, though elegant, were not feasibly manufacturable. If only the manufacturing engineers had been consulted... The goal here was to eliminate the barrier between design of the product and design of the manufacturing process.

It's easy to see how we confused the two. For reasons not cogent to this discussion, they conflicted, which hurt the program. Here's what we learned.

We vaguely knew that most of the money was committed early in the design cycle. By that we mean that major decisions were made, like "we'll make this out of plastic" (instead of aluminum) and this committed a great many other decisions that after a short while could not be undone. In other words, midway through the design, if someone said, "what about aluminum," and could actually make a good case, it was too late. We knew this, and thought that CE would allow things to be undone later in the game than normal. If we had just stuck to the first goal, leaving the manufacturing guys out of the picture, maybe this would have happened, though would still have had unmanufacturable products.

The problem was that the manufacturing guys were smart enough to map what they could do, or could get done, to the product. Once this happens, you need to start committing resources. The reason we couldn't change from plastic to aluminum was because we had already scheduled capability on an aluminum foundry and to back out would have incurred a cost penalty. CE didn't solve this problem; it made it worse.

Concerning the first problem, it turns out that reducing the design time is pretty minor compared to all the other steps in the process that an enterprise must address. For instance, we were worried that it sometimes took 18 months for the military to get a critical, but obsolete replacement part designed and made. It turns out that more than 90% of the time was in paperwork. This is an extreme example, but the typical case is that shortening the engineering cycle is not a great help; often that time is required for financial preparations, so that an accelerated finished design might have to wait for closing on finances. Our CE effort was a bust, at least so far as triggering a revolutionary improvement.

The experience taught us that the sharing of engineering data is easy. What is difficult is integrating design and manufacturing engineers from many companies, including a variety of business factors, and moving them in and out during the process. Added to the simple sharing of engineering data is the problem of recognizing a contribution and properly rewarding that contribution.

We finally evolved to research in support of the AVE. The key thing that we wanted to address was the ability to relax the time that binding decisions had to be made. The reason that we couldn't change from plastic to aluminum is because we had to get our aluminum foundry selected and committed early in the game. Suppose we had an agile virtual enterprise where these commitments didn't have to be made until much later in the game, or could be changed after being made?

So we ended up with the agile manufacturing program, but we went through a period where we thought enterprise integration was the answer.

Enterprise Integration

In Chapter 6 we mentioned SEMATECH, how we formed the Suppliers' Working Group to look at enterprise integration, and how a significant series of workshops dug into this issue. The idea was simple: If we could create an infrastructure that allowed players to plug in and unplug quickly and cheaply, we'd all be much better off.

The enterprise integration community was split into two positions. On the one hand was a top-down system where enterprise integration is accomplished by the means of creating a complete, rational enterprise model. Such a model is expensive, since it is comprehensive and must be constantly updated. Worse, such an approach requires that every player "play by the rules," by changing every single one of their processes to conform to the standard model. The questions here were focused on issues of what language was best for the enterprise model, and how many pieces it had and how did those pieces fit together. Enterprise resource planning vendors emerged out of this position, and indeed this specific activity.

On the other hand, we had the folks who knew that the "master" enterprise model would not solve the problem because it is too expensive and static. Regardless of the difficulty of the EI problem, we sought to define it well enough that we could address the issues in our research. By our second major set of workshops (Kosanke, 1997), we created a capability model for enterprise integration, which is now widely used (Figure 8.1). Five levels of integration were defined, with each level building on the capabilities of the previous one.

- Level 1 is the common situation, where almost every element in an enterprise is integrated with some other element. But there is no general ability to get information everywhere it needs to go.
- Level 2 is the situation where the enterprise is indeed integrated. Information can move as it needs to for good operation. But the cost is that everyone has to use the same information architecture (usually from a single vendor or consultant) and processes and tools must therefore be homogenized. This is the common state for today's integrated enterprises. Modeling makes this possible.
- Level 3 adds an important ability. Where level 2 allows information to flow, this level makes it possible for each process owner to understand how their processes fit into the whole. The information they gather can be used to optimize their process within the context of the whole system. Rational, ordered enterprise frame-

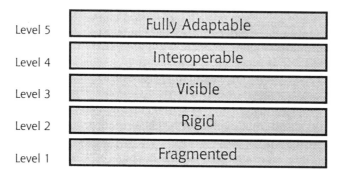

Level 5	Fully Adaptable
Level 4	Interoperable
Level 3	Visible
Level 2	Rigid
Level 1	Fragmented

Figure 8.1   The Enterprise Integration Capability Model

works for models makes this possible. This is currently the state of the art for advanced enterprises of interesting scope.

- •Where level 3 allows a process owner to understand and change her or his own process, level 4 allows a process owner to understand the dynamics of how that process and another process interact within the context of the enterprise's goals. Then it supports the suggestion to the remote process on how to change that remote process. This is a significant leap. It is one thing to optimize your own process for your own goals. It is another to understand the enterprise well enough at a high level so that you can optimize your process to those goals, even if it suboptimizes your local goals. This level allows you to understand not only the enterprise at a high level, but the enterprise at a detailed level, so that any combination of processes can be considered as a group and change so as to benefit the whole.
- •Level 5. Here, you can not only understand how a remote process should change (and presumably suggest those changes), you can actually (within some guidelines) *make the change.* Think about this a minute. It means that you no longer have control over the design of your process; if, collectively, your process needs to change to benefit the whole, the whole can actually change your process!

Levels 3 through 5 (and all the supporting definitions) support what we now call the AVE, and what was fleshed out by another workshop (as we described in Chapter 5). In a sense, what we've done is redefine the concurrent engineering agenda so that we are designing and redesigning both the product and the enterprise concurrently. So, the EI agenda evolved to become the technical component of our AVE program.

We'll take a moment here to note two other "techie" solutions that AVE infrastructure makes obsolete, product data management and object-oriented modeling.

Product Data

Much of what happens in the manufacturing enterprise considers the token being passed between entities in the enterprise as based on product information. This is a natural perspective in some sectors, especially the aerospace and automotive industries. The product data standard STEP (Standard for the Exchange of Product data) is based on this paradigm.

The problem that STEP was designed to solve was the ability to share computer-aided design among systems from different vendors, but only within a single discipline. For instance, it did not support the CE-inspired requirement of, say, thermal engineers sharing models with assembly engineers. It used a complicated methodology to specify a common language that had to be used. A problem with this was that each vendor used a proprietary representation not because they were trying to bring chaos to the world, but because that representation allowed special advantage to the user. Forcing them into a lowest common denominator forces the user to toss that special environment. We audited a major aerospace company that standardized on, and extensively exchanged documents by, STEP. The result was that essentially every engineering group was forced to use less than the optimum tools, to a measurable detriment to the product. In fact, we are aware of firms who are structuring themselves with their exclusion of STEP as a competitive advantage.

But if STEP is so bad, what is a better approach? The artificial intelligence (AI) community faced the very same problem. Different representations are created in products from different AI vendors, and there is a need to exchange these. Instead of creating yet another neutral representation, the vendors took a more sophisticated approach. They created a way of formally defining how things are represented. Then, when machine A sends something to machine B, it sends the information in machine A's form, and also the common language description of how machine A represents things. The mechanics are not important here, but that information allows machine B to sort things out. No one is compromised.

But the product data management community is substantially less sophisticated because their heritage is from the document management community. All this is to say that a great many people see the AVE as merely an integrated enterprise, and they see the integrated enterprise as one that exchanges and manages product data through STEP. We hope it is clear that we mean something else.

Object Orientation

The workshops that created the enterprise integration capability model dropped a real bombshell. They stated what in retrospect is common sense. There are some problems in life that are amenable to small evolutionary steps—the walk-before-you-run theory. Of course, in this approach everyone works the simplest issue first, by definition avoiding the hard problems.

And then there are the problems which are *not* amenable to evolutionary approaches. This is the group that says learning to walk may have nothing to do with, say, space flight, and a focus on walking might create a legacy that makes the ultimate goal harder. EI is this kind of problem. If you create a solution for level 3 EI, it not only won't help you with level 4, but will create a legacy that makes it much harder to advance to level 4. You really need to bite the bullet and address the hardest problem you can first, because its solution will change all the little stuff you otherwise would be working on.

A number of examples were given to the group, but the one that's worth mentioning here is object orientation. This is a really good idea in the area of developing programs. The problem was that the majority of all programming projects failed because of their complexity. In response, the programming community came up with a way of hiding complexity in programming elements called "objects." Objects are nice in that they are black boxes, you don't have to know what goes on inside, only what their external behavior is.

It works. It is good for application development. But there's a problem: The making of models for managers and enterprise engineers is quite different than building programs, though many of the same underlying principles can

apply. Object-oriented methods are so popular that without critical examination, they are being used in the modeling arena as well. And this actually can
help build level 3 EI services. The bombshell is that object-oriented methods
are a barrier to creating levels 4 and 5. They are actually a negative! The reason
is that objects hide their internal dynamics, but those dynamics are extremely
important for levels 4 and 5. We want to know not just that a certain outcome
results from a process; we want to know why that outcome happened. We want
to know the causal mechanics involved. Later on, after we deliver to you some
practical tools, we'll readdress this.

The bottom line is that if the AVE is part of your future, you're going to
need some awareness that is different from what you already, for possibly good
reason, are doing with activity-based management, business process re-engineering, concurrent engineering, electronic commerce, current notions of
enterprise integration, enterprise resource planning, flexible manufacturing,
lean manufacturing, object-oriented modeling, product data management or
total quality management.

NOTE

1. We are assured that every book has to pretend to coin a new word to be a success, so here's ours. The correct accompanying hand gesture is to intermesh your fin-
gers across your palms; they have to wiggle, and both thumbs should be up. The word
was to our knowledge first used by Ted Nelson to describe a particularly advanced
vision of hypertext.

Chapter 9

Issues

Time out for a roadmap check. Now that we have some more precise definitions of what we need, we turn to providing tools to satisfy those needs. In this chapter, we outline the strategy at a very high level and present the limits of the approach.

A TOOL STRATEGY

We need a set of tools that have all the capabilities that have been outlined. There are two key characteristics among those presented. First, agility is something you do *in addition to* other things, instead of *replacing* other things. The tools and methods should be rather flexible so that you can add them into the mix of your current tools without having to reinvent them. Second, our goal is to *engineer your enterprise* for agility. The tools can't be vague efforts at team building and awareness., they have to be solid techniques that present facts and reveal underlying dynamics.

We assume that you already have a strategy and market intelligence. You must know who you and your customers are and what you want to do. You must have a general idea about the nature of the change to which you wish to respond. In the ordinary case, this will be market-oriented, but we see many cases where the response is to niches in international regulation, monetary policy and new process technologies. The tools we provide do not help with this, but we developed a structured brainstorming tool that the Focus Group to assist in this phase. It will be reported in a future publication.

We really only come into play after you have a strategy. Our tools have three parts:

1. A breakdown of the whole world of your enterprise. You might use this in strategy development to understand yourself and your enterprise. But in the tool strategy, it is a way of defining and focusing in on a few critical processes that will define your agility barriers and your levers. Chapter 10 covers this strategy in detail (the Reference Model is also defined), along with several examples. This strategy should integrate well with existing methods.

2. The key processes need to be understood in some detail and modeled. Chapter 11 shows a way of modeling these. In this chapter, we use a somewhat unfamiliar modeling method because it illustrates the theory behind the metrics. If you already have those processes modeled using a well-founded modeling method, you can still use the metrics, subject to limitations.

3. Chapter 11 also outlines the theory we employ, and shows our method of computing the metrics, together with examples. We also talk about costs.

The last chapters show how we have extended this general method to measure trust, which is on-going research. Finally, the agenda for what's next in AVE research is outlined, followed by a description of what computerized tools are available.

SUMMARY OF THE METHOD

We focus on analyzing processes to evaluate their agility, their ability to adapt. We have developed a method to do so, based on associated methods which are required to support certain needs. What goes into this evaluation are models of ordinary processes within an enterprise or across partners. What comes out are numbers or functions which indicate the time and cost of change. These results could be used in one of two ways.

1. A pair of processes are compared (resulting in the time and cost of changing from one to the other). For example, you have two or more suppliers (or processes) and know what their cost, time of delivery, and quality are, and you want the relative time and cost of change. For instance, you are designing a product and have tentatively decided on making it from plastic. You have a bevy of suppliers that you want to lock in early because of production coordination (or some other strategic need). You know which is the best supplier if you go with plastic. But there is a very real chance (your product engineers tell you) that you will go with aluminum, perhaps even in mid-production. It may be that the partner which is the apparently cheapest one if you do not change would be very expensive comparatively when encountered with this need to be agile.

One agile response would be for the selected partner to have the ability to manufacture in both materials. Another would be that the partner has the ability to locate an alternative partner and to transfer requisite design information and bow out cheaply. In fact, there are a variety of agile responses out there. What you want to do is evaluate all your potential suppliers for the time and cost of change. Then you can add that in some way (depending on your strategy, how likely you think the change will be and how critical it will be) to the other metrics you use in selecting your partner.

2. Evaluation of a single process against a threat or a spectrum of threats to determine how agile the process is. For example, suppose you have a critical process in your enterprise such as a costly painting/finishing process for an auto part. Several threats could challenge that process (these are from a real case):

- Environmental regulations change that force you to modify the paint, a solvent, or some worker protective action;
- A subsidy in another country is targeted to attract specifically that process and you want to consider moving that and related operations to take advantage of the subsidy;
- An attractive, much cheaper new electrostatic painting process is being used by your competitor;
- A recent strike forced new featherbedding union rules that greatly increased costs; or,
- You discover that the painted product is a safety hazard because it releases carcinogens when the car is left in hot sunlight.

All are potential threats that you have brainstormed; none are real yet. What you want to do is re-engineer that process so that you are minimally impacted if one of these things actually does happen. The metrics can be used to evaluate the time and cost of adapting from an existing process, or potential process design to a new process that can deal with the new threat. With the metrics you are able get to evaluate the cost of the change compared to the cost of the changed situation.

To amplify: Suppose you are painting at $5 a unit and one of the threats happens. Some changes that you could make result in the items costing an amount that amortizes to 50¢ a unit and end up in a process that costs $6 a unit (including the cost of change). A different change might amortize to $2 per unit but end in a process that costs $2/unit. You'd want to know this, and how disruptive the change will be.

Most of the corporate users employ the metrics in the first mode, but more than half of the users in nonprofit sectors use the second mode.

Modeling

The bad news is that the metrics can only be applied where process models exist, or can be created. Where processes are not modeled, the models must be created. Where explicit models are difficult to capture, as in many important social interactions, the behavior must in some way be captured.

The good news is that essentially any modeling method can be accommodated, so planners and managers can incorporate agility considerations in models and tools created for other purposes. Moreover, an agility analysis only requires models of a few key processes in the organization, so incomplete existing models can be relatively cheaply supplemented in order to add agility considerations.

Concerning social and cultural change, Chapter 14 provides an approach that utilizes new formal methods developed under our effort. These can be used to sufficiently characterize explicit behavior whose causal processes are unknown.

The process we follow is simple at a high level. We start with models, the collected models of various processes, which incidentally can be modeled by diverse methods. And we end up with models; metrics in the formal view that we call *parametric models*. The method we develop is a transformation of the input model into the output.

We do this in large measure by constraining the input model in three steps. The three filters we use are intuitively describable:

1. Infrastructure breakdown. Here we force the process decomposition to fall into a standard parsing of the Virtual Enterprise. This normalizes the input models and directs the focus to the creation and change of infrastructure, the core phenomena of interest. The research we have done in this effort is novel, and it results in rigorous definitions of agility. But it could have been done by others. There could be some mild controversy here concerning our focused use of terms that others may use in more loose ways.

2. Communicative acts. This forces the representations into a standard form that sets up the next step. It results in a normal form that directly relates interaction with tools by others, by agent-based approaches, and by repositories of cases and agile processes. This research is adapted from others (Longacre, 1976; Parunak, 1996; Winograd & Flores,1988), and rests on well established, non-controversial foundations.

3. Agility features. This third filter is the most novel; it extracts five complexity measures from the processes that pertain to agility. It employs some advanced mathematics in its most complex form, as an input to strategic planning/simulation systems. But we have also developed a simple arithmetic method that requires no special skills or automation support for common situations.

LIMITS OF OUR APPROACH

Modeling for Utility

The approach that our project has taken depends heavily on modeling science; much of the attention has been oriented toward understanding the nature of the modeling approach and the resulting parametric model, the time and cost metric. What goes into the Reference Model is, by design, intuitive and simple. What comes out of the model, the time and cost information, is also by design very simple.

Constraining the design of the approach this way resulted in a "black box" of the features model being somewhat complex and non-intuitive. The term *modeling* is often used explicitly to capture and display processes and/or relationships. Often, the value of the process is in making things explicit and displaying the results so that relatively non-technical users can see what is going on. In other words, making the graphic display of the model clear, usually takes priority over the computability or formal utility of the model. We have opposite priorities: Essentially no effort is going into visualization of the features at this point, and everything into making them computable. The model is essentially a black box so far as the user is concerned.

In part, we make up for the need for visualization by presuming a precursor model. A user will ordinarily model their organization using techniques that are already in use for other management needs. The understanding of the processes from visualization is presumed to be provided by this precursor model, since we believe that the nature of agility is so different that it won't, by itself, be apparent.

Necessity for Strategic Modeling

The original intent of our project was to pursue two uses simultaneously, tactical and strategic. *Strategic* users would evaluate many options and a very large number of features to structure many elements of the enterprise. For example, a prime contractor would develop a strategy which accounted for agility, advising on the design of the supply chain: What gets bought and what factors govern. The result would include what agility features are of interest, what the relative weighting of those features would be, and the degree of agility desired in each of those features.

The *tactical* user is an empowered decisionmaker working later in the life cycle and implementing the strategy. For instance, a middle manager may be evaluating which of several suppliers support the enterprise's agility goals. This manager deals with a much simpler case than the strategic one; there are simply fewer variables. But there is a more fundamental difference in that the tactical manager is presumed to have the guidance, the agility requirements, set by the agility strategy. It appears that we cannot use the metrics in any meaningful way tactically without such a strategy.

This is another limit of the approach, at least tactically, and is a result of the unavoidable truth that *all agility is strategic at root*.

Second-Order Agility

We went back to many of our best practice examples to evaluate whether the metrics would have been directly useful. We were surprised to find many cases of second-order agility which were not captured in the original approach.

Second-order agility is a result of those actions that do not directly follow from the existing state of the enterprise. A second-order effect would appear if an early response to a change fundamentally changes the enterprise's ability to respond. For example, consider the simple case of physical agility in equipment and the simple dimension of increased capability. A first-order measure would consider the ability to increase the output of the existing equipment.

But what if the supplier has an outstanding order for new equipment which they accelerate as a result of the new demand. This is meaningful agility that is not apparent from examining the capability of the existing physical system alone. But this capability, the ability to order and quickly incorporate new equipment, can be captured if at the system level.

The lesson is that the knowledge that is captured must include features from a system-wide perspective. Our initial belief that local analysis would have some incremental benefit was false; in order to get any appreciable value, the features need to be evaluated system-wide.

The resulting constraint is that the metrics are not incrementally implementable. In fact, since the social and cultural factors have been excluded from the first phase of the research, the interim metrics are incapable of fully exploiting second-order agility. This limit on the approach also results from the fact that *agility is essentially a strategic, system-wide set of capabilities, not a state.*

Possible Lack of Quantitative Information

In future research, we intend to develop a modeling technique to insure the correctness and completeness of the knowledge capture process. But, until then, we have to depend on existing modeling techniques, under the assumption that enterprises will want to use information that is already captured, or to use methods with which they are familiar.

We need information that is captured in quantitative form, together with all of the relevant causal relationships. Both characteristics are desirable for the integrity of the approach. But we find that such information rarely exists in cheaply accessible forms, much more rarely than we initially thought.

Most quantitative information suffers from the accountant's syndrome: Effects are measured, usually in the form of time and cost, but the complex causal relationships that a robust model would capture are lacking. Another problem is the nature of the existing models where some dynamics and inter-relationships are captured. Models fall into one of three types: descriptive, qualitative, and quantitative. The first type are the most common and the least useful for our purposes. Usually, they just display relationships as an aid to help managers think more deeply than they otherwise would.

Our site visits revealed very little in the way of existing quantitative information, which means that the information collection process could be more expensive than originally thought. The good news is that the approach overall is tolerant of the type of input. One cannot get high integrity quantitative information out even if only descriptive information is fed in. But some coarse analysis can be done with notional, descriptive information so that one can determine where more apt information gathering is profitable. Therefore, this limit of the process is not so severe.

Agility and Evolution

The final limit on agility is perhaps the most basic. The concept of engineering agility is a radical idea which is already eminently useful in many sectors. But its radical nature can be a disadvantage. Agility is a simple concept to understand in theory, but conceptually it can be difficult to apply to specific cases. Four years of activity by the Agility Forum has underscored this difficulty.

The actual identification of agile needs or behavior in a specific application is the only major step that has thus far eluded us in pinning down a rigorous, comprehensive definition. Identifying such needs appears to rely on some art in the eye of the analyst as well as some fearlessness in abstraction. For example, according to the way we describe it, the whaling industry was agile, with some of its core competencies surviving to the present day and forming the basis of our largest contributor to balance of payments (movie making). But all that would be scant comfort to the by-passed candlemaking enterprises, to whom the whole affair appeared quite brittle. In the SEMATECH example, the idea that the manufacturing goal was in the fab (their term for the factory) and not in the chip could not be adhered to even after initially adopted by the sponsoring group.

We offer the following insight: Some problems in identifying agility behavior or needs boil down to insecurity about whether agility is a tool to *maintain* an accustomed *evolution* (in effect, the status quo), or to *enable* a directed *revolution*.

If an automobile company looked at agility as a technique merely to improve its competitiveness without fundamentally re-examining itself and what it does, it may have trouble coming to terms with what agility is. It will most likely see agility as much like other productivity/profit maximizing techniques, such as those collected under the rubric of lean.

If, on the other hand, an industry is undergoing revolution, and a company is looking for a way to continually reinvent itself, to change in order to take advantage of change, then agility is easily applied. The questions then become less intransigent, and the needs are more apparent. We believe that the aerospace defense community is unavoidably in such a revolution, and so is an apt candidate for agility.

The U.S. automotive industry (including workers, industry suppliers, and the follow-on repair market) is instead in the mode of working to preserve large, stable institutions and practices with a minimum of change, so they will likely perceive agility in a more limited way.

Essentially, it is a question of whether one merely reacts or intentionally builds an ability to adapt. We, of course, are promoting the latter. The underlying issue is whether the cost of much evolutionary change is actually less in real terms than the cost of possibly-small changes based on revolutionary analysis. Each enterprise must make that evaluation for itself in considering the engineering of agility.

Environmental/Social Measures

A final word on management methods that may not be so intimidating. We assume here that a primary goal of the enterprise is to be profitable. In fact, many of the case studies, especially those of the Suppliers' Working Group, were non-profit enterprises. Everything we mention here applies to non-profit organizations, except some of the details of the specific metrics we provide, which measure things in terms of cost.

But the fact remains that for-profit enterprises also have an effect within the fabric of society. In most cases, we find this as a constraint. For instance, a chemical company we worked with is a good environmental citizen, not because it is a moral good, but because regulations and public opinion make it bad business to not be so.

We do see enterprises where a need for agility derives from different goals, like our project with the Special Forces. And we've seen non-governmental organizations whose mission is to do good, and agility works well there too. In fact, the VE mechanics are probably cleaner because the risk/reward equation is simple.

We mention all this because we often get asked about the effect of the for-profit AVE on society. One way the AVE could be formed is that people and talents are pulled in and sloughed off at random times. This could be a bad scenario. Who handles medical insurance, pension, continuing education, and such? This question comes up in a different form in the Defense business since the point is not to create weapons per se at any social cost, but to ensure security for citizens.

AGILITY FORUM AND A3 AGILITY

We use traditional agility terms where appropriate, but it is important to note the few differences that might exist with assumptions of prior research and study by others.

The Agility Forum over the past four years has developed different sets of descriptive terms for agility. Some of those sets are more popular than others. Even though our vision of agility is quite a bit broader, it might be beneficial for our metrics if straightforward links with those terms and concepts are made. It certainly will register the metrics better with those accustomed to using those terms.

Problems arise, since the many existing terms are general and not formally definitional. That is, it is possible to find examples that fit all the terms but are not examples of Agility3 agile systems.

In one set of definitions (Preiss, Goldman and Nagel,1996), the Forum used the following four characteristics to define agility: Solutions provider; Collaborative production; reconfigurable organization; knowledge-driven enterprise. These characteristics don't discriminate between agile and non-agile cases with sufficient crispness on which to base the formal metrics studies. Therefore, our definition of Agility3, pure agility is a subset of what the Forum has taken as its charter. The difference, we believe, is simply that we've avoided the many good business practices that are not unique to agility—*the ability to respond to change.*

Nonetheless, the AVE Focus Group worked to make a mapping from a Life Cycle Dimension of the AVE Reference Model of the next chapter to descriptors that the Forum has developed for Agility1.

Older Agility Forum Study

Another legacy of agile terms has come from the Forum-sponsored Best Agile Practice Survey (Dove, 1995). This vision deals primarily with manufacturing processes, tools, and resources. Social and business process issues exist only to support change in those domains. This view is fine-grained, focused on individual items, practices, and tools. An implicit assumption in this vision is that agility is additive; a sum of agile tools and methods will result in an agile enterprise.

We look at the broader context; agility concerns any type of enterprise, though manufacturing has the most general utility. Its scope includes very early phases in the opportunity, and continues as late and as deep as the enterprise reaches. It includes all processes, not just those related to manufacturing. This vision looks for systemic principles and concerns itself with agile infrastructure.

A useful exercise is to reconcile these two approaches through the metrics. As a preliminary step, the terms of the Forum's Best Agile Practices vision need to be redefined in the context of our results.

The best practices study used four dimensions of agility that describe end benefits. They are cost, time, robustness, and scope. We find great value in these, but do not consider them as being in the same class. We've heard strongly, from our potential user base, that agility metrics need to be in terms of the time and cost of effecting change. The other two dimensions are part of the descriptions of the context. In other words, we expect that a manager will ask, given a specific context (which includes scope and robustness), what is the time and cost of a specific change. Time and cost are related by a function, so one of these will also be a constraint, depending on the situation. You may have constraints on the cost of the product but have freedom on how long it takes to address the customer need. Or it may be the other way around, with speed-to-market being the driving factor.

Our use of the term *context* is intended to subsume scope and robustness. Context is the characterization that is determined by strategic studies that specify the type and extent of agility of interest. For example, one context may be the agility associated with supplier contract arrangements, the scope being the ability to change from a specific small number of contracted units to a larger, specific number. We might be interested in the agility of that context. But if the larger number were twice as large, a different scope, a different agility metric would result. (Incidentally, we've discovered that some things which are agile in one scope are comparatively less so in a different context.) With this understanding of scope, the time and cost function captures the notion of robustness.

A second set of legacy characteristics from the Best Agile Practice Study is called the *eight change domains of agility*; they describe characteristics of agile tools and methods. They are creation, capacity, capability, reconfiguration, migration, performance, improvement, and recovery.

Our metrics do not use these as definitional of agile systems. Instead, we understand these to be expected characteristics in certain situations as brainstormed by bright people based on intuition. In their place, we expect that rules-of-thumb will appear from the use of the metrics. These should mirror and validate the cited change domains but with the applicable context.

Chapter 10

The Agile Virtual Enterprise Reference Model

We are now ready to begin a journey into the new tools and methods. Our first stop is a way of breaking the world of AVEs into smaller pieces. The good news is that one reason we do this is because only a few of those pieces need to be well understood for our purposes. But a well-founded breakdown is useful for anyone wishing to understand the relevant dynamics. Our support group, the Agile Virtual Enterprise Focus Group, devised the model that present in this chapter.

The Reference Model is a simple matrix, or table. Along one side are the decisions that are associated with all the life-cycle processes of a Virtual Enterprise. Along the other side are what we call *infrastructures,* or areas of application within an enterprise. Such areas, for instance, include your contractual and workflow infrastructures.

A useful characteristic of the Reference Model is that the defined pieces, the cells of the table, are all of the same "size." This is important. In particular, we require:

- •That there be a standard level of granularity for each complete process (each table cell). While many of the simpler uses of the metrics do not depend on such a standard granularity, the more interesting ones do (the trending and pattern matching of processes, for instance).
- •That process dynamics be cleanly segregated. This means that we cannot mix worlds that operate according to different principles; truth, for example, follows different laws in legal, physical, and business process domains. The same is true

of many principles. We avoid having to understand, manage, and map the differences if we carefully separate them.

The reference model is of the world of VEs. If certain things are done well within the processes the model describes, it will be an *agile* VE. Table 10.1 shows the major headings of the Reference Model. Don't be intimidated by anything that doesn't look familiar.

The vertical columns provide an important breakdown concerning the *infrastructures* of the VE, the major categories being Physical, Social/Cultural, and Legal/Explicit, the latter including Business Processes, Workflow, and Contracts/Regulations. The row headings focus on decision points. For clarity, two more levels of detailed breakdown are necessary for the columns and one for the rows.

Decision Point Breakdown:

Opportunity Identification
    Opportunity Strategy
    Opportunity Exposure
    Targeted Marketing
    Search
Partner Identification

Table 10.1 Major Headings of the Reference Model

	Social/Cultural: Human Dynamics	Social/Cultural: Community Cultures	Social/Cultural: Business Culture	Legal/Explicit: Business Processes	Legal/Explicit: Contracts/Regulations	Legal/Explicit: Workflow	Physical: Logistics/Warehousing	Physical: Equipment	Physical: Laws of Physics
Opportunity ID									
Partner ID									
VE Formation									
VE Operation									
Reconfig/Dissolution									

Opportunity Strategy
Partner Performance History
Partner Search
Virtual Enterprise Formation
Vision/Strategy Development
Partner Criteria and Selection
Enterprise Metrics
Capitalization
Product Liabilities
Risk/Reward Strategy
Operating Strategy
Dissolution Plan
Virtual Enterprise Operation
Performance Metrics
Customer Relations
Operating Practice
Virtual Enterprise Reconfiguration/Dissolution
Identification of Need
Residual Liabilities
Dissolution Plan

Infrastructure Breakdown

Social/Cultural Infrastructure
Social and Psychological Laws
Community Cultures
Business Culture
Legal/Explicit Infrastructure
Business Processes
Strategy Development
Supervise Risk/Reward Process
Supervise Engineering Quality
Work Scheduling
Depth of Customer Relations
Legal/Regulatory
Quality Assurance Agreements
Risk/Reward Contracts
How the Virtual Enterprise Is Represented
Assignment of New Technology
Labor Agreements
WorkFlow (Business Plan)
Planning Work Breakdown Assignments
Work Breakdown Responsibilities
Monitoring/Adjusting the Work Breakdown Structure
Arbitration/Adjudication

    Routine Exception Handling
Physical Infrastructure
  Warehousing and Logistics
    Virtual Enterprise Human Collaboration
    Virtual Enterprise Product Collaboration
    Customer's Pipeline, Product
    Customer's Pipeline, People
    Raw Commodities
  Equipment
    How Modular
    How Reconfigurable
    How Scalable
    How Relocatable
    How Storable
  Physics
    Geographically Limited Processes
    Scale Limited Processes
    Attention Limited Processes
    Time Limited Processes
    Accident Limited Processes

Definitions for this model have been freely and widely available in several formats, including at the Agility Forum's web site. We'll define each of these lines in detail in a moment; the important point is that it gives a structure for analysis such as our first target, agility metrics. Each cell in the model deals with a discrete decision (the horizontal rows) and involves a specific, discrete set of principles (the columns). Each of the cells defines the scope, type, and dynamics of a specific process or candidate process that a VE might be considering.

The number of cells can seem daunting at first, but, fortunately, this is not bad news. By studying best practices, the group discovered that successful agility strategies focused on a very small number of cells: one or two major focus cells, a half dozen or so support cells, and a few cells in which incompetence could create problems.

This was counterintuitive; we expected that agility would be a result of high scores in many cells, but that was not the case. Moreover, the cells that anchored a strategy varied widely, reflecting different leveragable strengths, business strategies, and market peculiarities. So there are few generic rules of thumb, no dummy list for painting by agility numbers. But for each strategy, only a few cells need to be modeled, as we've described above. This factor tends to make the system-wide evaluation of agility inexpensive.

Consider Table 10.2. Of the large number of possible cells to consider, using the art of consulting skills, we selected 20 that were likely to host an agility strategy for the example that we will step through later. This was done by comparing results from all of our case studies. The company is a real company, a defense aerospace prime contractor that we'll call Consolidated Aircraft. The numbering system will be explained later.

We wanted to show you this early because we want to underscore a point. Most consultants appear at your door with some sort of breakdown of the enterprise. In order to take advantage of their tools, you need to populate, in some detailed and expensive way, huge areas of the reference model in order to use their method or tool. That is not the case here. So far as agility is concerned, only a few cells matter. Less than 2% of the enterprise needs to be understood in detail in order to get complete results.

Since we've mentioned this big advantage, let's mention the biggest downside: While the AVE Reference Model is intuitive and simple, it is not the way most enterprises see themselves. Also, by identifying the process at this level to define the communicative acts (the next step), you need to fold in the agility strategy and, implicitly, your organization's understanding of the nature of change. These are matters that middle-level managers, one important target user community, may have trouble envisioning.

Also, interesting and useful agility involves partners, often suppliers. These suppliers are used to answering questions about how much things cost and

Table 10.2 Twenty High Value Cells

	C. Legal/Explicit Infrastructure a. Business Processes e. Depth of Customer Relations	C. Legal/Explicit Infrastructure b. Legal/Regulatory b. Risk/Reward Contracts	C. Legal/Explicit Infrastructure c. Workflow c. Work Breakdown Structure	D. Physical Infrastructure a. Warehousing/Logistics a.a. Human Collaboration
1. OPPORTUNITY IDENTIFICATION 3. Targeted Market				
2. PARTNER SELECT 3 Partner Search				
3. VE FORMATION 6. Risk/Reward Strategies				
4. VE OPERATION 1. Performance Metrics				
5. VE DISSOLUTION 1. Identify Need for Change				

how long it takes. They now sometimes answer questions about quality, but many may not be equipped to reveal process dynamics at the level we need. These three factors push the cost of using the metrics up.

We will discuss in detail on how expensive it is to address these problems. In other words, we'll detail how much it actually costs to use the tools to get agility metrics. Short answer: Not very much compared to other common tools being used for other strategic needs.

THE REFERENCE MODEL

The conventional views of the enterprise as a collection of *functions* (personnel, manufacturing, etc.) or *resources* (people, machines, intellectual property, etc.) are not particularly useful in considering agility. Instead, what is of interest are decompositions based on value-added processes and capabilities to provide that value-addition.

Toward that end, the life cycle of the VE has been broken down into its major processes. Each process involves decisions; these decisions use tools and methods which are informed by our metrics. Each of the categories and subcategories capture the process involved when a decision is made. A decision in this context is one that involves cost and commitment.

The model is usually represented as a matrix at its high level categories. The rows are key decisions, the columns are infrastructures. First we describe the processes. These are organized by the life cycle of the VE, from birth to death (see Figure 10.1). The major breakdown is roughly chronological, but the subdivisions are not.

Then we define the infrastructures. Differences among infrastructures require some special attention by the reader; a more rigorous breakdown and definitions are used here, and some terms may differ from their more informal meanings. The goal is to tease different underlying mechanics into different categories; for instance, the things that bind a VE culturally are quite different in nature than those that tie things legally or by business processes. The importance of making these distinctions pays off later.

In both axes of the model, we worked hard to fit all manner of business models and market sectors. The model at the high levels has been validated in a wide range of for-profit enterprises. The lowest level of detail in the infrastructure is domain dependent; details of aircraft enterprise infrastructures differ from those of movie or food sectors, for instance.

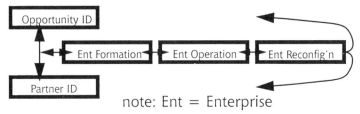

note: Ent = Enterprise

Figure 10.1 Major Life Cycle Categories

Finally, we give some examples of specific process decisions, specific cells in the matrix, which might be made by an enterprise. There are five main categories of life cycle processes, each with subcategories.

Process Category 1: Opportunity Identification

This category assumes that some agent, either a potential lead for an AVE or some tentative collection of contributed experts, has the charter to identify, refine, and/or characterize the opportunity. This could be a broker who has no capability cogent to the AVE's operation. The simplest case is probably the most prevalent today: Identification and refinement of an opportunity by one firm that has a key relevant core competency. That firm seeks to fully understand the characteristics of the opportunity to define the requirements of the AVE that must be formed in response.

Processes in this first category may proceed simultaneously with the those of the second, Partner Identification, with a better understanding of the capabilities of a future AVE informing an understanding of the market/opportunity. As an option, simulation (virtual manufacturing) can be used to support both of these two categories.

Opportunity Strategy

In order to identify an opportunity, the identifying agent needs to have a strategy. The strategy must be explicit and well reasoned, because results from the strategy need to be understood and adopted by potential members of the AVE. There should be no question of principles in the strategy; otherwise, each potential member would have to independently conduct their own analysis. The formation of the AVE would be unnecessarily encumbered.

Within the strategy, there should be a means for protecting the disclosure of details of the opportunity to potential partners, because full disclosure could mean empowering a competitor. The assumption is that market information will be distributed among firms, at least in the Type 1 AVE, so that a combined overview must be synthesized from several sources.

Relating to the above, early in the entire process there must be a consistent understanding of who is the lead for the AVE (at least for this phase). There may be brokers and consultants involved who are specialists in the strategy. The strategy should be based on a consistent method for defining and determining core competencies. There will probably be a simple relationship between characteristics of the opportunity (as defined by the strategy) and core competencies of the partners.

The strategy also needs to incorporate a vision of what constitutes success. This definition of success will form the basis for many of the processes that follow. Finally, the strategy must have a way of determining whether the opportunity is a strong candidate for being addressed by a feasible AVE. At this point, the AVE criteria are probably unknown.

Example attributes of this process that would make it agile would be:

•Responds quickly (appropriately fast)

•Forward, panoramic, view of market opportunity
•Explicit, well reasoned, and consistent process for opportunity ID/assessment
•Continually assess opportunity and competition
•Accommodates continual and unexpected change
•Repeatable method for applying competency definitions to partners

Exposure

Independent of the strategy (which is analysis oriented), there needs to be a collection of actions. This and the remaining subcategories represent various types of actions supporting opportunity identification.

The lead should have an exposure mechanism and use it to inform the customer(s) that there is an intent to address the opportunity. Ideally, the customer would have a role in the AVE. Simultaneously, actions must be taken to expose intent and information with potential partners. How this advertisement occurs may be different in the future. For now, it is likely to be critical in successfully forming the AVE and addressing the opportunity. It may be that an entity will advertise its intent to address a class of opportunity rather than a specific opportunity.

Agility will result if the exposure can be to many customers, for many trial situations, at low cost. It is also essential that fast action can be taken when the situation looks promising. Such speed infers that a pre-AVE situation can be evaluated by sufficiently high confidence metrics to commit resources.

Example attributes of this process that would make it agile would be:

•Multiple mechanisms to inform/expose customers (internal and external) that there is an opportunity and an intent to address the opportunity
•Individual core competencies advertised

Targeted Marketing

There is a collection of actions that may actually intervene in the marketplace to help incubate or firm up an opportunity. This process is where the customer becomes integrated into the AVE at an early stage to incubate conditions. The process will be more sophisticated than opening a communication channel, since many customers may not know what could be possible, or may not have recognized changing conditions.

This process includes the actions that clarify the needs and match them to core competencies in the AVE, effectively defining the need for AVE partners. The result is a solution in response to the need. The lead may go through a process of educating the customer(s) to help create the demand for an opportunity. Perhaps the definition can be directed to maximize the competitive advantages addressed by the potential core competencies of the AVE.

An AVE will almost certainly include the customer in the partnership in some way beyond a buyer-seller relationship. Ideally, some core competencies in the customer base will be leveraged to advantage.

Example attributes of this process that would make it agile would be:

•Insight to changing key buying factors
•Initiator may educate the customer to help create the market demand for an opportunity
•Leverage competencies

Search

Sometimes the opportunity is not apparent, as is implied in the two sub-categories noted above. Regardless, each firm (or stable partnership) should be constantly searching for new ways to leverage its competencies. Therefore, there will be a set of processes that scours new, perhaps unconventional markets empowered by new partnerships. This collection of processes will vary depending on the sector and the creativity of the organizations.

Apparently, the search in the AVE context will assume capabilities from new partnerships. These will come either from strawman partners or generic capabilities. There needs to be science employed (based on the strategy) in order to evaluate tentative opportunities. Because the costs of AVE are different from non-AVEs, this science (however implemented) may be a key competitive tool.

As with Opportunity ID: Exposure, an AVE will be simultaneously investigating many possibilities, including very unfamiliar ones. It will leverage many short-term relationships with various potential partners at reasonable cost.

Example attributes of this process that would make it agile would be:

•Simultaneous investigation of many possibilities
•Continue to scour new, even unconventional; markets utilizing novel analytical techniques
•Electronic opportunity search for possible solutions to current needs or problems that could lead to new products
•Use stakeholders to identify possible leads

Process Category 2: Partner Selection

This category generally addresses the selection of partners. Types 2 and 4 AVEs assume that the partnerships pre-exist, so they will largely omit this category. Types 1 and 3 may choose to perform these actions in parallel with the opportunity identification and crystallization because it could reduce the costs associated with the strategy and improve the relationship with the potential customer. But nominally the business decisions will be first associated with identifying an opportunity, then a partnership team.

Type 1 partners are envisioned more as partners, compared with Type 3 relationships, which may resemble traditional supplier relationships. It is currently debatable how distinct these two types of relationships are in the AVE context.

As in Category 1, an AVE will be promiscuous, forming and dissolving many partnerships among a large portfolio at low cost. The partnerships will have loose couplings, being limited only to the need to address the opportunity well. This might be accomplished by having each partner tend to be self-organizing in the context of the Virtual Enterprise. And it may be aided by some partners' migration of organization-building tools from prior AVEs.

Partner Qualification

As noted in Opportunity ID: Opportunity Strategy, there will be a strategy that can be commonly shared, and which has a standard method for defining core competencies. Also, the core competencies required by the opportunity will have been identified. This process concerns revealing, with a high level of confidence, the core competencies of candidates, together with other key business indicators.

A method is required for applying the competency definitions to partners. Problems could arise due to dishonesty and variations in the definitions. While core competency evaluation must be determined, there are other factors to qualify: Quality, technical, capacity, and financial criteria. These criteria will be evaluated somewhat differently in an AVE context than in a traditional context. There needs to be a quick, cheap method of getting this information with sufficient fidelity.

There may be methods for prequalifying partners, one of them being the reliance of a third party to precertify them. A question of liability arises from mistakes or misrepresentations made during this process. There must be a process to address this issue of accountability.

Overall, there must be available a class of metrics that address the ability of a firm to enter into an AVE, independent of the value its competencies bring to the AVE. This measurement will reflect *the ability of an AVE to form quickly and flexibly.* There also needs to be an independent class of metrics associated with the level of agility the firm will bring to the AVE during its life, *the ability to support agility in the AVE,* external to the firm. There may also be a third class of relatively independent metric that measures the agility within the internal operations of the firm, the *agility in own processes.*

If there are no qualified partners, or if an unqualified partner must be included for some reason, then there must be a provision to make that partner qualified.

Example attributes of this process that would make it agile would be:

- Evaluate factors such as quality, technical, capacity, financial criteria; must be done quickly and cheaply yet maintain sufficient fidelity
- Provision to make a potential unqualified partner qualified
- Minimum requirements (information system, communications, resources, etc.) identified as existing, needed, not needed

Partner Performance History

A key issue in forming AVEs is the matter of trust. This collection of processes facilitates trust. A method is required to reveal a partner's history based on proven quality, delivery, and other criteria. A related method is required to determine which of the traditional and new measures of a firm's history is cogent to the AVE. There could be a single AVE profile, or this could be situational.

This subcategory is differentiated from the previous one by focusing in on specific, historic information. The previous category spans many strategies for qualification. This one is concerned with data from the past. Special analytical tools will be required to map past situations to the current one since it is presumed that the situations will widely differ.

One agile strategy will be the sharing—possibly selling—of information among current and past AVEs. Historic information may be a sustained asset of dissolved AVEs, or there may be a new infrastructure. Generally, the issues are the same as with the prior subcategory.

Example attributes of this process that would make it agile would be:

- Has trust been demonstrated in specific areas, such as proven quality, delivery, ability to deal with/operate, and to share share/sell information without violation of trust
- Ability to apply/map past performance to new situations (look at historical data: Safety, strikes, performance responsiveness)
- History of face-to-face handshake (informal) agreements being trustworthy
- Is the potential partner able to form and dissolve many partnerships at low cost, relative to input?

Partner Search

The two previous processes presume that some candidates have been evaluated, but it is likely that a more exhaustive search for candidates will be desirable. It is advantageous to have multiple methods for searching for candidates, but it is an open issue of which are the best search criteria or search forums. It is debatable whether a firms' self-presentation will reflect the appropriate criteria. In other words, it is unknown whether widespread AVE formation depends on a not-yet-developed search infrastructure.

An agile lead will have strategies to search out many potential partners. Potential AVE partners will be agile by making themselves easy to be found and evaluated.

Example attributes of this process that would make it agile would be:

- Initiator should look both internal and external to the walls of the company— *outside the box thinking*
- Multiple methods/technologies (intelligent agents, brokers, etc.) for searching

Process Category 3: Formation (Business Case Development and Commitment)

Having identified the opportunity and partners, the AVE must fully build the detailed business case, make the multiple commitments required, and form the AVE. There are a substantial number of issues concerned with this process. To a large extent, everything until this point has been performed with the purpose of building the business case and making the commitment. It is at this point that major resources are committed. But it is also true that the AVE (in all its infrastructure) must be carefully established in ways to insure success in the future phases (operation and dissolution).

The key to agility in the Virtual Enterprise is in this category. An AVE will, in addressing the formation process, exhibit several agile attributes. The most notable are: Reusability (in infrastructure components from prior AVEs); scalability (in escalating core competencies of partners to the AVE as a whole); self-organizing (in distributing the binding infrastructure among the partners); and loose coupling (by lowering the cost of removing partners as conditions change).

Vision/Strategy Development

The AVE has to be founded on an explicit statement of purpose. This can be built on the foundation of the strategy noted in Opportunity ID: Opportunity Strategy. The strategy is likely to be mission-based and differ from the host organization's strategy in being based on partially temporary infrastructure. The strategy must incorporate a sense of the life-span of the AVE, how it is going to change in response to expected conditions, and how it is going to institute agile practices for unanticipated change.

A particular AVE will have to accommodate new types of agile practices, not needed in each host organization. The vision will have been presented as an early template for determining the feasibility of the specific AVE. While more detailed decisions related to formation are noted below, they should all relate to this vision. Unanticipated events/conditions may change some of those implementation details, so this vision is needed as the constant core. Included in the vision are some basic principles about the overall goals and roles. Agility will be seen in how readily and robustly the vision can be developed and shared among the partners.

Example attributes of this process that would make it agile would be:

- Explicit statement of purpose; built on the opportunity strategy; mission-based modified strategic plan
- Incorporate a sense of the life-span of the AVE
- Agreement on how to handle both anticipated and unanticipated change, including continual competition assessment
- Continual customer assessment (new and old)
- The customer will have a role in the AVE ownership (for example, Boeing involving the airlines in new aircraft specification)
- A common set of ethical standards (Code of Ethics) not legally binding, that is an expression of the values which facilitate an environment of trust and cooperation

Partner Criteria and Selection

This subcategory's process is the actual selection of and commitment to partners. In an ideal case, it should fall out of the processes that precede it. However, it is possible that things will not have proceeded in an orderly, slow fashion to this point. So there need to be a collection of catch-up processes of filling in the gaps and clarifying all the roles. This process is based on the go/no go decision and involves implementation details about the relevant infrastructures.

Agility will be seen in how quickly resources can be committed to close the partnerships with specific candidates. The commitment will be dependent on the agility exhibited in Category 2: Partner Selection.

Example attributes of this process that would make it agile would be:

- Core competency tradeoffs among AVE members for time and cost
- Go/no go decision shared quickly throughout the initiating organization and partners

Enterprise Metrics

Part of the formation process is in determining the metrics to be applied across the AVE. These will be based on traditional financial and operational metrics. They should be capable of identifying change downstream; that is, they should be capable of determining not only whether goals are being met, but also to anticipate problems/changes. Certainly, there are overlaps between these metrics and the agility metrics noted in Partner ID: Partner Qualification. One can be conceived as a subset of the other.

Note that the metrics of this subcategory are not the more general set of metrics addressed by our metrics project. Instead, these metrics deal only with the relationships and interactions that need to be addressed in forming the AVE by integrating processes from diverse sources. Agility will be exhibited not in the acceptance of these metrics, but in their facile use.

Example attributes of this process that would make it agile would be:

- Consistent roll-up (summing up through higher levels of abstraction) of heterogeneous metrics across the AVE
- Capable of identifying change downstream
- Anticipatory in nature

Capitalization

This process deals with the detailed determination of who commits what capital (and other assets) and with the commitment of those assets. It means that new financial/legal infrastructure must be created. Where intellectual property is involved, this needs to be evaluated as a contribution. It will be necessary to set the method by which the value of intellectual property (and other dynamic assets) is determined as the AVE is operated and the value changes. As with most of the allied subcategories, agility will be seen in how quickly, competently, and cheaply the processes are conducted.

Example attributes of this process that would make it agile would be:

• Better, faster, cheaper financial/legal infrastructure
• Dynamic assets—recognition that value may change

Product Liabilities

This process deals with assignment of all anticipated liabilities, including those which are improbable. This process also creates new legal infrastructure, which is related to the capitalization subcategory. Included in the process is the scoping of warranties: Who is responsible for what and how the warranty profile is presented to the customer. Note that there is a separate class of liabilities associated with the process (ecological or social suits, for example) that are not bound to the product. These are addressed elsewhere. Agility will be exhibited in the legal infrastructure. Speed and cost are not issues here; instead, the problems concern accurate anticipation.

Example attributes of this process that would make it agile would be:

• Assigned responsibility for anticipated liabilities
• Accurate anticipation for all potential liabilities is the key—not speed and cost

Risk/Reward Strategies

The previous two processes are related to contracted *commitment*. This process focuses on determining *rewards* in detail. Presumably, risks and rewards will be defined with reward based on risk; risk is one of the metrics that must be captured in the subcategory on metrics which follows contribution (see Formation: Enterprise Metrics). Those metrics should be capable of identifying failure modes as a way of assessing negative reward.

The process should accommodate the reality that the risk contribution may not be naturally reflected in a dollar amount. Examples include: name, image, goodwill, and market intelligence. Included in the risk metric should be a threshold at which the dissolve/reconfigure processes of Category 5 (Reconfiguration and Dissolution) are triggered.

In addition to the speed, correctness, and cost issues normal to Category 3, agility in an AVE will be improved if the risk/reward structure is itself agile, and thus capable of responding to change.

Example attributes of this process that would make it agile would be:

• Establish an atmosphere that all are viable value-added members of the business
• Inter- and intra- dependency/results

Operating Structure

The processes of this subcategory address the creation of the *operational* infrastructure to be used in the AVE. Infrastructures need to be created to support the relationships which partners have with one another. Reporting and supervisory relationships need to be established. The hierarchy of partners needs to be explicit. How top management spots are filled and with whom need to be determined. It may be that a role unique to AVEs needs to be established: That of scorekeeper/adjudicator. This role may be supplemented by processes that anticipate and neutralize conflict, possibly through team-building activities.

An AVE will be agile in its formation if both the aggregate and components of the partnership can bring the operating structure up quickly and cheaply. The resulting AVE will be agile in operation if the partnership has been designed with agility in mind. As a result, this subcategory provides the bridge between agile formation and agile operation.

Example attributes of this process that would make it agile would be:

- Permits intra-AVE member learning, leadership, team building, brain storming, empowerment, etcetera.
- Minimum corporate leadership, maximum AVE teams cooperation; profit and loss responsibilities at the team level within member companies
- Potential scorekeeper/adjudicator established

Dissolution Plan

AVEs (certainly Types 1 and 3) are presumed to be temporary, based on a specific opportunity. Therefore, a dissolution plan must be devised and the infrastructure for dissolution built into the AVE when it is created. As one necessary component, a trigger or threshold needs to be set to establish when the opportunity of the occasion for the AVE ceases to be productively addressed.

As mentioned in the introduction, a Virtual Enterprise must have this plan in order to be agile. The best practice expected will be in an AVE that has clearly thought out the plan and contingencies above and beyond a simple intent to dissolve.

Example attributes of this process that would make it agile would be:

- Built into the creation of the AVE
- Trigger/threshold established for Dissolution/Reconfiguration: Identification of Need

Process Category 4: Operation

Having established the AVE, it must be operated. It should look like a single organization from the outside. That is, the operation should have an external view that looks like a conventional organization. But there are likely to be operational factors unique to the AVE. These may be similar or identical to the operations of a large, decentralized manufacturing company (as in automobile or large aircraft enterprises).

Performance Measures

This collection of processes will implement metrics that measure individual components at the microlevel, the lowest level at which the strategy of the AVE is concerned. But these should combine at macrolevels: One of which are the enterprise metrics of Operation: Capitalization. Therefore, these metrics support the predetermined risk/reward structure. Some AVEs may integrate processes to the extent that boundaries between firms are blurred. In this case, the AVE's performance measures take on the additional responsibilities of managing tasks normally the purview of a member firm.

Agility in operation can occur only if managers can understand what is happening both within the AVE and within its context. A best practice would have in place sufficiently clear metrics to enable the manager both to understand and to control dynamic conditions.

Example attributes of this process that would make it agile would be:

- Responsive to dynamic conditions that require real-time or near real-time performance measures
- Federated metrics
- Delineation of AVE member boundaries required to identify bottlenecks, delays, etcetera, in order to maintain accountability

Customer Relations

The AVE must appear as a unified organization to the customer, so processes must be established to support this transparency. Presumably, some of the risk/reward structure will be based on customer satisfaction. This necessitates a metric that measures satisfaction and assigns traceability to the proper component. Processes have to recognize and ideally to measure intangibles such as goodwill. Also desirable are processes that support giving back to the community, society, and environment.

Conventional agility is supported in an AVE that has agility in this respect. By being in touch with the customer, presumably by their membership in the AVE, market changes can be better anticipated and understood.

Example attributes of this process that would make it agile would be:

- Processes to support transparency of the AVE; looks like one entity to customer
- Metric to measure customer satisfaction in order to assign within the risk/reward structure

Operating Practice

Once the AVE is up and running, in important ways it should function as if it were a single organization. Boundaries between firms should be minimized, so the processes used in some types of AVEs will be managing certain processes within the AVE's components instead of merely administering boundaries between firms. This subcategory is intended to incorporate all the best agile practices from other studies relating to agility in a single corporation.

However, there may be additional practices unique to the AVE. All of the best agile practices associated with the agile operation of an enterprise are incorporated here by reference.

Example attributes of this process that would make it agile would be:

• Integrated processes across the AVE's components to maximize process synchronization
• Continual ingraining of the virtual thinking at all levels of the AVE
• Scalable, reconfigurable, reusable

Process Category 5: Reconfiguration and Dissolution

At a predetermined point, the time will come when the opportunity has been fully satisfied or otherwise changes. It will then be time to dissolve or radically reform the AVE. This point is presumed to be mutually understood within the AVE, and may be tracked by a metric.

Moreover, that point probably is well outside the normally encountered dynamism addressed by agility practices of the previous category. However, reconfiguration may be a normal agile response in some types; for example, Type 3, Agile Supplier Chains. If the AVE is to be reformulated, this process will feed back to the first category.

It appears clear that agility here cannot be created; it has to be inherited from earlier processes as described, particularly in Operation: Dissolution Plan.

Identification of Need

The AVE will have predefined sunset conditions related to the situation of the initiating opportunity. A process is needed for monitoring those conditions, with special metrics in some cases, to identify when the formation of the AVE needs to be revisited. This process will trigger (and provide information for) fundamental change of both the nature and the structure of the AVE.

Once again, agility is tied to metrics. The metrics central to this process derive from the environment (*see* Opportunity ID: Opportunity, Strategy and Operation: Customer Relations) and the predetermined plan (*see* Formation: Vision/Strategy Development, Formation: Partner Criteria and Selection, and Operation: Performance Measures).

Example attributes of this process that would make it agile would be:

• Revalidate assumptions of predefined, mutually understood criteria for dissolution or radical reformation
• Human decisionmaker supported by intelligent decision aides coupled to trigger matrixes. The trigger matrix in this case is the matrix of all factors upon which the AVE was founded. Each will have a satisfaction metric. Some will be satisfactory or not, and it is time to review the status of the AVE when some combination of these dips into an unsatisfactory profile.

Residual Liabilities

Whether dissolved or reconstituted, there needs to be a set of processes to identify and assign responsibility for residual liabilities. Examples would include warranties, environmental concerns, employee benefits, and product liabilities. Note that even normal operations or changes in the AVE may require liability reassignments. It is possible that the assignee might not have been a partner in the AVE; it may instead be a partner acting in a new role, or it may be one or more successor AVEs. As with all issues in this category, the agility will have already been built in by this time, in the legal and social infrastructure.

Example attributes of this process that would make it agile would be:

- Validate assumptions and execute predetermined processes to identify and assign responsibility for residual liabilities based on current opportunity; this process may require a total rethink of the original plan
- Assignee may not have been partner in the AVE (may be partner acting in a new role, may be one or more successor AVEs)

Asset/Equity Dispersal

A series of processes are required to distribute assets and equities. This is similar to the liability assignment. But whereas liabilities are not precisely quantifiable, assets and equity should be, so the processes are likely to be more metrics-based, cost-based. However, assets could also include intangibles such as goodwill. This subcategory does not include profits dispersal, since that should have been handled in normal operations. Moreover, assets form the basis for reconfiguring or otherwise reconstituting the AVE.

This subcategory, as with the preceding one, will be addressed by previously determined agile mechanisms. However, both need themselves to be agile to respond to unexpected conditions in the dissolution, such as catastrophic failure.

Example attributes of this process that would make it agile would be:

- Validate and execute predetermined process of dispersal
- Dispute resolution, if necessary (mediation, arbitration, court system, etc.)
- Metrics or cost-based

INFRASTRUCTURE ELEMENTS

Infrastructure forms the second axis or dimension of the model. The idea in this breakdown is to separate the different dynamics that bind the AVE together. In agility considerations, we focus on the coupling of different entities in the enterprise. The laws and behavior of workflow differ fundamentally from those of, say, safety regulations, so we strive to make the differences clear in the model.

Unfortunately, some of the terms we use for these infrastructures are also used in functions by others to mean different things. There doesn't seem to be any way around this, since all the useful words have been overloaded, so careful definitions must suffice.

Information Infrastructure

This is not the collection of your computers and phones! Information infrastructure is a fundamental infrastructure dealing with the nature of communication. This is not to be confused with the arrangements for automated support for the other infrastructures. Automated support is implicitly in the other categories; for instance, computerized workflow support such as modeling and operating control systems are considered components in the Legal/Explicit Infrastructure: Workflow area.

This infrastructure deals with the underlying means for communication and coordination, and includes verbal, written, and graphical notations and the logics and abstractions which underlay them. The project has some results in notations and information-theoretic (meaning situation-theoretic) approaches to describe and partially understand the mechanics here. Since these are not engineerable at the VE level for the individual enterprise, we ordinarily do not include this infrastructure.

The addition of metrics to the disciplines of enterprise engineering and operation is at this level.

Social/Cultural Infrastructure

The infrastructures discussed in the next section deal with dynamics in the enterprise which are implicit while the two listed here are defined explicitly; elsewhere we call this the *soft* (meaning not fully explicable) infrastructure where the others are *hard*.

Social and Psychological Laws

This subinfrastructure concerns behavior that seems to be built in: certain personality types, interactions, and reproducible group dynamics. Some enterprise engineering can be accomplished here, but the understanding of the laws involved is relatively crude. Engineering often consists wholly of the evaluation and selection of individuals and teams that collaborate.

An example attributes of this infrastructure that would make it agile would be:

- •AVE leadership is attentive to and leverages basic patterns of human behavior, group dynamics, and individual/team motivation

Community Cultures

The community culture subinfrastructure deals with influence and communication networks and associations which are driven by identification with factors such as nationality, ethnicity, race, and gender. Many other identities are involved: club, religious, class, political and trade affiliations are examples.

Example attributes of this infrastructure that would make it agile would be:

• Methods for readily tailoring processes, contracts, and workflow to leverage special cultural strengths and weaknesses (e.g., Korean vs. Mexican autoworker schedules)
• Methods to proactively identify potential work flow descriptions due to cultural differences

Business Culture

Business culture is a special kind of community culture that may cut across (or federate) many communities. It is unique in being sustained, possibly consciously generated, by the enterprise.

An example attribute of this infrastructure that would make it agile would be:

• Synergism of business processes leveraging the diversity of business culture (allows heterogeneous cultures in the AVE)

Legal/Explicit Infrastructure

This infrastructure is defined by processes that are explicit and possibly engineered in the enterprise. *Explicit* means that they are articulated somewhere; it includes processes that deal with how the business is run, who manages whom, and who makes what decisions. The rules that influence job descriptions are included. In the virtual enterprise, this concerns who does what in supporting interactions.

Business Processes

The Business Processes subinfrastructure deals with such processes as the risk/reward system, the supervisory and monitoring relationships and ownership of various elements of the enterprise.

Example attributes of this infrastructure that would make it agile would be:

• Distributed ownership of the strategic planning process, including spread into the customer base
• Distributed responsibility for customer relations and modeling expectations
• Flexibility in how the monitoring for rewards is handled
• Ability to recognize and leverage risk by a partner when the reward is AVE-wide
• Ability to reconfigure supervision of product/service quality/completion
• Ability to redistribute who does what and when in terms of actual value-added
• Support system for innovation is established and in place

A more specific breakdown can be made. At this level, we find that the details vary according to different business models and market sectors.

Strategy Development: The conventional business strategy that would be included in a business plan, concerning specific approaches to markets, competition, partners, etcetera. A key component of this infrastructure is who owns/can adapt the strategy.

Supervise Risk/Reward Process: Addresses the explicit plans for who gets paid how much for what. A key factor is who owns/can change the risk/reward process.

Supervise Engineering Quality: Deals with who owns/can change the processes that match customer demands for quality with the VE's processes, and what the processes are to provide that supervision.

Work Scheduling: Who decides and can change who does what within the VE.

Depth of Customer Relations: Addresses who is and what processes are responsible for understanding, dealing with, and satisfying the customer. Includes the processes to change the customer and how they are dealt with.

Legal/Regulatory

This subinfrastructure concerns the processes that deal with legal instruments. Internally, these would be contract clauses; externally, they would be codes, laws, and regulations. Example attributes of this infrastructure that would make it agile would be:

- The ability to simultaneously manage different models of culture
- Use of contract templates based on case law and other precedents
- A proliferation of agents to fill legal needs of discovery, certification, and indemnification
- Flexibility in how contracts support fluid and flexibly scoped (e.g., partner vs. AVE) risk/reward scenarios
- Flexibility in who is the customer (e.g., licensing by Disney moving from films to tapes, parks, toys, etc.)
- Flexibility for how intellectual property is managed during and after the activity of the AVE
- Pre-determined, pre-prioritized dispute resolution processes.

A more specific breakdown of contracts and regulations concerning specific responsibilities and process follows:

> *Quality Assurance Agreements:* Involved with measuring, monitoring, and guaranteeing the quality of each partner's effort in the context of the VE.
>
> *Risk/Reward Contracts:* Associated with how each member gets reimbursed (or receives other benefits) for benefiting the VE. Naturally, penalties for harming the VE are included.
>
> *How VE Is Represented:* How each member contributes to the relationship with the customer.
>
> *Assignment of New Technology:* How new intellectual property gets developed, used in the VE, and used outside the context of the VE.

Labor Agreements: How the VE deals with workforce issues that are normally covered in continuing institutions; such as pensions, insurance, and continuing education.

Work Flow (Business Plan)

This subinfrastructure includes processes that are explicitly defined to determine the sequence of tasks. It differs from Business Processes; that group deals with processes in the enterprise that affect product (or service); this group deals with processes associated with the product that affect the enterprise. Physical Infrastructure: Warehousing/Logistics deals with physically determined procedures/rules; this group's rules are defined by business needs.

Example attributes of this infrastructure that would make it agile would be:

•Adaptability in who does what and when among existing and potential partners
•Adaptability in who tracks that performance
•Distributed responsibility for handling complaints and researching improvements
•A robust mechanism for handling exceptions to facilitate open communication
 A more detailed breakdown of the processes include:

Planning Work Breakdown Assignments: How the tasks of the VE are decomposed among the various partners to the benefit of both each partner and the VE.

Work Breakdown Responsibilities: Who is responsible for what tasks in the VE. The previous group dealt with planning, this deals with performing.

Monitoring/Adjusting Work Breakdown Structure: Who in the VE is responsible for monitoring the task distribution once the VE is in operation, and adjusting the assignments as conditions change.

Arbitration/Adjudication: How complaints are handled and controversies resolved, presumably early in the game.

Routine Exception Handling: How unplanned exceptions (other than those involving reassignment of responsibilities) are handled.

Physical Infrastructure

This infrastructure encompasses processes that are governed by physical laws.

Warehousing/Logistics

This subinfrastructure deals with issues associated with the movement and storage of goods, equipment, and personnel. Example attributes of this infrastructure that would make it agile would be:

•Real-time inter-operatable tracking system

•Location of human and physical assets independent of ownership or paymaster
•High-speed, low cost of document movement for generation/change (it's primarily a physical ownership and movement problem)
•Ability to sustain a high number of opportunistic meetings (unplanned encounters and self-directed agendas), which includes surrogates for physical collocation
such as electronic communication
•Redundancy of facilities and network creates lack of dependency

A more detailed breakdown of these attributes include:

VE Human Collaboration: How people gather and interact to support the
VE. This includes surrogates for physical collocation such as electronic communication.

VE Product Collaboration: How various non-human resources of the VE collaborate as if they were collocated, for example, as virtual workcells.

Customer's Pipeline, Product: How the flow of components and services
which constitute the product of the VE is physically linked to the customer.

Customer's Pipeline, People: How the individuals in the VE communicate
with the customer.

Raw Commodities: How raw materials which feed the VE flow into it.

Equipment

This subinfrastructure deals with physical resources (including facilities)
employed by the VE to accomplish its goals: Doing the task as well as creating,
sustaining, and changing the VE. Agile processes within this infrastructure
would be shared by a Flexible Manufacturing infrastructure model. Example
attributes of this infrastructure that would make it agile would be:

•modular, reconfigurable, flexible, relocatable, maintainable, and scalable equipment, skill sets, and team
•multiple sources of equipment

A more detailed breakdown of equipment and related processes includes:

How Modular: Common and standard interfaces so that equipment-related
processes can be defined in an encapsulated form as objects or agents. This
allows reconfiguration of collections of such processes.

How Reconfigurable: Individually reconfigure to perform a range of functions.

How Scalable: Support an increase in load, throughput, or complexity.

How Relocatable: Can be relocated from one site, cell, or VE partner to
another.

How Storable: Can be easily and cheaply set aside and recovered when
needed.

Physics

This subinfrastructure deals with those processes that are narrowly constrained only by some law of physics; for example, assembly sequences or geographic factors that effect properties of the materials. Example attributes of this infrastructure that would make it agile would be:

- Lack of dependency on processes that cannot be scaled for physical or time reasons (2.5 micron chips need clean rooms
- Epoxy curing requires a large autoclave and a set, long curing time)
- Lack of dependency on a source of raw materials (not the case with paper mills, aluminum smelting, raisin growing)
- Lack of dependency on a customer's fixed location (not true of fire stations, congressional lobbying, concrete plants)
- Lack of dependency on physical presence to detect an instant, short-lived need (unlike slogan tee-shirts for demonstrations)

A more detailed breakdown of the processes:

> *Geographically Limited Processes:* Tied to certain areas. For instance, ore smelting is limited to proximity to mines or aircraft servicing is limited to airports.
>
> *Scale Limited Processes:* Tied to certain physical scales: for example, semiconductor fabrication is highly defined by feature size limits or certain composite wing sections are constrained to the size of curing autoclaves.
>
> *Attention Limited Processes:* Influencable only if you are in the right time and place. Many market-creation activities (promoting shoes at the Olympics, reporting the news are obvious examples) depend on having alert agents when and where it counts.
>
> *Time Limited Processes:* Tied to certain physical time scales; for example, brewing, farming, and servicing life insurance.
>
> *Accident Limited Processes:* Depend on unpredictable (or nearly so) happenstance. Examples might be disaster recovery services; or fabrication of jewelry using extremely rare gems. Note: this is a type of process that presumes a competence in agility.

INFRASTRUCTURE OBSERVATIONS

Numbering

In most of the previous discussion, we chose not to include the numbering system because it might cause confusion. The lifecycle processes form rows in the matrix, the usual form of the model, and the infrastructures form columns. A standard numbering system that has evolved for lifecycle processes is:

1. Opportunity Identification

1.1 Opportunity Strategy
1.2 Exposure
1.3 Targeted Marketing
1.4 Search
2. Partner Selection
   2.1 Partner Qualification
   2.2 Partner Performance History
   2.3 Partner Search
3. VE Formation
   3.1 Vision/Strategy Development
   3.2 Partner Criteria and Selection
   3.3 Enterprise Metrics
   3.4 Capitalization
   3.5 Product Liabilities
   3.6 Risk/Reward Strategies
   3.7 Operating Strategy
   3.8 Dissolution Plan
4. VE Operation
   4.1 Performance Metrics
   4.2 Customer Relations
   4.3 Operating Practice
5. VE Reconfiguration/Dissolution
   5.1 Identification of Need
   5.2 Residual Liabilities
   5.3 Dissolution Plan

The rows (infrastructures) use an alphabetic scheme. The focus of the metrics project was on infrastructures C and D below, so they have been expanded to a level appropriate for evaluating an agility strategy. Note that at this level, the three digit level, the breakdown is domain dependent. The breakdown here is typical of our case study, a conventional defense aerospace supply chain.

A. Information Infrastructure
B. Social/Cultural Infrastructure
   B.a Social and Psychological Laws
   B.b Community Cultures
   B.c Business Culture
C. Legal/Explicit Infrastructure
   C.a.a Business Processes: Strategy Development
   C.a.b Business Processes: Supervise Risk/Reward Process
   C.a.c Business Processes: Supervise Engineering Quality
   C.a.d Business Processes: Work Scheduling
   C.a.e Business Processes: Depth of Customer Relations

C.b.a Legal/Regulatory: Quality Assurance Agreements
C.b.b Legal/Regulatory: Risk/Reward Contracts
C.b.c Legal/Regulatory: How the VE Is Represented
C.b.d Legal/Regulatory: Assignment of New Technology
C.b.e Legal/Regulatory: Labor Agreements
C.c.a WorkFlow (Business Plan): Planning Work Breakdown Assignments
C.c.b WorkFlow (Business Plan): Work Breakdown Responsibilities (WBS)
C.c.c WorkFlow (Business Plan): Monitoring/Adjusting the WBS
C.c.d WorkFlow (Business Plan): Arbitration/Adjudication
C.c.e WorkFlow (Business Plan): Routine Exception Handling
D. Physical Infrastructure
D.a.a Warehousing/Logistics: VE Human Collaboration
D.a.b Warehousing/Logistics: VE Product Collaboration
D.a.c Warehousing/Logistics: Customer's Pipeline, Product
D.a.d Warehousing/Logistics: Customer's Pipeline, People
D.a.e Warehousing/Logistics: Raw Commodities
D.b.a Equipment: How Modular
D.b.b Equipment: How Scalable
D.b.c Equipment: How Reconfigurable
D.b.d Equipment: How Relocatable
D.b.e Equipment: How Storable
D.c.a Physics: Geographically Limited Processes
D.c.b Physics: Scale Limited Processes
D.c.c Physics: Attention Limited Processes
D.c.d Physics: Time Limited Processes
D.c.e Physics: Accident Limited Processes

Naming

The infrastructure names must be carefully defined in order to avoid mis-
leading associations. Legal/Explicit, in particular, can give the wrong connota-
tion to an infrastructure of rules and policies which incidentally includes laws.
It was proposed that the categories be renamed to more closely express the
qualities that discriminate them; if those qualities are natural, more intuitive,
then the names will make sense. In the end, we chose not to change the
names, but the considerations help to define the categories.

A proposal was made to rename Physical to Explicit-Physical. This domain
deals with infrastructure issues that are physically real, and so have unambiguous, expressible characterizations which include the laws of physics. Legal/
Explicit, under this proposal, might then become Explicit-Procedural. What
characterizes this infrastructure is the explicit expression of the rules, procedures, and laws involved. It may not be fair to claim that this collection is fully
unambiguous, consistent, or internally correct, but it must be expressible. The

infrastructure may have non-deterministic mechanisms, whereas the physical mechanisms just mentioned are presumed to be deterministic.

Both cases, Physical and Legal/Explicit, might have some mechanisms that are not controllable (civil laws, physical laws) and some that are (business rules, plant layout).

Continuing the pattern, Social/Cultural appears as Implicit. It's assumed that some of the dynamics involved are hardwired into our genes and that other dynamics are the result of choices and learned behavior. Thus, this infrastructure category involves the balancing of these two types. Which issues are natural and which artificial, and whether this should reflect the difference by being two categories instead of one, are open issues.

It's also assumed that although the forces involved are not explicit, their principles can be understood and codified, though perhaps only by induction. Our effort in situation theory helps with understanding the implicit principles.

This leaves the Information Infrastructure. It has always been unique in the sense of being the most fundamental. Rather than being the set of computers in an enterprise, this set of mechanisms deals with the ability to represent, integrate in some fashion, and manage the various representations involved, and thus the suggested title of Representational Infrastructure. There are a host of issues that follow, but the discriminator from the others is simple. They deal with the actual applications, whereas this one deals with the underlying representations.

Ultimately, we decided not to make the name changes. We would have done so if the target audience were academics who might appreciate the more precise terms, but since the user of these tools is the management decision-maker, we went with their preferences.

The four infrastructures may be clean and distinct regarding the tools used to express and manipulate metrics (that remains to be seen), but they are not distinct in the way that decisions will be made. In particular, the four infrastructures are not in a formally *orthogonal*, but in a dependent relationship. Fortunately, the dependency seems to be straightforward and linear.

Each of the four infrastructures inherits some requirements from the preceding one and some representational constraints from the one following. That is, the methods used to represent information in the more explicit ones build on techniques used in the less explicit ones. So, for example, the representation paradigm used in the Legal/Explicit domain inherits properties from that used in the Social/Cultural domain.

This issue is important because of the implications for integrating and transporting information across domains. We'd like to have our cake and also eat it: While recognizing that different representation/application paradigms are a fact of life, we'd also like to use some principles that would apply across the enterprise. The metrics should be as simple as possible, leveraging the enterprise-wide issues as much as possible.

Dependencies

We took the infrastructure dependencies a step further, since there are internal dependencies that are generally recognized. For instance, Business Culture often affects Business Processes. These dependencies are spelled out in the following list and shown in Figure 10.2 and Figure 10.3. They help in selecting the few cells that are key to an agility strategy.

Social/Cultural Infrastructure
> *Social and Psychological Laws* are weakly affected by *Business Culture*
> *Community Cultures* are affected by *Social and Psychological Laws*
> *Business Culture* is affected by *Community Cultures*

Legal/Explicit Infrastructure
> *Business Processes* are affected by *Business Culture* and *Legal/Regulatory*
> *Legal/Regulatory* is weakly affected by *Social and Psychological Laws*
> *Work Flow* is affected by *Business Processes*

Physical Infrastructure
> *Warehousing/Logistics* is affected by *Work Flow and Physical Laws*
> *Equipment* is affected by *Work Flow, Warehousing/Logistics* and *Physical Laws*
> *Physical Laws* are not affected by anything

Example Cells

The best way to really give a feel for the AVE Reference Model is to suggest some examples for cells. We will now turn to the 20 example cells we discussed earlier in the chapter (see Table 10.3).

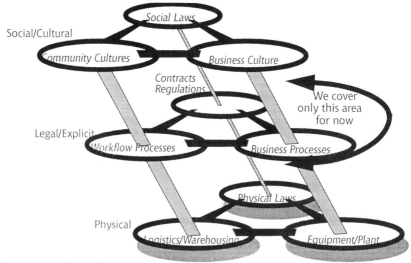

Figure 10.2 Key Infrastructure Breakdowns

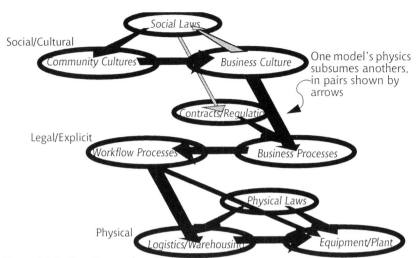

Figure 10.3 Key Dependencies

Table 10.3 Twenty High Value Cells

	C.a.e. Depth of Customer Relations	C.b.b. Risk/Reward Contracts	C.c.c. Work Breakdown Structure	D.a.a. Human Collaboration
1.3. Targeted Market				
2.3 Partner Search				
3.6. Risk/Reward Strategies				
4.1. Performance Metrics				
5.1. Identify Need for Change				

For each of these cells we've given a definition and provided three suggestions for agile practices. Note that these are not prescriptive; what cells are important, and what is the most agile *entry* in a given cell is directly related to strategic and environmental conditions. Of course, a certain type or extent of agility may not be at all beneficial to the VE.

Row 1.3: Opportunity Identification: Targeted Market and Column C.a.e: Legal/ Explicit Infrastructure: Business Processes: Depth of Customer Relations

This cell concerns business processes that support how new markets are identified, and existing markets are served and extended through establishing strong and meaningful relationships with customers. Examples:

- A business process that sends sales and marketing staff on *prospecting* missions, customer visits to learn what opportunities are nascent.
- VE marketing practices that encourage partners to bring market contacts to the VE even though they are outside the existing VE scope.
- Customer focus groups that are convened with the intent of exploring what-if scenarios.

Row 1.3: Opportunity Identification: Targeted Market and Column C.b.b: Legal/ Explicit Infrastructure: Legal/Regulatory: Risk/Reward Contracts

This cell concerns how partnership contracts are structured within the VE to reward partners for promoting the VE outside of their primary role, possibly penalizing partners in some way for not advancing the VE where it conflicts with their interests. Examples:

- Contract provisions which provide a *finder's fee* for identifying both promising new market targets and ones that do well.
- Provisions that subsidize partners to expand capabilities in such a way that the benefit accrues more to the VE in new markets than to the partner in increased profits.
- Provisions that withhold bonus payments from partners who siphon off new opportunities for themselves at the cost of the VE.

Row 1.3: Opportunity Identification: Targeted Market and Column C.c.c: Legal/ Explicit Infrastructure: WorkFlow (Business Plan): Work Breakdown Structure

This cell concerns how assigning or reassigning who does what can open new markets. Examples:

- Processes that recognize that by moving parts and assemblies from one partner to another serves a specific customer's future Just-In-Time workflow requirements to the detriment of the current VE workflow.
- Redundancy in assigning task requirements so that a backup exists in case of problems.

•Choosing a partner for a specific task package not because they are the best in that area, but because they offer a greater spectrum of VE-complementary possibilities.

Row 1.3: Opportunity Identification: Targeted Market and Column D.a.a: Physical Infrastructure: Warehousing/Logistics: Human Collaboration

This cell concerns the strategies for getting people in the VE together physically (or a virtual substitute) in order to identify, analyze, and pursue new VE (and individual) market opportunities. Examples:

•A central location, suitably designed and furnished, that hosts regular meetings of existing and potential partners for the purpose of market targeting.
•An email discussion group, or a paper memo distribution, that shares substantial information on leads with existing and potential partners.
•A dedicated roving person, perhaps an independent broker, who circulates among partners getting and sharing market ideas.

Row 2.3: Partner Selection: Partner Search and Column C.a.e: Legal/Explicit Infrastructure: Business Processes: Depth of Customer Relations

This cell concerns how relationships with existing and future customers are mined to identify best partners. Examples:

•A business practice that involves the customer in searching for and meaningfully evaluating partners to meet specific needs of those customers which may not have been explicitly identified in the original opportunity scope.
•Creation of an *experience database,* shared with competitors, of positive and negative experiences that a wide variety of customers have had in similar circumstances.
•A VE-subsidized activity-based costing analysis of a customer's enterprise to assure that the VE best benefits the customer's value chain in ways that may not be apparent from the VE's perspective alone.

Row 2.3: Partner Selection: Partner Search and Column C.b.b: Legal/Explicit Infrastructure: Legal/Regulatory: Risk/Reward Contracts

This cell concerns rewards that may go to partners for identifying new partners, even when that works against the original partners' conventional interests. Examples:

•A broker's fee that shares the cost of savings between the VE and a partner when that partner decreases its role in the VE to the benefit of the VE or the customer.
•A VE-subsidized risk fund that pays for studies within partners to explore ways of working with their competitors in precompetitive areas.

•Labor agreements which reward evaluations, and perhaps certification of partners with whom they have experience.

Row 2.3: Partner Selection: Partner Search and Column C.c.c: Legal/Explicit Infrastructure: WorkFlow (Business Plan): Work Breakdown Structure

This cell concerns how it is decided who does what within the VE. Examples:

•Agreements with the customer that give them insight into the process of and final say over how and to whom the task is assigned within the VE.
•Dynamic agent systems that quickly and cheaply support bidding among many ready potential partners who are competitors who can do the same task.
•A process for creating spin-offs from the VE or partners that have key capabilities that are only available to the VE and successors.

Row 2.3: Partner Selection: Partner Search and Column D.a.a: Physical Infrastructure: Warehousing/Logistics: Human Collaboration

This cell concerns support for physical space wherein representatives from potential partners can come to be evaluated. Examples:

•An assessment center for potential partners to evaluate how well they fit in with others projected on the team, and how they respond to change within the engineered VE. This presumes that performance on the actual task is known.
•Maintenance of a centralized database of prequalified partner information.
•A regular retreat location where customers, brokers/consultants, and prospective partners explore not what they do, but be aware of what they might do.

Row 3.6: VE Formation: Risk/Reward Strategies and Column C.a.e: Legal/Explicit Infrastructure: Business Processes: Depth of Customer Relations

This cell concerns how the relationship with the customer is exploited to incentivize behavior deep within the VE that benefits the customer, the VE, and the partners. Examples:

•Training sessions that increase the awareness throughout the supplier chain of how the VE supports the customer, and how each function results in profit.
•A partner within the VE whose primary mission is to act as advocate for the customer (or the customer's customer), and which provides input to the initial partnering negotiations.
•A simulation tool that exercises several models of reward strategies and breakdowns with the intent of optimizing continuing linkage to the customer.

Row 3.6: VE Formation: Risk/Reward Strategies and Column C.b.b: Legal/Explicit Infrastructure: Legal/Regulatory: Risk/Reward Contracts

This cell concerns the actual contract support for the risk/reward strategy. Examples:

- Contract negotiations for forming the VE are conducted by an outside legal contractor whose remuneration is tied to the success of the VE.
- A major portion of each partner's payments are tied to shares, or percentages of the VE's profits.
- A major portion of the capitalization of the VE comes from the partners in rough distribution to the profit to each expected.

Row 3.6: VE Formation: Risk/Reward Strategies and Column C.c.c: Legal/Explicit Infrastructure: WorkFlow (Business Plan): Work Breakdown Structure

This cell concerns the linkage between determining who does what, and who gets paid how much. Examples:

- A pricing system that is not tied to extra-VE market pricing, but instead special intra-VE value-added analysis.
- A system that accords influence over the management of the VE (controlling votes), based on the value added by each constituent.
- A flexible system for rewarding partners for suggesting ways to improve the work breakdown (and other VE roles).

Row 3.6: VE Formation: Risk/Reward Strategies and Column D.a.a: Physical Infrastructure: Warehousing/Logistics: Human Collaboration

This cell concerns how human interaction among VE partners is managed to assure that trust is maintained. Examples:

- A regular retreat where partners' representatives can not only relax and socialize but also air problems and misunderstandings.
- A dedicated consultant who travels from partner to partner to brief what the other players do and to carry concerns from one to the other, presumably also conducting team-building exercises.
- A partner dedicated to arbitration, using a central database of performance metrics on each of the partners.

Row 4.1: VE Operation: Performance Metrics and Column C.a.e: Legal/Explicit Infrastructure: Business Processes: Depth of Customer Relations

This cell concerns the method of using customer satisfaction to evaluate how well each activity in the VE is performing. Examples:

•An activity evaluation that determines not only whether each member is doing what was expected, but also the extent to which it adds to customer satisfaction.
•Benchmarking to compare what-if changes in the VE to competitors' offerings.
•Quality of life audits to determine whether market forces are optimizing the well-being of the customer and the VE.

Row 4.1: VE Operation: Performance Metrics and Column C.b.b: Legal/Explicit Infrastructure: Legal/Regulatory: Risk/Reward Contracts

This cell concerns the level of connection between partner reward and real-time monitoring of performance. Examples:

•Quality metrics tied to partner payments.
•Customer-generated agility metrics tied to partner payments.
•Metrics that weight reimbursement for investment based on the level of risk involved.

Row 4.1: VE Operation: Performance Metrics and Column C.c.c: Legal/Explicit Infrastructure: WorkFlow (Business Plan): Work Breakdown Structure

This cell concerns how the work is divided in order to be monitorable by the VE. Examples:

•A *lingua franca* within the VE that allows each participant to understand the performance if its partners.
•A set of product and corporate responsibility boundaries that corresponds to measurable process boundaries.
•A generic, comprehensive set of performance measures that can be used to advertise and contract for services from a pool of new partners.

Row 4.1: VE Operation: Performance Metrics and Column D.a.a: Physical Infrastructure: Warehousing/Logistics: Human Collaboration

This cell concerns how human collaboration within the VE is measured. Examples:

•Qualitative measures for the level of quality in collaboration among team members.
•A specific assessment center for evaluating (and improving) intercompany collaborative team functioning.
•Support for extracorporate, extra-VE teams, such as labor unions.

Row 5.1: VE Reconfiguration/Dissolution: Identify Need for Change and Column C.a.e: Legal/Explicit Infrastructure: Business Processes: Depth of Customer Relations

This cell concerns the way the VE gets indications from the customer that the VE needs to change (or blink out). Examples:

•Dedicated agents (persons) in key partners whose primary job is sensing the customer for changes in the opportunity which mobilized the VE.
•Agents who deliberately destabilize the market in controlled ways to sense and create new trends.
•Processes that examine unrelated markets for analogies which may indicate general technical, economic, and social trends.

Row 5.1: VE Reconfiguration/Dissolution: Identify Need for Change and Column C.b.b: Legal/Explicit Infrastructure: Legal/Regulatory: Risk/Reward Contracts

This cell concerns how partners get reimbursed for sensing, communicating, and acting on the need for change. Examples:

•A reward pool for agents, perhaps deep in the supply base, who report suspected changes that are later validated.
•An investment pool that subsidizes internal research and development in a partner who could effect that partner's role, someone else in the VE, or the customer.
•Disincentives for partners who focus on a narrow, inflexible customer need that is susceptible to change.

Row 5.1: VE Reconfiguration/Dissolution: Identify Need for Change and Column C.c.c: Legal/Explicit Infrastructure: Work Flow (Business Plan): Work Breakdown Structure

This cell concerns how the VE is decomposed in a way that eases the identification of change and the change itself. Examples:

•A work breakdown structure that is designed in such a way as to make processes relatively independent; processes and players can be swapped without major change among other partners.
•Work breakdown of VE control functions that makes it difficult for each partner not to be alert to change; for instance, by having each process responsible for its own comparative value-added audit.
•Elimination of a dominant prime, so that the roles of leadership is forced into innovative reinventing in order to preserve the frangible institution.

Row 5.1: VE Reconfiguration/Dissolution: Identify Need for Change and Column D.a.a: Physical Infrastructure: Warehousing/Logistics: Human Collaboration

This cell concerns how partners interact to identify the need for change and planning for change. Examples:

•A simulation center where partners use role playing to identify future problems in the market, and in external change forces.

•A process where employees are shifted from one partner to another for long periods with the primary goal of cross-fertilizing ideas for improvement.

•Workforce collaborative and educational practices that produce high performance workforces (that is, those which support a culture likely to drive innovation).

BEST AGILE PRACTICE EXAMPLES

The Focus Group created the Reference Model and associated definitions in concert with a major effort in surveying best practices in agility. During the conceptual stages of the project, we also decided it was essential to have some real cases to discuss. In addition to the important task of helping with the model, we discovered a few things:

•There are practically no cases where an enterprise has deliberately engineered agility into the system. The tools, such as metrics, did not exist, so such engineering was impossible. So we captured agility, even when it was accidental.

•There are no cases that we found where the VE was wholly agile. We captured cases where agility was manifest in some notable area.

•There are no fully Type 1 or 2 VEs. We surveyed relatively conventional VEs.

•All were agile in either VE formation or operation, but not both.

About 50 cases were identified based on insights from the group and the larger virtual group. These were interviewed by phone and/or email, and nearly 20 were visited. Eight were deemed useful cases for discussion outside the group, half of these insisted on anonymity. More than half of those surveyed overall had concerns which would have resulted in similar restrictions. Specific case details are found in Table 10.4.

Anonymous Railroad

This case concerns a major railway. We surveyed its ability to partner with a potential industrial firm to locate at a site which would be served in perpetuity by the railroad. It is a qualified Type 2 AVE.

The strength of railroads, like local phone and utility suppliers, is built on growth. Some growth comes from increased use from the existing base, but the most important growth comes from new users. With railroads, this means attracting certain industries to sites that are or can be served by their rail. In other words, stockholder value can only be increased if the rails' customers grow.

This rail company has been remarkably successful in matching sites and firms, thus strongly outpacing its competitors in growing its sustaining base.

The best practices is this case are in the opportunity identification and partner selection. A full-time staff is dedicated to these tasks. They are independent of the traditional sales/marketing staff, and enjoy a high status and priority in getting resources in the firm.

There appear to be several facets of how these best practices are executed. A set of long-lived partnerships have been established to support the needs of the short-term VE partnership. These partners are of two types: those who share the goals of the VE (local utilities, municipal/state economic development authorities, local chambers of commerce, possibly unions), and those that provide supporting analytical and consulting services. This team is entirely opportunity driven.

The rail company employs a staff (which uses consultants) to keep current a collection of knowledge about trends in certain industries which traditionally use rail service. State-of-the-art market prediction tools are employed. In some cases, this mirrors (but is independent of) similar forecasts going on the firms in those sectors. The purpose of these analyses is to anticipate an industrial need which is likely to be served by assets in the rail's geographic area.

The rail company does not wait for a firm to take action on a need, but actively seeks them out with their results. Often when the businesses are approached, they have independently determined the need (opportunity). But sometimes they have not and are surprised, in which case they often welcome the information.

Because the rail line has good operations research skills from its running of the railroad, it has developed good operations research-based tools to keep the focus of expensive analyses narrow and the approaches limited to high payoffs. This is the key to the entire endeavor and could form the basis of Opportunity Strategy metrics.

Agility comes into play here. The nature of the tools is two-fold: one edition of tools looks at long-lived trends. The other edition is optimized to analyze surprises, and to look for new niches opened by such surprises. This latter set is adapted from tools developed by a commodities speculation firm.

Table 10.4 List of Case Studies

Name	Type	Sector
Anonymous Railroad	2	Service
FlexCell	4	Manufacturing
Sikorsky	1 (in formation)	Manufacturing
Anonymous Electronics Manufacturer	1	Manufacturing
Westinghouse	3	Manufacturing
Anonymous Airline	4	Service
Anonymous Shipyard	3	Manufacturing
Taligent	1 (in formation)	"Manufacturing"

One feature of the tools is remarkable. Each analysis needs to have two faces: one that shows risk/reward of the core business of the (at this point unknown) manufacturer; and another that shows the risks/rewards to the rail company.

The rail company does not approach a partner until it has been identified by its in-house processes. (Of course, there are cases where a partner is out looking for a site and calls on the rail company or municipality, but that's another situation.) Hardly anyone, much less the rail company's competition, knows the extent of the behind the scenes analysis.

The rail company learned early on to limit its target markets to only those industrial situations where their geographic strengths (supplemented by the efforts of the cities, etc.) are clearly strong. A best practice appears to be that the target market determination is largely made by each partner before introducing themselves. The partner-specific spins on this determination form the basis for all VE decisions that follow.

One winning feature of the evaluation is the weighting in favor of foreign firms who do not yet have U.S. plants, and therefore regional entanglements. Maintaining the capability of addressing this involves having staff or available consultants who can speak several languages (and understand the partner's local business signals). The same operations research-based metrics come to bear on the need for marrying non-U.S. business practice to those of the U.S.

There is no partner search as such. It appears to be a best practice that the search criteria are built into the opportunity strategy and are not an afterthought. For example, the opportunity analysis determines not only that a new fertilizer plant can be justified, but also which firm is the strongest to succeed at it.

What results is the formation of a temporary VE with the intent of getting the target firm established and operating. Many interesting stories were reported involving core competencies specific to the occasion, but no generic characteristics were perceived except the strength of the local VE to handle the unexpected issues thrown at the newcomer. Once that newcomer is established, it begins its normal business, and the VE is dissolved.

Legal agreements are "light" like the whaling case study, and often largely overlooked.

FlexCell

FlexCell is a collection of small businesses, banded together for collective business development. Their business is focused on small lots of machined/manufactured parts and associated services. They are a Type 4 AVE, using conventional practices for most of the reference base subcategories with the following exception.

The partners are nearly exclusively drawn from a closed group, geographically limited. Membership in the collaborative is built around decisionmakers in the firms. Prequalification is achieved by history and trust, incubated by encounter-group like techniques and socialization. The key best practice is the assignment of a full-time person whose goal is to build and maintain that trust over several years. The link is exclusively within the Social/Cultural infrastructure.

This practice leverages local, agriculturally-based values of honesty and constancy. It also appears to depend on a rare, high energy individual. There does not appear to be an indication for a metric. The metric is binary: If you compromise the trust factor incubated by the group, you are likely to be shunned.

This group is trying to develop some legal infrastructure through a shared financing mechanism, but there is no track record or legal best practice yet.

Sikorsky

Sikorsky Aircraft, a $2.3B corporation, manufactures both commercial and military helicopters. The VE effort surveyed here examines how a permanent Type 1 VE, still in creation, is leveraging a specific, valuable best practice.

Sikorsky, as with essentially all helicopter manufacturers, had in the past relied on a stable base of military orders. That military base sharply declined, and its future was in question. The firm responded by designing a helicopter with potentially broad appeal to commercial and international users. Sikorsky realized that they must respond to a price-driven market yet still deliver quality products with high performance on time.

This craft, the S-92, was not wholly new, being derived from their successful BlackHawk series. The new design primarily added internal cabin space and modified subsystems so that the derivatives could be brought to market relatively quickly and inexpensively.

However, a new product requires customers, and in the S-92's case, key customers are international. These international concerns required that at least their machines be manufactured in their countries in some sort of joint venture. Therefore, Sikorsky is necessarily in the Virtual Enterprise business. Sikorsky is familiar with teaming and had recent experience integrating product and process with Boeing on the Commanche. But partnering with the S-92 partners was very much more difficult because of cultural and technical barriers as well as the need for speed.

What was novel about this case was the specific infrastructure investment that was being made. This investment greatly improved the ability to agily form Virtual Enterprises and was a best practice of an early phase of the VE.

The problem was one of transferring key elements of some manufacturing practices to a partner and integrating those with other practices of Sikorsky, who would act as prime contractor. In that role, the prime contractor is responsible for quality throughout the aircraft. Cases in similar (non-Sikorsky) situations, has demonstrated that the detailed definition of and integration to processes is a difficult job which has not yet been done well

Sikorsky has an ambitious effort underway to introduce small knowledge bases to key processes associated with manufacturing engineering. Rule-Based Technology (RBT) is used to create a tool to perform some special, bounded function associated with an engineering process. This tool is usually embedded in the 3-D CAD environment. Therefore, it has a dual nature: It is both a part of the process and contains explicit, expert knowledge about the process.

About two dozen of these knowledge projects were underway. Some relate to supervisory or oversight functions, and most concern the relationship among design, manufacturing engineering, and the manufacturing process. Typically, a knowledge project was scoped at 6 months and 2000 hours for the first benefits. The effort was well past the stage where management was identifying isolated problem processes. Individual engineering managers were growing the projects into adjacent processes so that knowledge about communicating processes was captured.

The most difficult areas were being addressed first. The effect of this preparation was that key processes were being super-modeled in knowledge-based tools that could be leveraged for the AVE. Two effects were apparent. First, the tools literally replaced expertise, usually held by a group of cross-functional experts. Since the expertise was packaged, it could be quickly transferred to a partner in the form of tools. Obviously, the resulting fabric of processes which incorporated these tools would strongly resemble Sikorsky's, making team integration and reconfiguration much easier.

The second effect was an extension of one well-known benefit of modeling: By making the expertise explicit in the knowledge base, Sikorsky gained insight into the process itself. This allowed for benefits in a number of dimensions. One cogent to Agile Virtual Enterprises was that the boundaries between processes, and their metrics, became more formal and trackable. These boundaries would be essential for fine-grained assignment of the work balance among partners.

Note that the coarse division of the aircraft among partners would be based on largely political factors, not on an informed analysis of the manufacturing processes. It makes the integration of fine-grained processes much more difficult. This is especially so considering that the responsibility (and liability!) for the craft resides with the prime contractor.

Certainly this early investment would reap major payoffs as the VEs were formed. It is interesting therefore that none of the investment was justified in terms of the AVE benefits. Instead, a rigorous return on investment case was made for each knowledge project with benefits on existing, in-house tasks within a year. Those cases that were completed had resulted in substantial savings when considered locally: that is, without consideration to the S-92 and the VE.

The best practice here was assigned to Partner Qualification, but could be spread over at least a couple reference base subcategories.

•Operating Structure covers the processes of harmonizing cultures, integrating processes, and establishing what in this case is the supervisory role of the prime contractor over quality. The best practice is in making those three elements explicit and portable before entering into the confusing period of actually establishing the VE.

•Partner Qualification. This case adds something to the Focus Group's understanding of this subcategory. In this case, the partners are selected for reasons that are not primarily based on capability. Thus, Sikorsky assumes some responsibility to make the partners qualified. The greater Sikorsky's ability to insert technology into partners, the greater the pool of potential partners and therefore the larger the number of countries that can be addressed.

We would expect, with further study, to find some leverage for metrics here. The place to look is the boundary of the knowledge project. We noted that these projects are often rescoped to make them larger or smaller, so that they represent a meaningful process module of a handy size on the order of our reference base's cells.

This case study hasn't yet addressed the four infrastructures. We expect that the major impact will be on the cultural infrastructure: The use of these tools by the partner(s) will necessarily bring most of the manufacturing engineering (but not manufacturing) processes into harmony with Sikorsky.

The Information Infrastructure role is indirect: Rule-based representation tools are in a support role, not as a driver. But Sikorsky is finding that legacy systems may be problematic. For instance, the S-92 is based on the BlackHawk, much of which was not exclusively designed using CAD methods. Therefore, a conversion of legacy data to 3D CAD models may be required to take full advantage of the best practice.

Probably, this practice would only function in a matrixed organization, where functional responsibilities across the company are well defined. The result, in a firm like Sikorsky, is that each rule-based technology knowledge project is dual-use, equally applicable to military and commercial aircraft.

Sikorsky managers expect many of these projects to be portable to other industries as well. Chrysler, for example, has a similar rule-based technology initiative. Their CAD checker project is being used in eight other firms, most not in the auto business.

Anonymous Electronics Manufacturer

This case concerns a large consumer electronics manufacturing firm (only certain features of the VE can be discussed). The example involves this firm entering into a Type 1 VE in the key best practice, and a Type 2 otherwise.

The background is that many consumer electronics markets require very fast ramp-ups of manufacturing capability to take advantage of a need, a niche, or to round out a product line. A fairly large, promiscuous base of suppliers exist to help address this need. Some only manufacture for others, and some are firms who manufacture their own brand names in the same markets. In many cases, this firm, and many like it, would job out the entire product, adding only the brand name (and some design).

In the past, the firm would use fairly simple criteria to select partners: Cost and schedule. Quality was an issue, but only insofar as requiring the partner to meet certain minimum standards. Notably, strategic issues have not been a factor; such issues might include selecting a supplier to keep it away from a competitor, or not selecting it because of fear of creating a future competitor.

What's new in how partners are selected is that liability is becoming an issue. Two kinds of liability are considered. The product carries a liability. Generally, that liability is of two types which overlap. The simple type deals with product failure: The downstream cost of products that fail for reasons not covered by negotiated specifications after the VE is dissolved. The more dangerous product liability is the potential that the product will cause damage, resulting in costly suits or recalls.

Another type of liability is also important: Liability associated with the process. Generally this consists of the risk of latent environmental damage, workplace suits (harassment or discrimination), and intellectual property infringements.

This firm now performs analyses on potential partners to evaluate all these liabilities. They are combined with other, traditional measures in selecting partners.

This best practice, therefore, is in the subcategory of Partner Qualification, though it impacts Product Liabilities and Risk/Reward Strategies processes later in the formation process. What's so interesting is that the practice directly employs (actually creates) metrics.

These metrics are quantitative (in the sense outlined in Chapter 7) and can be easily converted to dollars. The techniques used were derived from actuarial techniques developed by insurance actuaries. This involves a special methodology for modeling the processes of interest. The processes are captured in this specific way, which often involves field surveys. Then, special analytical tools are used. A large, historical database (including information from other actuarial domains) is also used.

It's notable that, while the firm sponsored the development of the metric and process, it was developed and is wholly performed by a captive, but independent consulting firm. My understanding of the process is that it would be applicable to a wide variety of AVE applications, but it may be difficult to blast it free since it is a very valuable competitive tool. Obviously, the impact is on the legal infrastructure more than the other cases.

Westinghouse

This case involves a division of Westinghouse (since sold to Northrop Grumman) that supplies complex electronic products. The dominant customer is the U.S. government. As with many producers of complex goods with a large supplier base, Westinghouse has begun to reduce and prequalify its supplier base. The firm is probably in the world-class category in how they manage this process, independent of agility.

The best practice of interest to the VE is related to how they take advantage of their supplier base. The sector in which Westinghouse competes is characterized by many bidding situations coupled with a remarkable need for keeping up (or leading with) advanced product and process technologies. In conventional supplier relationships, technology and bidding strategies trickle down to the suppliers, having been determined at the top. Westinghouse, however, has well-developed mechanisms to involve their suppliers as partners in both strategic technology planning and competitive bid development.

As the supplier base has narrowed, supplier liaison personnel have increased their scope to include the entire product development cycle. Suppliers are continually surveyed for potentially advantageous new skills and processes which might add to the overall competitiveness of the Type 3 VE. Once an opportunity to bid has been identified, the portfolio of new processes is surveyed for advantage.

Therefore, when the bid is developed, the suppliers become involved in a more peer-to-peer way than their competition. The ability of a supplier to collaborate with Westinghouse in this closer manner is one of the criteria used in searching, evaluating, and prequalifying partners.

Anonymous Airline

The VE effort surveyed how a Type 4 VE is employed to provide market guidance using partners which are also partnered with competitors. This case involves an airline.

Domestic airlines have lost a lot of money in the past few years, and this airline has been heavily hit. Most airlines are substantially constrained in the changes they can make in costs and price. Costs can be squeezed somewhat, but only to a point. The price charged is a matter of a game largely unconnected to what to the product costs. One airline has to meet another's price, while lowering prices on other routes offensively.

In this environment, airlines are desperate to differentiate themselves, and to create brand loyalty. The frequent, business traveler is the target. To this end, all major airlines have frequent traveler programs. All these programs partner with essentially the same set of hotel and rental car corporations, in a near-Type 4 VE.

However, this airline was able to use its partnership to develop market information which it will use to enhance its competitive position, while preventing similar information from flowing back to its competitors. The result is a marketing strategy which could make a big difference in saving the airline by creating greater business traveler loyalty (the specific strategy is not mentioned here). How this was accomplished constitutes a best practice.

Each frequent traveler point program, in air, car, and hotel industries, is fully computerized. The typical business traveler is assiduous in assuring his points are tracked, so gathering information on who went to what kinds of places and how often is an easy task. Each partner sells that information, usually for a discount against the traveler's benefits.

This airline wanted to go much further, to do some targeted marketing research to identify an expected unmet need that they could address better than the competition. They wanted to get this information without direct airline-to-traveler interviews for various reasons. At the same time, they realized that car and hotel firms routinely identify and address needs similar to those they sought.

The question was: How could they use their partners (primarily hotel) to reprocess old information and collect new information without letting that information fall into the hands of their competitors? The situation is similar to many shared intellectual property problems in design/manufacturing VEs.

The Risk/Reward Strategies subcategory is supposed to address ownership of newly generated intellectual property. But it fails to address the situation when that property originates in the second-tier partners, but takes on added value through the VE. This case indicated an expansion of the definition of that subcategory.

In this case, the airline negotiated some very sensitive legal instruments. Individuals (by name) in each organization were compartmentalized: each could only function in the context of the VE and its successor, and could not contract with a competitor for specified number of years.

The hotel partners were limited to two who compete in different markets to avoid friction and confusion. These hotel partners were granted preference in cooperative marketing when the new service began, in addition to some financial recompense.

Some physical separation of workers and records was required, as well as some co-location. (Unknown to the airline, this mirrors a solution to similar intellectual property problems in the defense and aerospace industries.) The legal agreements treated the employees (for the sake of intellectual property) as if they were employed by a joint venture. A line of supervision, populated by the partners, was established just for these issues (policy, arbitration). No other joint venture management structure was created; all else was managed under conventional buyer-supplier frameworks. While the legal and physical infrastructures were affected, the information and cultural infrastructures were not.

The VE was truly agile in the sense of disassembling after the need was met, to be replaced by a more conventional relationship. However, the effort went so well that the arrangement may be revived in the future for more market intelligence needs.

Relevance to metrics exists in the nature of the legal documents we were told, but we were not able to examine those agreements. It was explained that statistical methods were used to determine what percentage (or portion) of the intellectual property was generated new within the VE and which originated in a partner. We got the impression that these methods were derived from activity-based costing methods, meaning the cost and not the value of the information formed the basis of the metric.

Anonymous Shipyard

This shipyard was until recently was mainly involved in U.S. Navy contracts. The VE effort surveyed here is how a Type 3 VE was used to bring core competencies to bring to bear and accomplish a switch to commercial business.

The firm surveyed once was largely a commercial yard. But for the last few decades, no new-ship commercial construction had occurred, following the unfortunate national trend. The Reagan buildup kept the yard busy until recently. A combination of predicable and largely non-predicable (political) reversals forced this firm to seek an agile introduction into commercial contracts.

What is novel about this case is how they leveraged a pool of suppliers for government contracts into a VE to address commercial contracts.

Building a naval ship is an interesting business. The shipyard acts as a prime contractor for a weapons system, and a large supply chain is involved. This supply chain changes from ship to ship, but consists of a limited, fairly well-connected community. Many of the practices involved in installing and integrating a component on a ship are co-developed between the prime contractor and the supplier.

In this case, the prime contractor had lost its corporate knowledge concerning commercial practices. But that knowledge largely existed, in a distributed fashion, in the supplier base. If the yard failed, the supplier base would suffer. So the prime contractor/supplier relationships were supplemented by a VE to transfer commercial skills to the prime contractor.

In normal commercial yards, the job of estimating the job (building a ship) is relatively disconnected from the actual planning and building of the ship. In military contracts, the two are more closely connected. The process plan is sketched out for the estimate, then fleshed out for the actual building. This provided leverage for the prime contractor to commit to a supplier base, conditional on getting the contract. Then those suppliers came in and helped develop the process plan (supporting the estimate), working side-by-side with the yard's planners.

The VE was opportunistic, based only on the one buy. Risks were shared—a radical change for the supplier base—but their later marketing expenses were reduced.

In the first case, the buy was successful, and commercial ships will be built by the yard, the first VE reverting to a traditional supplier/prime contractor relationship. Plans are underway to use this mechanism to identify and address unusual and niche market commercial contracts. The idea is that they can address these new and unusual situations faster and cheaper by relying on their suppliers to help develop the at-risk process plans for confident bids.

There is a lesson here for military contractors who feel hampered by an onerous upfront planning culture. It can be turned into a mechanism to bring new, commercial skills from the supplier base into the organization via a VE.

The best practice here focuses on Operating Structure. Besides the novelty of the idea, the yard developed a way to coordinate the cacophony of bottom-up planning. (They were used to a more top-down philosophy.)

The development of the bidding-level process plan was seen as a manufacturing task in itself. A process plan for that (a *metaprocess* plan) was developed with identification of who would come in when, for roughly how long, to help develop what piece of the shipbuilding plan. This idea of planning for the creation of a working structure for a VE is powerful one, which we were not able to expand beyond the scope of the shipbuilding sector. But it seems generally applicable. We would expect, with further study, to find some leverage for metrics here.

Conventional supplier/chain legal infrastructure was used with the exception of early selection for at risk assistance.

Physical infrastructure was important, with facilitated temporary collocation being essential. Socialization was moderately encouraged. Participants think that more of this would help next time, since the one-time pressure could not be sustained. Information infrastructure was not a factor, in the sense of requiring new capability.

Taligent

Taligent is a joint venture, a Type 1 VE (excepting that is it a permanent joint venture), whose charter is to provide a radical improvement in the ability to develop and use software in enterprises. The company is developing a next generation object-oriented (OO) application system that is portable across all major desktop hardware and operating system environments. It was originally formed by IBM and Apple nearly three years ago.

Several major changes have been made since its formation. A new major partner, Hewlett-Packard, was brought into the VE. The development reference platform was changed from Apple Macintosh 68K to IBM AIX RS6000, a technical enhancement in response to developer requirements. The mission of the company was changed, based on customer feedback, from deploying a single integrated OO environment to providing both a portable application system that rides on many operating systems and a separate OO operating system.

The focus of this case is how Taligent has been able to listen to and respond to their customers, the three investors, as partners and outside customers, while juggling the realities of competitive versus precompetitive issues.

Three internal policies contribute to this ability. Taligent's investors and partners must cultivate a trust relationship with Taligent while they also compete with each other. Taligent's workforce needs to collaborate closely with a respective partner in either the shared domain or various proprietary domains. For Taligent to proceed, it must scrupulously maintain the confidentiality of the information shared by its partners. No single set of procedures could cover all the conditions which arise in unexpected ways. The VE's solution is to provide leadership by example from above. A strong, ethical tone is set by the senior management and permeates the corporate culture, which is unique.

We were not able to gather anecdotes to illustrate the practice. But numerous discussions with the sponsors underscored how prominent and visible this feature is in the corporate culture. It greatly eases the potential for mistrust and allows focus on the mission.

Recent Events

Here's a chance to underscore a point made earlier. Agility in one dimension does not necessarily ensure agility in another. That is, if you have the ability to respond to a specific type of change, you have no guarantee that you can respond to a different kind of a threat. All of our examples were agile in a sort of accidental way; they hadn't engineered agility, they just intuitively stumbled into it. So one would expect them to be vulnerable to other sorts of unexpected change. That indeed happened in the few years since the original study.

- The railroad's competitors just couldn't match our example's strategy of building profitability by lowering their cost of money. So they changed the rules by instigating a huge acquisition. Our company had to match it, or die in the minds of investors and lenders. So they had to ditch the very fine strategy we outlined and play acquisition catch-up.
- The division of Westinghouse we surveyed was unexpectedly acquired by Northrop Grumman as a strategy to consolidate contracts. This has little to do with delivering value to the customer; in the defense business, you usually bid a story of capabilities and that feeds consolidation. Also, the defense market is strongly influenced by congressional lobbying, which also drives consolidation. Northrop Grumman's supply chain practices are substantially less modern, so the system we described has been dismantled.
- The nature of the airline business has changed, as monetary policy has unexpectedly increased the value of transatlantic traffic. Also the booming economy (also unexpected) has made the business traveller a less pampered commodity. A major partner jilted our studied airline and this indirectly increased the visibility of labor costs. That forced our surveyed company to abandon the improvement we tracked.
- The shipyard we cited competes commercially with international firms and is hampered by exchange rates which have shifted. Some eastern European yards became productive much faster than anticipated. Also, union rules, created for the relatively fat defense environment, proved to be more unyielding than planned. This is a case where the padding in the system was agile in one dimension, but unagile in another. Losses on the first commercial effort are in the hundreds of millions, and the commercial business has been abandoned.
- Finally, the internet so radically changed the market for operating systems that many of the fundamental assumptions of Taligent no longer fit. Taligent has been dissolved.

These are hard lessons which underscore the fact that it is a dangerous business world out there. Agility is required, but accidental or intuitive agility just will not cut it, since the wrong kind of agility can actually hurt you. You need to carefully engineer your agility strategy.

Chapter 11

Communicative Acts and Information Theory

In the grand voyage toward engineering your VE, by this point you should have:

- Determined an agility strategy by employing your existing planning tools, supplemented by brainstorming and intelligence about the market and potential partners.
- Broken down your enterprise conceptually into the framework we described in the last chapter. You have only done this breakdown superficially, unless you—like many—employ the framework in your strategic planning. (Some planners do this because the Reference Model helps identify leveragable strengths, what used to be called *core competencies*.)
- Within that breakdown, you have identified the few key cells that are relevant to the agility threat and your possible options in addressing that threat.

Let's give an example. We were approached by a European phone company. They are going through three simultaneous revolutions: First, they are going from being a publicly-owned monopoly to being privatized; second, their customers are fair game for other companies, and they can likewise target anywhere that makes sense; and, finally, it is unknown exactly what the nature of the telephone business will be in the future. To name but a few of the uncertainties: will they be a wholesaler of "long lines," and thus an entertainment delivery company, an internet throughway, or a content provider?

For these companies, and their siblings in the U.S., there are a great many options. The stupid way to hedge the future is what most are doing: Invest in all options so as not to miss the boat. This is stupid for a few reasons, including having to fund the shotgun investments by repetitive downsizing, and doing that downsizing with no idea what future capabilities will be needed.

Our telecom wanted to do things better. They knew that they could not determine the future, and they could not burden the company by competing in bidding wars in all directions.

It is a very simple case but a good example to illustrate steps of the process. The enterprise to begin with is a single, stable, monolithic company. They want to be world class in their business but they do not know what that business is. They can, however, identify types of strategic possibilities and for many of those possibilities the best strategy is partnering with another firm. Also, those potential partners are easily identified. They will want to team with the telecom because of the large existing installed base of customers.

The telecom did strategic studies on a variety of what-ifs concerning how profitable and risky certain options would be. They wanted an additional evaluation of how fast and costly it would be to enter a market by partnering. At some point, partnering too late will be inordinately expensive in order to take advantage of the emerging situation. On the other hand, it pays to wait as long as possible so that all your reserves can be called to roar into the window of opportunity. The telecom wanted to know where the breakpoints were—what were the times when partnering must be made if you are going to chase an opportunity.

So we had a strategy, the first on our list at the start of the chapter. We applied the Reference Model to the strategy, the potential partners and the possibilities. This was less difficult than it would be in many cases, because the number of partners were few, their processes were well understood, and they were used to novel types of partnering.

We then extracted the cells, those processes that could have supported various instances of the strategy. In this case, they were cells concerned with financial evaluation of rewards among the partners, and contractual clauses to support them. This was a viable strategy because if you can wait until the opportunity is clear before partnering, you can better target how your partner is rewarded. The competition has to enter into partnering earlier, and so has to deal with a more generic strategy which is less attractive to the partner financially.

Now what would you do as a next step? That's what this chapter is about. You need to *model* the processes. That is, you need to understand in some significant detail what those processes are and also represent them in a formal way. Here's where the magic happens—we can turn those models into numbers that tell you the time and cost of change.

LEVERAGING INFORMATION THEORY

The magic behind this modeling-for-numbers is actually a simple trick. We employ a body of science from information theory and practices associated with that science. There are two parts to this: *information theory* and *communicative act modeling*. Fortunately, the ideas behind each of these are easy to grasp.

The corner of information theory that we are interested in was developed to understand the complexity of certain computer operations. When a computerized method is applied to a problem, that method is called an *algorithm*. People who create programs are simply in the business of structuring the right collection of algorithms against specific problems and it is valuable to know how well the algorithms match the problem.

A practical problem in computer coding is the reusability of algorithms. It would be really great for programmers if there were a vast collection of algorithms already coded and validated and in a library somewhere, that could just be assembled tinkertoy-like.

One problem in this ideal vision is that some algorithms are very good for very specific problems. Others are good enough for a wider variety of problems. There are a couple dimensions to the tinkertoy problem. The first is simply: Can a specific algorithm address a problem at all? If so, the second problem concerns how much it will cost (in computer time). This aspect is what is of interest to us: The science of figuring out how much an algorithm costs in a given situation.

Take time for an example. The way we deliver mail is based on a simple algorithm. You locate the place the letter goes down to a country, state, city, street, and specific mailbox. (Coding a shorthand for the first four of these in a ZIP code is a mere implementation detail.) But it is entirely possible to use a different search algorithm. One could address a letter to an individual based on, say, a telephone number. The country and area code (city code for outside North America) and exchange code have geographic significance. But the remaining digits are essentially random. The search algorithm required would be bad for the post office. But if some of the messages come by post, and some by email, this address-search algorithm may have some real merit.

Some information scientists (Asperti & Longo, 1991) can tell you the cost of using an algorithm in a given situation. The trick here is to model the algorithm as a collection of formal entities (incidentally called types and functions, using something called category theory). If this is done carefully, the number of these and the way that they are related indicate the complexity of the algorithm in a specific context. The complexity of an algorithm is directly related to its cost—how many computer cycles it will take.

We use this same idea, and many of the same mathematical tools. For us, a process is the same as an algorithm and is applied against a problem, which in our case is the tactical goals of the strategy. Where the information scientists have measured the cost of adapting an algorithm to address a problem, we want to measure the cost of adapting a process (actually a collection of processes) to address a new situation.

COMMUNICATIVE ACTS

The key to bringing the weight of this information science to bear on management problems is all in how we represent, or model, processes. When information scientists model a process, they use something called category-theoretic types. *Category theory* is the theory of how things are abstracted and how the resulting abstracts (*types*) are similar to one another (in *catego-ries*) and are transformed into one another (by *functions*).

We've worked with category theory and real-world models for some time. It is a very esoteric and mathematical art, and certainly not anything one can insert into the everyday world of business. It simply costs too much, but there is a more severe limit: What we are talking about is making important business decisions that may affect many lives, cost lots of money, and put the enterprise at risk. In such cases, the method must be visible and intuitive. If you cannot understand it, how are you expected to trust it?

Fortunately, there is a modeling method that is understandable and simple and that can be employed in a category-theoretic manner. You can use this method to model the half dozen processes indicated by the cells of the framework you have identified. It is an easy method to understand and use, so much so that we can introduce it fully in a few pages. First, we'll give you an overview, then a more detailed look.

Basics

In this view, there are only two main items: agents and the communicative acts that transpire among them. You could make it quite complicated, of course, adding subtle distinctions and dynamics, but a simple version of this basic concept is all you need; it is what we use. Agents are simply people or small functional groups in most cases, and the communicative acts are just what they "say."

For us, the world of communicative acts completely describes information-based collaboration. In this information world, it is important that what each agent does as its task—what the communication is—is captured at the lowest level possible. We do this by breaking each action into one of a very few basic communicative acts (see Figure 11.1). The taxonomy we use has been common for decades.

Because our domain is business, we can get by with only a few non-speech acts, the two on the right hand side of the chart. When we employ the theory to measure the agility of, say, commando forces, we need a more complex non-

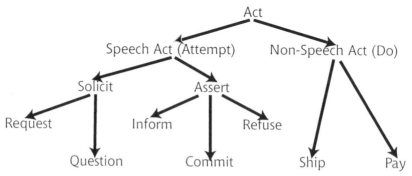

Figure 11.1 Communicative Act Taxonomy

speech act breakdown than ship-and-pay. Relatively speaking, business is a simple collaboration, because the primary driver, at least at the enterprise level, is to make stuff (including services) and to get paid. Non-business collaborations are more complex, and we have separate non-speech acts for schools, military task forces, emergency response teams, and even evangelical organizations.

The reason we go to the trouble of modeling in this way, and at this level of detail is simple: If you take a business process and break it down into its agents and communications, the complexity of that representation correlates well with the cost of changing the process. And the relationship is well behaved arithmetically, so that resulting metrics can be directly folded into your other metrics of time, cost, and quality. Thus, agility can be considered with other metrics in strategic planning, risk management, and enterprise engineering tools.

MODELING BY COMMUNICATIVE ACTS

In addition to the Reference Model, the metrics depend on a few fundamental foundations, one being the use of a canonical decomposition of processes. Such a decomposition is required because we look at the structure of processes rather than the details of their content and meaning. Taking this approach both highlights the dynamic couplings of interest within the VE and avoids the comparatively high cost of semantic (meaning-based) modeling.

But what decomposition to use? The bewildering variety of process modeling approaches is only an indication of the variety of theoretical approaches we could take. One goal of the project was to discover the best approach.

We settled on one that is close enough to the mainstream that a great body of existing science could be inherited. On the other hand, some elements of the approach are still under development and freshly incorporate new thinking about *agency* (who does something) and *effect* (what is done). The parts of the theory that are still being worked out help us with the "soft modeling" agenda we'll introduce later. What's important is that the parts of the theory we need for our formal metrics are well understood, rock solid.

The Emergent Systems Influence

One of the reasons we chose this specific modeling technique was because it supports not only conventional modeling, but new ideas about autonomous agents. In the conventional view, you model to support decisionmaking; there is circuit of sorts where the real world provides facts out of which you build models. The models support decisions which are implemented in the real world. In this normal mode, the models do not control any part of the enterprise.

In a more active view, on the other hand, the models are part of an agent architecture that actually controls part of the enterprise. This is a particularly attractive view when addressing agility, because assumptions that you know everything you need to no longer hold. The solution is to build processes that are adaptive enough to somewhat automatically adjust. The challenge in this case is to design not just a system of processes (agents) that is optimized, but to design an environment where they are self-adaptive, where the optimal solution "emerges."

This is where we wanted to go after fully developing the metrics, so it influenced our choice of modeling theories. We'll have more to say later about this way of enterprise engineering. For now, let us just note that the considerations of choosing a modeling method are not trivial; one must follow several threads and several of these take you to uncharted territory. The three threads we were concerned with merging are:

- •The notion of *information*. All models and enterprise management techniques are based on facts. That is simple enough. But since some of the facts are unknown (the definition of the agility threat), some of the dynamics aren't well understood (clash of business cultures for instance), and some of the processes you may be working with are nondeterministic, the information thread quickly takes us from wading level to very deep water indeed.

- •The notion of *logic*. Surprisingly, the coupling between information and logic is not as tight as one would assume. We let you know in the Preface that we are concerned only with methods that are not only rational, but formally so. This allows us both to computerize some of the tasks and to audit decision processes in detail. Keith Devlin (1991) provides a good overview of the murky relationship between logic and information.

- •The notion of *action*, where the water gets not only deep, but turbulent and treacherous. It turns out to be very hard to forge a useful set of concepts that is action-based, relies on information in the ways that we want, and is logical in the clean, formal manner we require.

(If you are a student of these issues, the problem between action and information is that we require actions to be first class citizens in the logic, and to be definable purely in terms of information units which also are first class citizens. Check out Devlin's book.)

The communicative act method we describe here solves those problems. We are firm believers that solving the most difficult problems first—rather than the simplest—is always the best strategy. In this case, building a foundation for the next step also helps us with the relatively simpler problem of metrics.

For managers, metrics are only a starting point. Planners will want to not only know how agile a process/system is, but also how to improve it. It's only responsible of us to choose a representation that supports this need, that reveals the behavior of agility.

Breaking things down by behavior defines *agents* in a way that agent system theorists can use directly to model, predict, and validate emergent behavior. *Emergent behavior* in this context is behavior that the system automatically assumes because of the way it is constituted. The extent to which it adapts, the cost of adaptation (extended from our metrics), and whether the result is desirable or not are all results for which we a groundwork. Key concepts are:

- *Emergent behavior* as the adaptive mechanism that constitutes agility
- *Agents* as the units which exhibit this behavior. For our purposes, an agent is something, usually someone, who does something useful. (We defined what tasks are of interest through the Reference Model)
- *Speech acts,* or Communicative acts, which is the exchange of information that allows agents to collaborate

Anyway, we wanted to tell you some future capabilities that this line of thinking may buy us. Modeling processes, in particular process cells of the Reference Model, using speech acts is key to identifying and evaluating the adaptability of the enterprise.

The Need for Federatable Executables

Stick with us through one other minor side trip. Another reason we went with speech act based modeling concerns what you can do with the models. The models should:

- Be directly executable in whatever computerized systems you may have. *Directly* is the key word here. No translations with all their glitches. We want the models to live in the computer, the same way they live in your mind.
- Be able to *control* whatever parts of the enterprise make sense. This is tricky. To "take action" with information needs a model which is formed around exactly those principles. If you, for some reason, use a different methodology, you are effectively translating its internal representation into information-motivated action.
- Be able to turn these processes loose with some constraints removed so that we can see what emerges. In this scenario, some of the agents (the processes, that are the models themselves) become autonomous. The beauty is that the enterprise can be simulated using the real control models the enterprise uses to operate in real life. Most simulations are worthless because of the imperfect translation between the "real life" control code, and the models that represent them; there is difference here.

Regardless of whether one invests in the emergent systems paradigm, important planning and control systems are computerized. It seldom occurs that all of an enterprise's knowledge, models, and code are well integrated. This becomes less true as business models involving many partners become more useful, as in an agile supply chain. The state of integration reaches a disastrous state in the Agile Virtual Enterprise.

What the AVE needs is a collection of methods and tools that will allow it to quickly and cheaply federate systems and knowledge among players regardless of whether there are appropriate standards in use. Developing general federating principles for the AVE was well outside of the scope of the first step; however, history shows that when a relationship is formed, and collaboration is desired, metrics form the basis for framing that collaboration. Integration is only needed to support collaborative goals. Thus, there is an intimate relationship between metrics and integrating infrastructure.

We need to be sensitive to these issues; we cannot simply devise a strategy in ignorance of its context if it is to become useful. Our focus on speech acts supports the most promising approach to this federation problem. The approach identifies the agents and certain principles of how they communicate. Awareness of the context which other agents use allows an agent to adapt its communicative act appropriately to effect federation.

Multiple Representations

Similarly, we need to practice federation within the enterprise's normal representations, because users have different needs and want different presentations. Users in this case may be humans who want to see and understand, humans who want to relay information to an external analysis, or applications which directly access the format. Users tell us that there is a need for four representations:

1. *Tabular* (or field or spreadsheet) representation. We've found this type of representation to be the most accessible to nonprofessional modelers, our target audience. In part, this is because it's a necessarily two-dimensional, ordered means of entering and recovering data elements common to paper and screen layouts. The familiarity is because this is how databases deal with information: Each *row* (the way we present it) is an instance, each *column* is a data type. The accessibility is because each entry is distinctly bounded and cleanly defined. The cells in our spreadsheet view map from our AVE Reference Model.

2. *Graphical* representation. When looking at a process as a system, one needs a representation that conveys the whole picture and key relationships at once. We've chosen a specific graphical representation called a *Dooley Graph,* which is described in some detail later. It is not a graphic logical notation for robust modeling, as one would find within an ordinary modeling methodology. Instead, it is a simple presentation (nodes and arrow) which reveals the structural elements of interest to us regarding how the agents are coupled.

3. *Parametric* representation. This consists of numbers and arithmetic relationships among them. It is essential that this model exist. We believe that few users will consider agility in a vacuum. They will be dealing with the costs and benefits of agility within the context of other business factors, and the common way for these to be balanced is as numbers in parametric models, usually as dollars in spreadsheets. If we cannot present a format for this process, the agility metrics cannot enter the mainstream.

4. *Sentential* representation. While many of our initial users will deal only with the parametric model, a whole new class of planning tools are emerging. These tools understand much of the underlying logic of processes and systems, differing from the tools that reference mere numbers. Formal statements, or sentences are required, statements about processes or related dynamics. The nature of this representation, its capabilities, and possible future uses are the topic of the section on soft modeling.

These are not just different views of the same data; they are different models. Some algorithmic transformation is required. The sentential is the most complete, while our parametric model has the least information, containing only specific arithmetic results. These four models would ideally be federated within an agility planning tool. See Figure 11.2.

Federation would allow a user to explore options in any representation and see the effects in another. The likeliest of these scenarios would be for a planner to enter a collection of real or possible processes in the tabular form, seeing the numbers that indicate agility of each process and the total system. Not liking the number, the planner may choose to look at the graphic format and ask what changes would make the process or system more agile (or equally agile at a lower cost). The tool may call externally using the sentential format, getting back results that show differing graphs and their respective numbers. Chapter 14, dealing with Tool Strategies, explores some useful directions in this regard.

Formal Foundations

Everything we do has to have a foundation that is rigorous. One reason is that we simply cannot support the useful agenda that we have layed out. Another is that business planning is not a casual affair. Where an auditable logic chain is sought, we should be able to deliver.

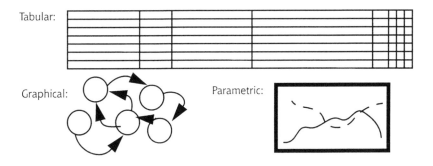

Tabular:

Graphical: Parametric:

Sentential: $S \models <<acts, p1, t, m, <seeks, Or, Ot, 1>, g, 1>>$

Figure 11.2 Four Different Representations

dical idea; the engineering of enterprises to be agile systems
anner is even more so. Conventional foundations can only
cannot afford to create new science, so a strategy was
.age solid science from other domains into this new one where
..te. Some terms and binding needed to be developed.

Among the insights that were integrated, one is central to the method: Modeling processes in the enterprise as *conversations*, then measuring the complexity of the resulting structure.

The Conversation Metaphor

Our representation utilizes a conversation metaphor. The basic idea is that agility is a matter of dynamic coupling, which is accomplished by information transfer. A convenient way to see one specific information transfer is to view it as an *utterance*, which is originated by a single agent and directed at one or more agents. A collection of related utterances is a conversation. Each process in the enterprise involves a conversation which reveals its information structure—the dynamics of how it is coupled internally and with other processes. (The utterance is what we also call a speech or communicative act.)

There's a fairly deep epistemological reason why this approach works for us, which we won't examine in depth, but a simple explanation is that we are interested in the dynamics of collaboration, and what some information values are within a complete system. By defining our primitives as single acts, originating from single actors, we reveal a topology of the collaboration within that system. This representation has a number of benefits:

- It reveals what we need, requiring the minimum (read: lowest cost) data collection.
- As we've noted, it can be directly used for simulation, each actor specification being expressible as executable code.
- As a result of this, it can specify and predict (some) behavior in nondeterministic systems, and reveal emergent behavior.
- The metaphor is intuitive in that many of the harder processes one models are business processes; here model "conversations" map literally to what is said.

Its primary disadvantage is that it is unfamiliar to business analysts and planners, our target audience. The case study in Chapter 12 evaluates the costs associated with this unfamiliarity.

Background of Speech Acts

A common sense view of a simple statement is that it contains information and is either true or false. Much has been built around this idea and we now have elaborate and useful notions of the truth, information content, and meaning of statements. Generally, modeling approaches separate the notions of a task from the information about that task.

This is seen also in the conventional distinction in computer science between data and programs. Data is information that is often shared among machines and humans. Programs, on the other hand, are relatively immobile, often seen as black boxes. They do things, but you don't know how or often even what.

But another view merges the two classes. An utterance by someone is part of the task that is being done, a rather significant part of the overall task if the activity is highly collaborative. Formal thinking on this view has been around for 35 years or so (Austin, 1962). This idea fortunately has been elaborated by the agent community which began within the artificial intelligence community and has since flourished (while generally AI has languished). A substantial percentage of the key sponsorship for this research was by the Advanced Research Projects Agency, one example of which is KQML, the Knowledge Query Markup Language (Cohen & Leveseque, 1995). This represents a decade of refinement of the ideas.

Hereafter, for consistency, we'll try to use the term *utterance* where we have also used *communicative/speech act* and *statement*. A coherent collection of utterances will be a *conversation*. The types of utterances are *performatives*.

Relevance to Agility

Before we get into details, let's review what we are doing and why. Agility is not concerned with everything that occurs in an enterprise; it's concerned with how things are coupled, how they interact, and how readily that coupling can respond in a beneficial way. In this, we are following the thinking of Ken Preiss (Preiss, Goldman, & Nagel, 1996).

That coupling is the same, if we are careful, as the set of utterances among agents within an enterprise. The Reference Model helps us with taking this care. By adopting the foundations of agent theory, we'll be able to express the Reference Model and have a formal basis for looking at the nature of the coupling in the enterprise.

A Candidate Dynamics of Speech Acts [1]

Utterances are of different types and this is important. The type of utterance that says: "Can you paint a widget tomorrow?" is different from "Painting a widget tomorrow will cost eight dollars," and "I painted your widget." The nature of the what is intended is different.

If the goal is to paint widgets, then the first utterance, the query, requires a response, which implies a different type of coupling than the others, which are more informational. The different types of utterances are called *performatives*, meaning loosely the different forms of performing a task.

Many recent process modeling methods and indexing strategies use this technique of defining performatives. Also, much of the research in the collaboration theory area, such as the research at MIT (Malone, Crowston, Lee, & Pentland, 1993) is close in its philosophy.

Major differences are in how many performatives there are, and what constitutes a useful primitive set. One approach is KQML (Finin, Fritzson, McKay, & McEntire, 1994) which defines 42 performatives, but there has been discussion that many are ambiguous and redundant. Another view (Cohen & Leveseque, 1995) suggests a much simpler approach which introduces the notion of a hierarchy and keeps performatives few and atomic. We've adopted this approach.

Speech Acts

Figure 11.3 shows the basic types of performatives, which have already been discussed. All acts are presumed to be attempts to accomplish something, so the top of the hierarchy is "attempt." All acts are subtypes of attempt. The following list is a brief dictionary of the types, which are also called performative.

> *Solicit:* A solicit is an *attempt* by a sender to achieve mutual benefit with an addressee. The sender wants the addressee to do something which the sender wants done. The sender defines both what is done and what constitutes completion.
>> *Question:* A question solicits the addressee to *inform* the sender of some proposition.
>> *Request:* A request solicits the addressee to *commit* to the sender concerning some action.
> *Assert:* An assert is an *attempt* by a sender to achieve mutual benefit with an addressee. The sender wants the addressee to believe the asserted statement.
>> *Inform:* An inform is an *assert* to get the addressee to believe the content.
>> *Commit:* A commit is an *assert* that the sender has adopted a persistent goal to achieve something relative to the addressee's desires.
>> *Refuse:* A refuse is an *assert* that the sender has not adopted a persistent goal to achieve something relative to the addressee's desires.

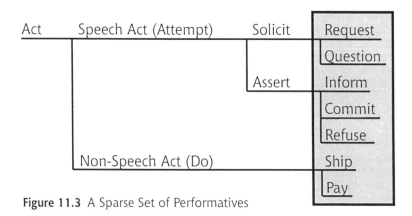

Figure 11.3 A Sparse Set of Performatives

There are some tasks that are not associated with speech. In the general case, these performatives are many, and difficult to define. Fortunately for us, our strategy makes this part of the problem trivial.

Our scope deals with for-profit business enterprises; we assume that every partner and every process adds value to a goal of creating wealth. What is important is that each process has a cost and it adds value; that's all. So we add two non-speech acts to our performative vocabulary.

Ship: A ship is the transfer of value the sender has (perhaps partially) created by executing some portion of the action promised in an earlier *commit* and a *request* that the addressee *pay.*

Pay: A pay is the transfer of wealth between the sender and the addressee. In some contexts, implies an *assert* that the addressee agrees that the sender has (perhaps partially) executed the action promised in an earlier *commit.*

Needless to say, we can come up with innumerable combinations and special cases of these performatives, as we do in everyday life. For instance, there could be a type parallel to assert called *command,* where the control over the content is with the addressee's desires rather than the sender. Or one could, for example, construct something called *propose,* composed of an inform of the sender's willingness to take some action on specified terms with a *request* that the addresses *request* this action of the sender. But for the metrics, we insist on this atomic breakdown because it is simple, complete, and gives us a neutral basis for comparisons among processes and systems.

However, we note here that these atomic performatives can be composed to theoretically map to any formally based modeling method based on information exchange. We expect that within certain applications the addition of composed items may emerge either as an aid for interpreting or as a path to mapping from established models.

Sequential Relations

Another component of the theory deals with the sequential relationships among performatives that constitute a conversation. For some time, *reply* and *resolution* have been considered the basis of repartee (Longacre, 1976).

Van Parunak (Parunak, 1996c) proposes that two others, *response* and *completion,* will also be useful. The four together establish relationships among the agents that we will exploit both in creating a graphical representation and in calculating the metrics. Each of the four is discussed next, in order from most connected to least.

Respond

It follows from the definition of a conversation that each utterance, except the first, responds to a previous one. The response linkage is the fundamental binding that constitutes a conversation in the larger sense; this also is true in the more limited sense we use of a conversation bounded as a process within an enterprise. An utterance (2) responds to another (1) if:

(1) was received,

(1) *caused* (2) (further investigation of "cause" being taken up in our research on Soft Mathematics discussed later), and

There is no other prior series of utterances which (could have) caused (2). Essentially this means that (1) was the first utterance to be received that could have caused (2).

It is necessary that the utterance one responds to be addressed to it; but it is not necessary that the response go back along the same path. The response could, and often does, involve another party. So if A sent an utterance to B, B could respond to that by sending an utterance to C. But B couldn't respond if A's utterance had been to C. A single utterance can respond to multiple preceding utterances.

Reply

Reply is different than respond. Not every utterance after the first is a response. Respond denotes more of a trigger, while reply concerns the *answer* utterance that is triggered. An utterance (2) is a reply to another (1) if:

(1) was received

One of the addressees of (1) is the sender of (2)

The addressee of (2) is the sender of (1)

(2) is the most recent response from that addressee to (1). This condition simply means that the most direct responses are the only one we recognize, not responses through intermediaries.

It is possible for replies to differ from responses. A could send an utterance (1) to B and C; then B could send an utterance to A. In this case (2) could be both a reply and a response to (1). Then C could send an utterance (3) to A that is triggered by (2). In this case, (3) is a response to (2) and a reply to (1).

Resolve

Resolve is a subset of reply. Some utterances presume a reply in the same way that in normal speech a question presumes an answer. This is a result of an utterance controlling some part of the conversation, and the resolve breaks down or completes that temporary control.

A *solicit* not only communicates a mental state, but also proposes rules for how the next steps of the conversation will proceed. A reply can accept or ignore those rules.

The sender of these kinds of utterances establishes the ground rules for the resolution and thence directs to some extent the flow of collaborative information. Since we presume that our conversation is a process that is engineered to accomplish a certain task, this temporal control is important. Presented with this type of control, an addressee can defer resolution, in order to discover more about the context or other agents. Tracking resolution helps illuminate these dynamics.

Only some of our performatives can be resolved: An appropriate *inform* resolves a *question*, and an appropriate *refuse, commit,* or non-speech act (*ship, pay*) resolves a *request.* Note that if an utterance has several addressees, it can have that many resolutions.

It also should be noted here that the whole theory is still being refined, and where new uses and contexts are discovered, changes may be made. For instance, it may be useful in modeling soft processes (those governed by social/psychological laws) to introduce new relations that track how the addressee chooses to deal with this imposed control. What strategy is used and why (assent, defer, ignore, assert) may be important as the scope of the metrics grow (into second order agility and soft modeling). But this is sufficient for many of the most immediately applicable cases.

Complete

Completion is similar to resolve in a way. Where the resolve mechanism captures how the conversation is controlled, the complete mechanism tracks control over the actual task which is the point of the conversation (process).

When one agent commits to do something, it is an important event in the conversation. It's the task that gets done within the bounds of the players that we've constrained in our Reference Model. Details of that task don't show themselves in the conversation, but how the conversation exerts control over the task does.

Only *commits* can be completed. When a party commits, they assume certain things about the environment, which is another way that constraints are composed over the conversation. But as we've noted, the target is not the form of the conversation, but the nature of the task. A commit can be completed by any act.

Resolve and complete are important to us because they capture the two methods by which agents control the conversation (process) toward a goal. The complexity of those control mechanisms relates to the process's adaptability, hence its agility.

PARALLEL TRENDS IN THEORY

Several parallel trends were folded into the effort. These also had the effect of expanding the impact and leveraging the funding of the project.

Linguistic/Syntactic/Situation Theories

The metrics depend on understanding dynamic couplings of processes through the structure of how they communicate. Real vibrant science of communication is full of differing perspectives, esoterica, and emerging results. The dominant thread has always emphasized semantics, the meaning of communication. But there have always been alternative, complementary branches of linguistics, language, and mathematics which focus on the structure, syntax, and context of communication.

In particular, there has been a branch of information science that is interested in the complexity of computer programs. Questions of interest are the intrinsic computing cost and adaptability of computing languages and algorithms.

Another pertinent area is the line of thought originating in studies of cognition and communication, and is a central part of much thinking in artificial intelligence and knowledge representation. It is particularly useful to those working in Multi Agent Systems.

The final of these trends is Situation Theory. Originally this was developed as an alternative to Chomsky grammars, which place primary emphasis on the structure of an utterance. Situation Theory emphasizes more indirect and contextual communication. The Stanford Center for the Study of Language and Information was the focus of this research. This specific line of thought is actually pretty important, so we revisit it in some detail later.

The union of these trends, through our BAST (Business Applications of Situation Theory) workshops accomplished within the project, provides us with a basis for decomposing processes *and their contexts* into speech acts; understanding and reasoning about the processes and contexts; and measuring their complexity and adaptability

Category Versus Set Theories

Early in the history of logic, the mathematical foundation of logic became identified with the mathematics of sets via Set Theory. Essentially all of the implemented engineering principles in programming follow this tradition. Yet mathematicians have developed a parallel tradition based on notions of types and functions, called Category Theory. This theory also can be used as the basis for logic and language, equivalent to set theory. But it has advantages in identifying the transformative process involved.

Category Theory, while relatively unintuitive compared to Set Theory, works well with the linguistic ideas just noted, because the structure of the process is more clearly revealed. As a formal basis, Category Theory also better supports the implementation strategies we note next, for similar reasons.

Group/Graph Theories

Syntactic approaches with categoric underpinnings have been used in the research context for some time. A problem that has limited the approach is the complexity of the underlying mechanics. This is a result of approaches that allow many types of abstractions to be easily created and supported. Without some sort of constraining methodology, the complexity of implementations becomes nasty and unsupportable for real world use.

We've spent a lot of time on this problem on prior projects, and feel that constraining the abstraction strategies by group-theoretic means is the answer.

In computerese, this translates to constraining the typing strategies so that they have an internal structure to which you can apply a simple vocabulary of functions to rigidly simplify constraints. In *real-speak*, it means that the terms of the model (the abstractions) need to be formed in such a way so that we can operate on them without changing them. The "conversation" modeling approach we outlined does this somewhat automatically. And that fact is the magic we employ to map the conversation to a graph that allows us to measure agility.

We've been developing this idea in a tool strategy. The mechanics that an implementor can use have been well developed on the theoretical side of the physical sciences.

As an extra bonus, we've found that group theoretical abstraction (i.e. symmetries) helps visualization of complex situations by a user/modeler, as well as supporting a decomposition within tools that componentizes them. Group theory, in fact all this math stuff, sounds difficult, too professorial to be in a book on practical management tools, but it is not really. In one of the last chapters we give a nontechnical overview of the concepts and why it matters (see Figure 11.4. for the relationships among them). Now, we begin to get closer to a strategy that can form the basis of mission critical, manageable information infrastructure.

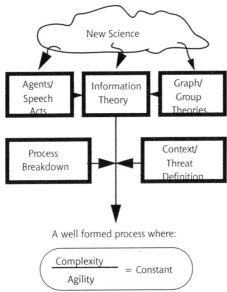

Figure 11.4 Several Contributing Components

BOTTOM LINE

Here's where we are. We described the problem and outlined a three-step solution. We described the Reference Model framework as step one and, as step two, a method for modeling a few of the key cells in the Reference Model. We indicated that this way of modeling not only helps with our immediate problem, but some other problems we'll note later.

But we haven't shown you the speech act modeling in action yet. And you are probably wondering what the third step is. Your waiting is over. The next chapter walks through some examples of the modeling and metrics (the last two steps).

NOTE

1. Information in this section was influenced by research at the Industrial Technology Institute (Parunak, 1996 a, b, c), which was a partner in our project.

Chapter 12

Examples

USE OF THE METRICS

As promised, we now present examples. These should be taken only as a demonstration of the mechanics of evaluating the metrics because there are a variety of ways that the metrics might be employed. The easiest, and most likely, is the one examined in our case studies, that of building a managed supply chain with a specific type and extent of agility. In this case, you presumably know the general type of change and have a general strategy for response that leverages corporate strengths.

The prototype problem that concerned our defense sponsor was a common problem with complex enterprises of many types: The development time of the product is much longer than the rate at which new, important technologies evolve. Best practices dictate that you build your supplier chain early and involve them intimately. But, as the product evolves, that supply chain needs to be agile, not artificially limiting the product and manufacturing processes to commitments made too early. Because the product in this case is a military weapon system, we also have the possible requirement for rapid refinement of its mission profile, which is just the same as shifting market windows in the commercial sector.

In this use, the metrics tell you which processes, among those available to you, are more agile (based on your local definition of the need for agility). Where you are building an agile supplier base, it can tell you which supplier's processes give you the agility you need, both as individual processes and within the VE-level systems context.

If you've evaluated agility a number of times in your situation, you'll build up a case base of instances from which you can draw. In that case, the raw agility numbers can be converted to instant time and cost numbers for a related use. Suppose that you wanted to evaluate the time and cost of changing from one set of processes to another; for example, from a prime contractor's current processes, plus those of a tentative supplier set, you may want the time and cost of changing to another set in response to change. (This would include the savings of the agility gained within the capability of current processes.) In this use, you supply a process and you get back a number measuring its intrinsic agility.

In the system-level view, one would combine all the key processes of all the potential suppliers—according to their weights—to evaluate the agility of the enterprise (for that one change). A simple spreadsheet can do this, but we and others have spent energy on other system-level visualization tools.

Because you won't be certain what the exact threat/change will be, you may want to do a *statistical analysis* of the likely changes to be encountered; in our experience, these might be based on the tools used by the insurance industry to model risk. A spectrum of potential needs will result, with a spread of potential processes and process needs that might be brought into play. Sophisticated tools already exist to perform cost/benefit analyses using extrapolation and simulation, if the responses are well formed functions. Our metrics are: continuous agility functions resulting from a family of related processes.

The way you'd look at a supplier or an enterprise in this view is not based on a single threat or opportunity, but a statistically distributed collection of possible events and options. The movie industry does a similar type of analysis when putting together production VEs, and when evaluating the potential profitability of certain firms, the investment community also performs similar tasks. The key in the investment community is knowing how likely a firm is to be profitable in the future, never mind now (which everyone knows). In many sectors, this means the ability to survive agily and thrive in turbulence.

The most interesting use of the metrics is to go beyond evaluating existing processes to suggest the design of new, more agile processes; or one can in time play with new or changed processes, then simulate/validate the results. That is the direction planned for our future research, which will leverage other tools, including some under development by the sponsored agility community.

The Dooley Graph

Consider Table 12.1. It shows a simple process at the level of complexity we find in a cell of our Reference Model. The process modeled is simple: A prime contractor (*A*) has suppliers (*B, C,* and *D*); the prime contractor needs 50 widgets by next Thursday. We model the process by a specific *instance* which has all of the features of interest. The prime contractor advertises, gets and commits to less than what it wants; changes its mind when it discovers that it can get what it wants by negotiation; ends up *not* getting what it wants; and has to take corrective action. Finally, it pays.

We have selected this instance of the process to capture all the important features of the process that bear on the agility analysis of interest, supposing that the type of agility we're evaluating is the ability to uncommit from one supplier when a more adequate one appears. There would be one conversation like this for each cell of the Reference Model, possibly different conversations for differing strategies or agility-defined conditions of change.

Table 12.1 Breakdown of an Example Process

Sequence	Sender	Receiver	Utterance	Type	Responds to	Replies to	Resolves	Completes
1	A	B C D	Please send me 50 widgets at your catalog price by next Thursday	Request	-	-	-	-
2	B	C	Are you bidding on A's RFQ?	Question	1	-	-	-
3	C	B	Yes, I am	Inform	2	2	2	-
4	B	A	I no bid	Refuse	3	1	1	-
5	C	A	How about 40 widgets at catalog price by next Friday?	Inform, Request	1	1	-	-
6	A	C	Please send me 40 widgets at catalog price by next Friday	Request	5	5	5	-
7	C	A	I plan to send you 40 widgets at catalog price by next Friday	Commit	1	1	1	-
8	D	A	I plan to send you 50 widgets at catalog price by next Thursday	Commit	1	1	1	-
9	A	C	I've found a better supplier, and am not relying on your Commit	Inform	7, 8	7	-	-
10	C	A	I am abandoning my Commit	Refuse	9	9	-	7
11	D	A	Here are your widgets. Please pay me	Ship	1	1	-	8
12	A	D	You are five short. Please send the difference	Assert, Request	1 1	1 1	-	-
13	D	A	Here are five more widgets. Please pay me.	Ship	1 2	1 2	1 2	-
14	A	D	Here's your moola	Pay	1 3	1 3	1 3	

As explained in the previous chapter, the table has a column for each of the sequential relations: respond, reply, resolve, and complete. Each row in the table is a specific utterance based on one and only one of the performatives.

Note how each relation works. Respond is pretty intuitive. Reply is pretty much the same as respond in most cases, but see utterance 4 where we've created a situation where it's different. *B* has decided not to compete with *C*, so *B* tells the contractor in 4 that they are no "bidding" (which may or may not be true). Utterance 4 was triggered by (*responds* to) 3, but is a *reply* to 1. It also *resolves* 1, since that's the end of party *B* for now.

The rest of the relationships are pretty straightforward. Figure 12.1 shows the overlap of the relationships for the example.

There are several ways of graphically representing the example conversation. We want our graphical representation to reveal the specific complexity of the conversation in terms of the features that are costly to both execute and adapt. This graphical form is called a *Dooley Graph,* after the person who first described it.

To introduce Dooley Graphs, we suggest the idea of *states.* In this view, all the players in the enterprise (*A, B, C,* and *D*) collectively form a state machine. Winograd and Flores (1988) developed the idea of a state machine) that would use speech act performatives of the type described previously. A version of their proposal adjusted to Parunak's formalized performative is shown in Figure 12.2. (The Flores version of this has been successfully commercialized by Action Technologies and has been validated in useful business contexts).

A Dooley Graph combines the qualities of *states* and *utterances* into one representation, showing both the effort to support or move the conversation (the utterance component) and the effort effected by the conversation (the state component). It is a simple node diagram, consisting of nodes, or circles and links or arrows. As a hybrid, speakers can occupy more than one node,

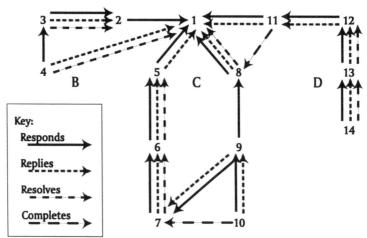

Figure 12.1 The Example's Combined Relationships

depending on the state of the conversation. The Dooley Graph of this example is shown in Figure 12.3.

See how A is in two nodes. A_1 is the role A plays in the first part of the conversation, advertising and eventually buying widgets. A_2 is the second part of the conversation which involves the commitment for an incomplete purchase and later cancellation of that purchase. The process of which this is an instance has additional complexity to be able to support these additional roles of the actors. The Dooley Graph reveals these roles.

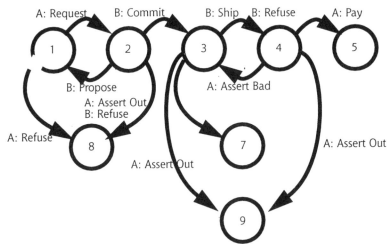

Figure 12.2 Winograd/Flores Model with Formalized Performatives

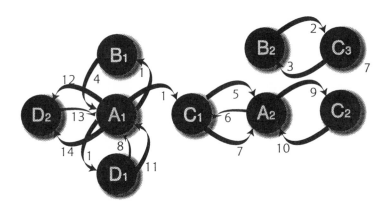

Figure 12.3 The Example's Dooley Graph

The method for creating a Dooley Graph from a table is not intuitively obvious; it is the only link in the process that is not, so we have created a prototype graph calculator, Pomegranate, and associated class libraries to do so automatically. This, which is still generally available, was widely distributed among partners and test cases. It goes from the table to the graph and then takes the step of evaluating the metrics by the counting technique we'll describe later in the chapter.

An Example

Our initial task was to find, among the various complexity features of the Dooley Graph that information theory defines, a small number of features that have the following characteristics:

- They capture the various relevant notions of complexity that relate to dynamic adaptive coupling (agility).
- In doing so, they don't require unneeded, expensive-to-obtain information about the enterprise.
- The number of features is minimal.
- Each feature is independent of the others.
- They are useful for the types of analyses business decisionmakers perform.

In mathematical terms, the features of interest are complete, sparse, and orthogonal; the characteristics make possible the useful mathematical operations that we need (including the arithmetic of accounting). We have found those complexity features that relate to agility; combined, they provide a basis for that black box that business analysts and enterprise engineers need—they put a process in and get back numbers for the time and cost of change.

To describe the interesting features of the graph, we'll use the following example. Table 12.2 shows a typical example process entered in a standard tabular form, slightly more complex than the earlier example. Each row in the table denotes one of the standard communicative acts.

The process modeled is a candidate case for delegated, distributed marketing by an Agile Virtual Enterprise's subordinate partners. Agents *A* and *B* are agents somewhere in the supply chain. *A* is a particularly astute monitor of a potential customer. Agent *C* is within the prime contractor, say a senior marketeer. Agent *D* is a potential customer. This is a particularly promising process for agility, one which enfranchises a partner, even a minor one, to market a customer on the behalf of the combined AVE, even one that cannot at the moment completely meet the customer's need. It could be one of a few key processes upon which this AVE could build an agility strategy.

In this scenario, Acme Grinding (*A*) finds a new need, a new jet engine thrust nozzle design (*N*), of which the customer, Department of the Air Force (*D*), might not be fully aware. The AVE, which contains *A*, *B*, and *C*, currently cannot meet the need. But it might if some processes change. Perhaps Basic Casting Co. (*B*) can satisfy part of the new need by developing a new process,

B'. Or maybe something less, a smaller change, *B"*, will do if *A* itself makes a change to *A'*. In both cases, it is unknown to *A* whether the prime contractor, Consolidated Aircraft *(C)*, can fill in the other blanks, either by itself now, by changing its own processes, or by finding or changing other partners. So Acme Grinding has to do some discovery and present tentative results to the prime contractor, *C,* for its action.

Let's say Basic Casting makes nozzles of (the fictitious) *nonamium* for Consolidated's new aircraft, which Acme cleans and treats. Consolidated and the Air Force selected nonamium over (the equally fictitious) *newstuffium* because of the finishing costs. Acme learns of a new finishing process (*A'*)

Table 12.2 Breakdown of an Example Process

Sequence	Sender	Receiver	Utterance	Type	Responds to	replies to	Resolves	Completes
1	A	D	Might you have a need for N?	Question	-	-	-	-
2	D	A	Now that you mention it, we might	Inform	1	1	1	-
3	D	A	Tell me more	Question	1	1	-	-
4	A	B	Do you have skillsets B', needed for N?	Question	2	-	-	-
5	B	A	No, but we have B"	Inform	4	4	4	-
6	B	A	Do you want us to develop B'?	Question	4	4	-	-
7	A	C	If I do A' and B does B' or B" can we do N?	Question	2	-	-	-
8	C	A	Yes; looks good; can do; only need B'	Inform	7	7	7	-
9	A	B	We only need B'	Inform	6, 8	6	6	-
10	A	B	Can you commit to B'	Question	6	6	-	-
11	B	A	We can commit	Inform	10	1 0	1 0	-
12	A	C	Both A and B can commit to A' and B'	Inform	6, 11	8	-	-
13	C	D	Would you like us to address your need, N?	Question	12	-	-	-

which might change that decision, and greatly reduce the cost of the aircraft, so much so that a competitor to Consolidated could (in the future) design a better, cheaper aircraft.

But Acme has to discover whether Basic can learn to make a clean new-stuffium part (B'), or a more dirty part, using a less radical casting process B". We've chosen this example because it assumes trust and novel reward strategies; these would be covered in another process that would be evaluated in a similar way. It also assumes that Acme can discover the cost of change within Basic, probably by using the metrics.

Table 12.2 shows Acme (A) going to Basic (B) and finding out what Basic can do, then reporting the results of potential opportunity and capabilities to Consolidated (C) for following up.

Figure 12.4 shows the same process in the Dooley Graph form, which reveals the structure of the communicative acts within the process. The letters in the circles are the players. Player A (A_1, A_2, A_3) appears several times, because it performs more than one role. An arrow denotes each utterance, which is also a line in the table. As with the previous example, to make things easy to follow, we put the line number from the table next to each arrow.

Note in the Dooley Graph that some nodes are linked by lightly shaded links which are not communicative acts within the scope of the process. These are virtual acts, presumably supported by other processes or contexts in the enterprise. The number and type of such *virtual linkages* forms the basis for a related set of metrics we have investigated, to measure trust. We'll get to that in the next chapter.

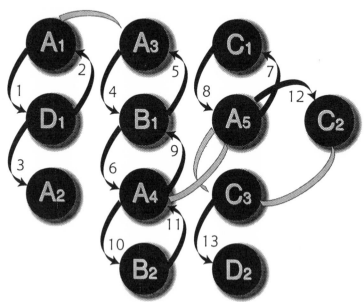

Figure 12.4 Dooley Graph of the Example

Recall that the complexity of this graph is directly related to how adaptable the process is. Metrics of this complexity give us measures of agility. One beauty of the approach is that the complexity of the graph is purely in its shape. Because it is the shapes and links we are concerned with, we can now forget about the fact that the upper left hand circle represents a specific actor, and that an arrow represents a specific utterance, or even which direction the arrow goes.

There are two measurable features of this graph which reveal its complexity: The number of nodes and the complexity of each node, and the number and complexity of the links. They are complete, sparse, and orthogonal, constituting a raw measure of agility. They are:

The Number of Nodes and Their Complexity

The complexity of a node is the number of other nodes to which it has a communicative link. Figure 12.5 tags the graph's nodes and links with these numbers. The node in the upper left, for instance, is a two-node, since it has two (solid black) connections, even though they are to the same node.

This example has 12 nodes, four of which connect to one other node, four of which connect to two, two of which connect to three, and two of which connect to four. The metric derived from this information is a simple sum of the number of each node raised to the power of its type. For instance, there are four two-nodes; since these are two-nodes, the four gets raised to the second power, 4^2 equals 16. As a colloquial shorthand (providing a name rather than a formal definition), we call the sum the *distance* metric. The example's distance

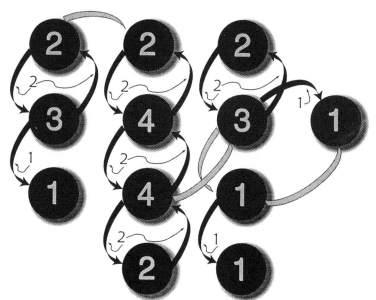

Figure 12.5 Counting Topological Features of the Example

metric is $4^1+4^2+2^3+2^4=44$. (The first number records that there are 4 nodes from Figure 12.5 that are labeled 1; they have only one link associated with them. The number of linkages is also the power to which the count is raised, in this case, one. There are four labeled 2, so that produces our second term, four raised to the second power. Two of the disks have three links, and two have four links, which gives our third and fourth terms.)

The higher the sum, the higher the cost and/or time of changing the process. One can see this intuitively: the more *actors* involved, and the more each one does, the harder it will be to change the process.

The Number and Complexity of Links

A strict application of this metric defines a link or loop, by the number of communicative acts (represented by arrows) there are before the utterance is resolved. We have found that an accurate approximation simply counts the apparent loops. For instance, in Figure 12.4, acts 6 and 9 appear visually as a two-part loop, though strictly speaking they are part of a more complex communication. Defined this simple way, the example has three one-loops (one-way arrows) and five apparent two-loops. These are added in a weighted fashion similar to the distance metric, so what we call the *Time Delay* metric for the example would be $3^1+5^2=26$. This is calculated in a way similar to the node-oriented equation except this time the arrow structures, or loops, are counted. Figure 12.5 shows that there are 3 arrows that are dead-end acts, noted with the number one to show that they are loop structures constructed of one arrow. These three raised to the first power are our equation's first term. There are five loop structures composed of two arrows, producing our second term, five raised to the second power.

The way to intuitively understand this metric is that the more tasks a specific subconversation (a "loop") has to do, meaning that more players are involved in the collaboration, the harder it will be to change.

The resulting two numbers (the distance number 44 and the time delay of 26) are simply added together to give a raw metric of the process's agility; the higher the number, the less the agility. This composite metric would be used in comparing the agility of processes which differentiate foe example, two potential partners.

There are associated metrics. Suppose that you wanted to evaluate the cost and time associated with making a specific change from one process to another, and you have a model of both. You would do a *topology match* between the two graphs, which measures the cost of changing from one process to another. The starting (or *before*) process is the baseline. Here we count nodes only, the percentage of nodes in the target process that have exact type matches in the baseline. The left side of Figure 12.6, using our example as the *before* process, while the right side represents a process with a different topology as an *after*. Six of the twelve nodes of the process on the left have matches with the process on the right, so the metric is six divided by twelve or .50. (For the four one-nodes on the left, there is one on the right; for the four two-nodes on the left, all find matches on the right; of the two three-nodes on the left, one finds a match on the right; and there are no four-node matches on the right.) A higher number indicates lower cost.

Here's an interesting observation: The relative cost of adapting from the right to the left instead of the other way around is .86, indicating that the adaptation would be easier going the other way. (For the one-node on the right, there is a match on the left; for the five two-nodes on the right, there are only four matches on the left; and for the one three-node on the right, there is a match on the left.)

The metrics of that example deal with individual processes. But a collection of agile processes does not necessarily add up to an agile enterprise; there's a second-order metric, which we noted in Chapter 9. But in many cases—essentially all cases where the extent of agility can be predicted and controlled—dealing with the first-order agility we've described is sufficient. Nonetheless, every process carries a different weight in the system. The following two metrics characterize that weight:

- *Importance* is the informal name for the comparison of the distance of the process to that of the enterprise, a comparison of the complexity of the nodes. In our example, let's say that the entire enterprise has an (unweighted) number of 423 (a number completely picked at random), then 12 divided by 423 is the relative importance of the process within the enterprise's agility profile. That number, $^{12}/_{423}$, gets compared with similar weights of other processes to evaluate the agility of the entire enterprise within the context being considered.
- A similar calculation takes place to determine what we call the *frequency* of the process, but this time, the process's number of loops is compared to that of the enterprise (see Table 12.3).

These two numbers summed provide the weighting function used when adding individual key processes across an enterprise to understand its relative agility. The latter two numbers do not require that all processes in the enterprise (or projected enterprise configurations) need to be modeled this way in order to get the enterprise-wide *distance* and *timedelay*. Because the *impor-*

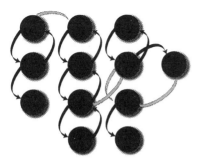 

Figure 12.6 The Cost of Mapping from the Process on the Left to the Right

tance and *frequency* are used relatively, the roughest of approximations will suffice.

We've now validated the metrics both by formal reasoning, by retrospectively applying them to the Agile Virtual Enterprise Best Agile Practice cases interviewed as a project of the Agility Forum, and by direct application.

The key metrics are the first two (distance and timedelay). These produce a raw number that can be used as a relative measure of agility of the process. Once the well-indexed case bases of agile practices now being built by MIT, the Agility Forum, and others (large consulting firms) are finished, we will be able to:

- *Calibrate* the raw agility numbers to time and cost numbers in specific sectors. This will allow managers to register agility with other cost/benefit calculations in a balanced strategy.
- *Extrapolate* numbers into functions. This will allow managers to follow process design guidelines in engineering the ideal agility into processes, again following a balanced strategy.

APPLICATION IN THE REAL WORLD: A CASE STUDY

What we've just described seems mechanical and sterile when taken by itself, out of context. How would tinkering with circles support a real-world strategy? Here we run through another, similar example, but this time at a higher level. The case study we now describe, had fairly modest aspirations. We took a typical Type 3 AVE, led by a conventional prime contractor. We targeted agility in the supply chain and had a specific ideal in mind.

The U.S. Defense acquisition system is based on the idea of designing and manufacturing the right system. That system is supposed to be apt for their missions and reflect the most beneficial product and process technologies when fielded. Essentially all defense manufacturing research has been design research, to increase the chances of getting it right the first time.

Concurrent Engineering (CE) and Integrated Product and Process Development (IPPD) are two examples of this thinking. They address the well-accepted "wisdom" that most of the cost of the system is set very early in the life of the design. CE and IPPD allow more iterations and alternatives in that short period,

Table 12.3 Summary of the Intermediate Metrics

Distance	Total number of weighted nodes
Time Delay	Total number of weighted loops
Moveability	Topology match, internal
Importance	Nodes compared to the VE's total
Frequency	Loops compared to the VE's total

and carefully provide for insight into the downstream implications of early decisions. This was discussed in Chapter 8.

But these two approaches can never be sufficient in dynamic situations where technology and missions continue to change throughout the whole life cycle, not just the first 20%. History shows that essentially no major weapon system since World War II has been right the first time. And odds are that getting it right will be even more impossible as missions evolve more quickly than in the past and as the technology changerate increases exponentially.

Our case study addressed lowering the cost of getting it right the second (or third) time, by relaxing the period of time that design decisions need to be frozen. Typically, in the defense environment, all major design decisions are made in the very early phases, because of the perceived need to lock in suppliers (and their processes). It's the way the system works. We change that.

The work breakdown—who does what—becomes a part of the legal fabric of contracts and responsibilities. If the supply chain were agile, if the members and processes could change in midstream, then basic design decisions could be changed much later at low cost—indeed all the way through. We did not make such unrealistic assumptions changes in how the world might change, for instance that acquisition law might change. Instead, we wanted a scenario that a prime contractor could implement today, which is how this case study came to be.

Background

In this scenario, you are employed by an aerospace prime contractor that supplies tactical missiles to the U.S. Department of Defense (DoD). The situation is highly competitive, and you are going head-to-head with a competitor for an important air-to-air missile contract which may affect your chances for survival.

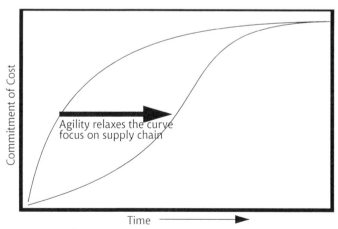

Figure 12.7 An Agile Supply Chain Allows Design Changes to Be Made Later

You and your competitor compete on cost, which hurts you both. But you could get extra points for advanced technology in your product in the contract-awarding evaluation. However, your DoD customer is sensitive to and avoids technology-induced risk in its projects.

Both of you are starting with similar, low-risk technical approaches, but you have a smart, inventive engineering staff. It's probable that they can come up with design alternatives late in the design life cycle, well past the ordinary time it takes for you (and your competition) to adjust your supplier chain.

If you have agility built into your supplier chain, so it can adjust to major redesigns late in the game, you can win the contract, and win it on advantageous, higher-cost terms.

Your Company's Possibilities

Your company has decided (through the strategic planning process) that competitive leverage can be gained by focusing on technology improvement in the design of the steering system. Both you and your competition were planning on using metal fins, which is a low-risk decision. However, your company's engineers have two design possibilities that would greatly increase the performance of the missile and improve your chances of winning the contracts, but both design options won't be ready until late in the development cycle, well after you normally freeze your production assets, in this case your supplier base.

The missile, as originally designed, is controlled by metal fins at the rear of the missile tube. The first option is to replace the metal fins with ones made of an advanced composite material, which would be both lighter and capable of standing higher temperatures. Most important is that because the material is far stronger and lighter, the fins can be larger, making the missile more maneuverable. The customer's evaluation criteria value that performance improvement. If you could use the new fins, it would mean that you would be competing on product performance rather than cost—your company would much rather have a high chance of winning on performance, and reap the benefits of higher profit.

The other design option is to do away with fins altogether, making the rocket nozzle out of the same composite material and gimbaling it so that steering fins aren't needed. Adoption of this option would guarantee winning the contract on merit and also open possibilities for profitable growth in the product line.

Unfortunately, your engineers will not be able to design sufficient risk out of these alternatives until 200 days before production in the first case and 100 days in the second. Your normal best date for freezing these decisions is 300 days, which is controlled by lining up and preparing suppliers. At the 200 and 100 day marks, your engineers expect to be able to tell you for sure whether the options are viable.

Therefore, your company seeks sufficient agility in the supplier base for this section of the missile to allow them to adapt to the alternatives if your engineers can get the designs ready by engineering out unacceptable product risk.

(Incidentally, the strategic planning that determined these levels of probability was a directed series of simulations, conducted at different levels of detail. The idea was to discover the strategies that are most beneficial and include conventional non-agile features, as well as the agile ones we add.

But such simulations are now directed by senior management largely on the basis of intuition. Our investigations of the dynamics which support the metrics have also indicated a structured brainstorming method that can better direct the strategic simulations. In this system, participants adopt memes that are contrary to their nature and argue from unanticipated perspectives.)

It was through the strategic planning process that the engineers' decision dates and associated probabilities were established, as well as the profitability of pursuing this agility strategy. The engineers have given you certain information concerning the options:

- Which transactions with potential suppliers are expected to be important (this comes directly from the simulations).
- Which features (described later) of those transactions are important, with a weighting factor for each.
- An agility bogey (or goal) for each instance—meaning the extent of change required in the supplier chain.
- An agility budget—meaning the time and cost allowed for that change while still maintaining a competitive product cost.

Your Agility Budget

The budget that you have been given is 25% over the baseline cost of the metal fins. Included in this budget is the cost of changing suppliers from the one planned to supply the metal fins. The LandFin Company is the supplier initially selected for this job, being the best (in terms of cost, time, and quality)

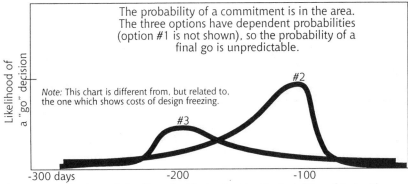

Figure 12.8 Design of the Supply Chain for the Probability of Late Changes

when only the metal fin design is considered. They have no experience with composites, so might not be an agile choice, but they are your baseline.

The 25% budget does not include added cost to the product proper; that is considered in the decision by engineering/management in whether to go with it or not. But it does include the cost of having a ready supplier base. You can spend the money as you wish to accomplish the goal. Examples of how you may chose to spend your budget:

- Increasing your internal ability to support the change, for example, in acquiring specifications related to composites so that you can direct unknowledgeable suppliers like LandFin.
- As contract termination fees to discontinued suppliers, so that a simple supplier swap is feasible, from LandFin to an alternative.
- As fees to keep suppliers hot, in which case you are buying capability that you may never use, like an alternative to LandFin.
- As funding to help suppliers learn/hire consultants or insource skills.
- As funding for your cost to transfer skills, processes and equipment to a supplier.

Probabilities of Change

Management has now consulted with the engineering staff and determined a balance for deciding to go with either of the two options. The composite nozzle option has a cutoff date for when the risk will be engineered out of the system design. That date is 200 days before production. A similar cutoff date of 100 days is given for the composite fins, later because it will perturb the overall design of the missile less. The strategic planners believe that there is a 20% chance of going with the novel nozzle and a 50% chance of going with the composite fins. Your job in effect is to design the risk out of the supplier base of making these design changes late in the game.

Your Alternatives

In order to address this problem, you've decided to investigate four alternatives using the agility metrics to determine the one that is most agile (together with other metrics which measure conventional time and cost criteria):

- Alternative 1: Stay with LandFin and pay them to develop/insource/outsource the needed capability.
- Alternative 2: Reselect a single supplier based on agility and engage with them to support the needed changes.
- Alternative 3: Reselect 2 or 3 suppliers based on pure capability, paying all to stay hot, and planning to terminate two. Pure capability means just their ability to make metal fins only or composite fins only, or gimbals, regardless of their agility.
- Alternative 4: Reselect 2 or 3 suppliers based on both capability and agility, and also engage with them to support the needed changes.

The practical use of the metrics will be in evaluating candidates for the alternatives, and in evaluating the alternatives themselves, against the company's agility strategy

The Target Cells

Creating and managing a Virtual Enterprise is a matter of creating and managing infrastructure. Your first job is to parse the infrastructure using the Reference Model (or similar breakdown) and identify the key processes. In this case, you've decided that the strategy should be contracts-oriented, as opposed to culture or workflow.

The contracts subinfrastructure in your company, the part that deals with your relationship to suppliers, is further broken down, for example, into the following kinds of concerns (as well as others):

•Quality Assurance (QA) Provisions
•Liability/Benefit Accrual
•Issues Associated with Intellectual Property Development
•How to Insert New Technology
•Disaster Recovery Plan

Each one of these will be handled as an individual, contributing component with metrics that evaluate its agility in the strategic context. At the end, the components will be added using the weighting factors passed down from the strategic planning effort. The resulting metric will only tell you the time and cost associated with change. Those time and cost figures will be added to other, conventional time and cost metrics that measure each supplier's effec-

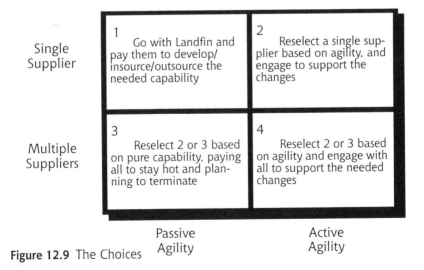

Figure 12.9 The Choices

tiveness at production. The result will tell you in quantitative terms which is the least time and lowest cost.

Modeling the Quality Assurance Process

Fortunately, parsing the infrastructure into these "cells" results in very simple processes. In this example, we'll focus on one of these processes: contract support for QA (that's just the contract support, not the entire QA process). In the baseline case, where you are buying the metal fins from a single supplier, LandFin, your QA is driven from above. From the point-of-view of the contracts, the sole purpose of the QA process is to satisfy the customer and indemnify yourself against claims.

In the baseline case, you use a conventional (at least for defense contractors) approach: You get a first article from the supplier, you destructively test it, and then you put into place an inspection/certification process that ensures that the supplier is meeting the relevant military specifications. By the terms of your typical defense contract, if you do these two things, you are indemnified from future damages. In this case, you understand how to test the fins and you own the test equipment. Your source model will record:

- Request for QA items (example items and relevant documents) from LandFin
- Receive the first article
- Test the first article
- Accept or reject the design
- In the case of acceptance, get the process certification plan (which tests for mil-spec compliance)
- Evaluate the plan for its ability to protect you and satisfy the customer
- Accept or reject the plan

You'll also model the QA processes of the alternatives from the contracts perspective. But either of the composite options are quite different. Let's say that your company has no experience with composites. In particular, you own no composite test equipment, nor do you have any related test experience. You can specify performance of the composite part, but you have no way of testing it; you'll have to count on the supplier for that. Also, DoD has no relevant specified processes for composites of this type, so you'll have to ask the supplier to guarantee processes.

Note the radical difference here. In the baseline case, all the contract processes are geared toward indemnifying you through the customer. In any of the alternatives, all the contract processes are geared to ensuring indemnification through the supplier. This is quite a change.

The alternatives all share the same model, recording:

- Request for indemnification plan
- Receive the plan

•Examine the plan to see whether the guaranteed performance of the product meets your needs, and to ensure that their plan indemnifies you
•Accept or reject the plan

In Alternatives 2 and 4, where you have decided to take action in case of a deficiency in the supplier, the model goes on. In these cases, the action would be to help them acquire a competency that makes them capable of indemnifying you. For example, you may loan them money for test equipment, or use search skills to find them a subcontractor to fill their need. The extended model for these cases is:

1. In the case of rejection, get help from a third party
2. Install the assets, loop to the second bullet, receive the new plan

Capturing the required information for you was easy because it used intuitive concepts, didn't force you to model the entire VE in order to understand contracts, and allowed reuse of diverse models.

The Graphs

The graph (see Figure 12.10) for the baseline case has six nodes arranged this way:

•Contracts (AC_1) asks for and receives the first article from the Supplier, LandFin (B_1)
•Contracts (AC_1) has engineering (AE_1) test and report on the first article
•Contracts (AC_1) notifies LandFin (B_2) that the design is acceptable
•LandFin (B_2) accepts engineering (AE_2) in-house to monitor mil-spec conformance
•LandFin (B_2) delivers an acceptable plan to contracts (AC_2)

The graph for both alternatives 2 and 4 (see Figure 12.11) has five nodes arranged thus:

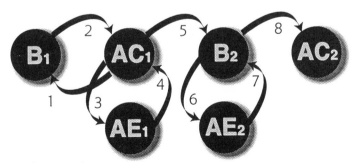

Figure 12.10 The Base Case

•Contracts (AC_1) asks supplier (B_1) for an acceptable design and indemnification plan
•Contracts (AC_1) has engineering (AE_1) evaluate and report on the plan and design
•Contracts (AC_1) sees a discrepancy in the plan and goes to another company (C_1) to supplement the plan
•That company (C_1) installs the missing competency to the supplier (B_2)
•The supplier (B_2) reports back to contracts (AC_1) with an acceptable plan

You may have noticed that this example has coarser nodes than the last, that each "utterance" performs more tasks. In fact, speech act modeling is an art like most modeling. Different styles can be implemented by different modelers, and how detailed one gets in breaking down the speech acts is one of these style choices. For our purposes, it doesn't matter which level of detail is used, so long as all models have the same style. As it happens, there is a formal way of mixing models that are coarse (to save modeling costs) and those that are fine (to capture important details). This is called Layered Formalism and Zooming (LFZ) (Devlin and Rosenberg, 1996). As before, the metrics result from a simple counting exercise.

Calculating the Metrics

Distance. The (weighted) number of nodes. The weighting is by the power of each node (the number of two-node is raised to the power of two because of the simple power law of complexity), so the distance (from zero) of the base case is $1^1+3^2+0^3+1^4+1^5+0^6=12$. The distance (from zero) of alternatives 2 and 4 is $0^1+4^2+0^3+0^4+0^5+1^6=17$. The relative distance between them is 17-12=5. The time and cost of adapting from a distance of 5 is less in a predictable way than the time and cost of adapting a distance of 20. With a large number of instances, we can calibrate this number to time and cost.

Time Delay. The (weighted) total number of loops. The weighting is similarly by the power of the loops, so the delay (from zero) of the base case is $2^1+3^2+0^3+0^4+0^5+0^6=11$. The delay of alternatives 2 and 4 (from zero) is $0^1+2^2+1^3+0^4+0^5+0^6=5$. The relative time delay is -6. A greater number is correlated with a greater sum of time and cost.

Adding 5 and -6 gives -1. The second process is more agile.

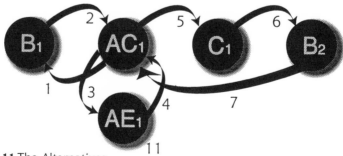

Figure 12.11 The Alternatives

Moveability. This metric is a topology match between the two graphs and measures the structural difference of the support for communication. It is calculated as the ratio of nodes that match to baseline nodes. The baseline case has one 1-node, three 2-nodes, no 3-nodes, one 4-node, and one 5-node. Alternatives 2 and 4 have four 2-nodes and one 6-node. Of these, three of the six nodes in the base case can find matches in the target case; this would be three of the 2-nodes. Since half of the nodes have matches, the moveability metric is 50(%). It's a crude measure of the topology match but very effective: a greater number indicates a greater match and a lowered time and cost to adjust.

Importance. This metric is the ratio of nodes to the total number of nodes (weighted sum) in the contracts subinfrastructure for the entire Virtual Enterprise (in this case, the supplier chain), normalized by 10,000 (just to make the results more friendly). Suppose that the total number of nodes in that area is 13,669 (a number picked at random for the example) for the base case and 8,085 for the alternatives. Then the importance of our example in the base case is $12 \div 13,669 \times 10,000 = 8.8$, and that of the alternatives $17 \div 8,085 \times 10,000 = 21$, a much higher importance. This means that although the first process is by itself more agile, the second process both supports a system that overall is more agile (by this measure) and plays a lager role in that agility.

Frequency. Calculated in the same way as importance except using weighted loops. Employing the same arithmetic, the frequency distance metric between the two is 194.5, supposing that the base case's loop sum is 4,890 and that of the alternatives is 220. (($11 \div 4,890) \times 10,000 = 22.5$ and $(5 \div 220) \times 10,000 = 227$). The greater this number (227 compared to 22.5), the greater the time and cost of change.

Summing the Metrics

We've given an example of deriving metrics for one of the small components into which we've decomposed the situation. You'll have many of these for each of the three Legal/Explicit infrastructure domains under consideration for the missile fin problem. These will be well-behaved arithmetically, and we want to add them according to the importance of that component to the enterprise. For example, it may be that the QA contracting area is expected to carry three times as much weight in computing the cost of change than, say, the component related to retraining document editors.

This relative weighting is one of three important pieces of information that the strategic planners provided you at the beginning of this exercise. They derived that information from simulation exercises using dynamic forms of the same metrics. The three insights they passed on were:

1. The relative importance among the components of the enterprise.

2. The breakdown of time and cost. You'll have created graphs which relate the five features to relative agility. Your planners will correlate the function you derive to the breakdown between time and cost, because that relationship is a matter of strategic priorities.

3. Finally, they'll have given you the probabilities to assign to each of the alternatives so that you can weigh how important agility for the composite fins is compared to the metal fins and the composite nozzle. We've already noted that those probabilities are: 20% for the nozzle, 50% for the composite fins, and 30% for the metal fins in absolute terms, but each of these probabilities is time-related. Everything changes, for instance, once the deadline for selecting the nozzle passes at minus 200 days.

Alternatively, you could get the same information from a large, robust case base on collected calibrated agility case studies, from your regular consultant. This assumes that they have used these metrics a large number of times already and can predict the results without actually "running the numbers."

You are now able to perform several simple arithmetic calculations: (1) Applying the time and cost functions to break your many component numbers into their time and cost equivalents, and (2) Using the weighting function to sum all the components for each alternative. On those totaled time and cost curves, you locate your agility bogey. We use the horizontal axis for this (see Figure 12.12).

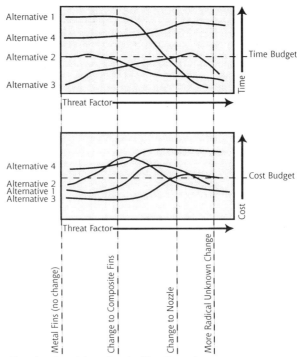

Figure 12.12 Graphs Combine the Agility Functions

What you have now is a total time and cost of change for each of the four alternatives, multiplied by however many candidate companies you have (combinations of companies in the cases of alternatives 3 and 4). But you are not finished yet! It's not enough to go with the candidates and alternatives that offer the lowest cost of change if their product cost is high. You now add on your agility time and cost of change with separately derived time and cost metrics of their basic products and services.

Finally, you weight the costs by the 20%, 30% and 50% weighting for possibilities that you are given and you have indications for the lowest cost design of a supplier chain under the engineered conditions of change.

DEEPER INTO A CASE STUDY

The previous example was part of the research done for a detailed case study with the following characteristics:

- focused on the supply chain, assuming practices current or possible without presuming unrealistic change in acquisition law;
- centered on problems of a real tactical missile manufacturer as defined by the DARPA-sponsored Affordable Multi Missile Manufacturing (AM^3) program;
- the cost portion audited by a third party experienced in enterprise engineering, the Aerospace Agile Manufacturing Research Center; and
- devised to evaluate the *cost* of applying the metrics in a practical case.

Did Akio Morita (see Chapter 5) have it right? Is Hollywood an exemplar of the new way of building organizations which are especially attuned to customer's needs, even more deeply than they themselves know? Is this extractable from the exotic movie sector and applicable to the primarily high-value manufacturing domains which concern us in the agility community? Is this agility?

With due regard to the limits of pressing analogies too far, we're inclined to think so, and we framed our Defense Case Study in the context of a (fictitious) High Concept enterprise. The chain of logic/chain of events we followed was:

- Start with a succinct problem statement, such as a *High Concept* for a missile.
- Use the AVE Reference Model to identify agents that result from the High Concept. The High Concept mechanisms in this sector are contractual and deal with responsibilities like the QA responsibility of the example.
- Apply the metrics as we've outlined in this chapter.
- Apply the system-level agility metric at the High Concept level to evaluate the relative time and costs of supporting the High Concept by those agents and strategies.

The purpose of all this was to confirm that not only can agility be understood and managed, but also that agility can have a beneficial effect on a new strategy based on High Concept. We went to much trouble in Chapter 5 outlining such a vision (the section that made big demands on your tolerance for buzzwords).

Application Domain

We present now another case study (which insists on anonymity) that had several interesting characteristics. By now you may be tired of hearing about the defense world, but many features of this case study are relevant for many large commercial supply chains. This domain has the following characteristics, which would imply a need for agility:

- The prime contractors are consolidating and sloughing off capability; creating VEs within the prime at some level; and investment cycles (investment changerate) within the prime contractors are being disrupted. So multiple products must be created with the same assets.
- The product is complex with a very high technology component; rate of change of basic technologies (technology changerate), in both products and processes is high and increasing.
- The *supply chain* adds a significant percentage of the product's value, with many niches of product and process specialization. That supply base is becoming less rich over time.
- The customers are changing: Where the U.S. military used to be the primary customer, now foreign sales are becoming more important.
- More variants and derivatives are required because the product/customer expectation changerate is increasing. The missions are more unknown.
- To an increasing degree, the product must be integrated into larger systems whose basic designs and integration strategies are not under the control of the prime contractor but which are jointly owned by several peer prime contractors and the customers.

In addition, the domain has the following two characteristics which may be unique. These make the case study manageable and a cartoon of the general commercial world:

- The acquisition laws and regulations that govern the customer to prime contractor, and prime contractor to subcontractor relationships, are different, more limiting, than those in the civil sector. Competitive pressure exists, but the mechanics are different than conventional free market forces.
- The defense manufacturing base in general is often managed as a *strategic* asset. The customer, DoD, performs various roles as conventional consumer of products, specifier (often designer) of products; often controller of work breakdown,

processes, and indemnification; and as occasional manager of strategic design and production assets (see Figure 12.13).

The Strategy and the Reference Cells

When we ran through one cell of this case study, we skipped over the step that we outlined in the last chapter: Going from a strategy to a few cells in the Reference Model. We saved that for now, because we want to indicate how use of the metrics can shape a strategy.

Experts familiar with the business and Reference models, considering the High Concept (feature-based manufacturing) idea as a goal, quickly zeroed in on Group 4 of the Reference Model's Life Cycle, *VE Operation*—specifically *4.1 Performance Metrics,* as the primary target. These are the measures used in operation to determine that each partner is doing its job.

Everyone knows that it would be much better to deal with change at a more fundamental level, earlier in the life cycle. But that is an unaffordable luxury for nearly all existing businesses. So we deal with a less revolutionary, more realistic fulcrum for change, later in the life cycle.

In the infrastructures, we settled on *Identifying the Need to Change*, process 1 of group 5. The focus on this was a direct result of AVE Focus Group attention on trusted agents (discussed later in Chapter 13). An element of that trust is confidence in the ability to recognize the need for change in the VE. Table 12.4 is the same subset of the Reference Model we've used a couple times. The one cell of primary interest in the case study is highlighted.

A total of twenty high-value cells resulted. The thrust of the case study was to investigate how difficult, how effective, and how costly it is to discover sufficient information about each of those twenty cells to allow us to compute our

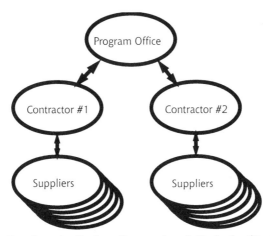

Figure 12.13 Two Supply Chains: Conventional Chain (agility benefits the contractor); DoD Chain (agility benefits the nation)

agility metrics (for each alternative for the cell). In doing so, we were guided by the following suggested agility strategies.

Strategy 1

(Refer to Figure 12.9 for a graphical expression of the local versions of these strategies.)

Let's suppose that DoD wants to lower the cost of missiles, and it has determined that high costs are due to specialization. A major symptom that is apparent is the one missile type—one plant/design team/supply chain problem. But underlying this is the high cost of moving across business practice boundaries once a project is rolling, affecting the ability to mix supply chain expertise and processes. This also prevents DoD from inserting technology into existing products for upgrades, variants, and special editions.

DoD might pursue an agility strategy that builds a supply chain that has trusted, empowered agents in key positions. These agents are particularly integrated into DoD's systems for determining need, or making cost/performance trade-offs. They would be able to bring information to the table about the need to adapt processes and the cost of adaptation.

Table 12.4 The Case Study's Focus Cells

	C.a.e. Depth of Customer Relations	C.b.b. Risk/Reward Contracts	C.c.c. Work Breakdown Structure	D.a.a. Human Collaboration
1.3. Targeted Market	■			
2.3 Partner Search				
3.6. Risk/Reward Strategies				
4.1. Performance Metrics				
5.1. Identify Need for Change				

This is a specific agility strategy that DoD, as the owner of a supply chain might devise. A way to support this strategy would be to focus on cell C.a.e (Business Practice Infrastructure to Support Depth of Customer Relations in the Supply Chain) and 5.1 (Identifying the Need to Reconfigure the Supply Chain). This is the set of processes that establishes trusted agents for change by both providing them with insights/feedback to the customer's needs and the wisdom/ability to make appropriate changes in the supply chain.

You could put together a support strategy in which these cells dominate in their support:

C.a.e/4.1: Business practice infrastructure that bases the way the Supply Chain is measured in its performance on how well they listen to and respond to the needs of DoD.

C.b.b/3.6: Contractual infrastructure that supports the above by building appropriate risk and reward strategies into the supply chain.

C.c.c/1.3: Infrastructure which identifies the mapping of processes in the Supply Chain to specific product goals in DoD.

C.d.a/2.3: Infrastructure which provides for sufficient collaboration among agents in the existing and potential supply chain.

Strategy 2

Alternatively, DoD may wish to optimize the supply chain to address a specific shortcoming in its contracting practices that has hampered agility (and has other deleterious effects). Weapons in general have very high performance requirements. In the past, DoD has intrusively monitored the performer and the process to assure high quality in this regard. But DoD could look for other ways of managing this performance equation.

The DoD might be interested in an agility strategy that lets the supply chain flexibly sort out who does what, so long as there are adequate performance metrics that travel with the work package, and those performance metrics are directly linked to system-level performance goals monitored and changed by the customer.

Instead of having to look into every component process when a system-level specification is examined, the supply chain is self-correcting to parcel out the tasks and measure performers appropriately.

The basic cell in this case is C.c.c/4.1, infrastructure which parses the complex product, the tasks that need to be performed, and the measures that guarantee quality to respond to DoD's needs without requiring DoD's intervention. This strategy would be supported by:

C.a.e/3.6: Business practice infrastructure that ties how risks and rewards are monitored to directly support DoD's needs for the system.

C.b.b/5.1: Contract clauses that rewards suppliers who recognize and instigate change that benefits DoD, but adversely impacts their conventional business role.

C.c.c/2.3: Infrastructure which identifies (and perhaps prequalifies) the skills and qualities needed in suppliers to support this agility strategy.

C.d.a/1.3: Infrastructure which supports a continuous collaborative structure between the key elements within the supply chain and the DoD customer to assure that there is a good mapping from the DoD's system-level performance goals to the detailed work-package measures.

Strategy 3

Alternatively or coincidentally, the prime contractor will have need for agility strategies that benefit it as a business. We'll explore two examples of this.

Suppose that the prime missile contractor understands that essentially all new missile business will be based on current designs in some way. That means extensions of current processes and supply chains. Also suppose that their fastest growing areas of opportunity are foreign sales, and each foreign customer has some special tweak it needs.

You want a supplier chain that is built to respond agily to this large class of different and changing opportunities as a simple business matter.

This strategy will be built on cell C.b.b/1.3, which concerns contractual infrastructure support within the supply chain so that each supplier is rewarded for helping you identify and address opportunities by modifying/updating internal processes. The supplier may be rewarded even if the opportunity doesn't mention conventional business sense.

Note that this is different than what we noted before, where suppliers get rewarded for benefiting the (existing) customer. (Here agility benefits the contractor over a customer if there is a conflict.)

In addition to the primary cell, a strategy along these lines might be supported by:

C.a.e/2.3: Business practice infrastructure which continually identifies partners who can help identify and evaluate opportunities by understanding (potential) customers.

C.b.b/4.1: Contractual infrastructure which harmonizes performance metrics with new business rewards, thus combining agile new business identification with agile manufacturing.

C.c.c/3.6: A work breakdown process that gives each partner rewards for seeking new opportunities, even those quite different from the current product type.

C.d.a/5.1: Infrastructure which builds a team among key agents in the supply chain to share intelligence on and collaborate to reach new opportunities.

Strategy 4

Finally, one other example which could be described among the many that a prime contractor may pursue. This one relies on C.d.a/3.6 to set up a collaborative infrastructure so that trust is built among the key players of the partners. The rewards benefit the players in a more self-organizing way than the previous strategy. There, the supply chain is engineered to benefit the contractor. Here, the partnership is engineered to help each member (including the contractor). Since this is an opportunity-seeking strategy, rather than a partner-seeking one, it tends to a Type 4. This agility strategy is supported by:

C.a.e/1.3: Business practices that encourage players deep in the supply base to probe the market, alert for opportunities for the VE, perhaps representing same.

C.b.b/2.3: Contract support for a partner to benefit if it finds a way to identify new partners, even competitors, if it will bring the aggregate closer to new, good business.

C.c.c/5.1: Provision for a partner in the supply chain who is not biased to the prime contractor and who equally represents all the partners in seeking new opportunities. This partner presumably does nothing else.

C.d.a/4.1: Operating metrics that track and reward the quality of support to sustaining the VE above and beyond merely producing goods and services.

Cost and Benefits

We chose to show you a cell that is common to all these strategies, because we found that the most effective strategic change we could make was one that kept as many strategic options as possible open. At the same time, we chose to show you one that, if well implemented, would greatly reduce the requirement for being extraordinary in another, more strategy-specific cell.

It turns out that tweaking how partners are selected using agility measures for this one cell has a significant effect. QA issues have an awful lot to do with liability and how the supply chain is managed. Lean manufacturing offers one solution: Force your suppliers to conform to QA processes that you understand, control, and certify (or have a third party do so).

This idea of High Concept or agility offers another approach: Certify the ability of a supplier to adapt its own decentralized QA procedures to satisfy your needs. A key to that certification is confirming that it is in the supplier's local financial interest to speak to system-level QA requirements.

This in fact was the result of our case study. Control of the environment (an agile concept) did in fact prove more profitable than control of the supplier (a lean concept). This closes an open question, at least in this sector, about the relative merits of *agile* versus *lean* that we posed many pages back. The reason for the advantage of agility is because of the underlying memes of collaboration which we illustrated with the colorful differences between the English and the French.

Costs

There is still the question of how costly the whole process is. After all, these types of management ideas have not only to be useful and realistic—they have to be cheap and easy as well.

We did a cost study with another prime contractor, working in a virtually identical area. This was audited by the Aerospace Agile Manufacturing Center at the University of Texas-Arlington. We addressed the problem by formalizing the questions that a modeler would ask in the form of a questionnaire. We did so because the normal case is that a modeler engages in a form of collaborative dialog when interviewing a subject matter expert. In the past, we've found that test cases used talented expert interviewers, so this made the process look cheap and easy.

In order to get a better feel for real costs, we put an arm's length between the needs of the interviewer and the various people in the prime contractor and various subcontractors who would know what we need. This was a simple questionnaire (reproduced here). Our main goal is to illustrate the costs of capturing the speech acts for key cells, but we expect that showing the types of questions will be educational as well.

Questions (Long Version)

Structure

There are two primary groups of questions. The second group contains the ultimate questions about costs, with the first group providing context. In each case, the normal form is: "do you have a such-and-such;" followed by questions that presumed that you did. We expect that in many, probably most, cases the responder will *not* have a such-and-such, for instance, a procedure to adapt a QA process to meet system-level goals. But we encouraged them to answer the questions as if they did have a such-and-such, presuming that they can reasonably imagine having one.

The questions were written as if they were to be repeated for each of the 20 example cells of the narrowed-down model. We expected their responses to be identical for many of these.

Questionnaire

Group 1: Existence of Controlled Processes

Please review the AVE Focus Group Reference Model. We've selected twenty example cells which, based on initial interviews, appear to be cogent to conventional prime-supplier relationships in the defense aerospace sector. Use these or a self-selected set that is more cogent to your business.

We expect that there will be many cells for which there is no *real* process, even in agile enterprises. A *real* process is one to which costs are allocated. What cells do you have real processes to support?

Probably there are a number of cells for which you do not have processes, but for which you can easily imagine a process set up and supported by your company and suppliers. What cells fall into this category?

The remaining cells are ones which your enterprise would not naturally support as it is. Which of these fall into the following categories:

- It is too hard; we know enough about how to do it to know it's unrealistically difficult.
- It is too expensive; we know how to do it, but it just doesn't seem worth it.
- It is too alien; we haven't an idea what you're talking about.
- It is contrary to our corporate culture or strategy; getting into this process contravenes or negates some other cell or philosophy on which my company depends.
- There is some other barrier (for example, a regulation).

Next, presume that you have one or more candidate processes in mind for each of the cells. If you were evaluating an existing supply chain's agility, these would have to be existing processes. If you were evaluating various options for a future, engineered supply chain, they could be notions, but notions of realistic processes.

However, we'd like these processes to be engineered processes. In addition to consuming costs, a requirement from above, they should each *require management attention,* they would be controlled processes.

For the processes from above, are they planned, engineered, and controlled to achieve best effect, regardless of agility? Or are they largely default processes, evolving of themselves. If they are not engineered, can you imagine them to be so?

Group 2: Representation of Processes

Review

Let's review. What you should have now is:

- A threat or opportunity. The suggested opportunity for the missile prime is how to fill the customers' need for missile variants while only generally knowing the nature of changes in missions and technology.
- One or more themes for your strategy; you may call these high level or general strategies. Such strategies are based on your strengths, on business strengths and goals, and on specific peculiarities of the situation.
- A breakdown of each strategy into a small collection of relevant cells of the AVE Focus Group Model.
- Possibly several candidate processes for some of the cells.

There are many ways to use the metrics. In this example, we assume that you will be using the metrics to evaluate both:

- Which processes being considered for a cell are the most agile; and,
- Which small combination of populated cells provide the most effective agility strategy.

The Leap

The main task in using the metrics is to make a transition in how these processes are represented. We need to get from however they are currently represented and understood, to a specific representation we need to evaluate the metric. The good news is that by working with the AVE Reference Model, as you have to identify processes and cells, three hard issues have been addressed.

> 1. Processes with different underlying mechanics have been separated; the underlying mechanics of what goes on in, say the contract universe, is different than those in the physical world. Breaking things down by our infrastructure columns takes care of that.
>
> 2. Each process must support a decision. We are engineering the control structure of creating and operating agile enterprises. Processes only have meaning where they affect this control. Working with the Model's rows takes care of that.
>
> 3. We need to have a standard level of granularity for each of the processes we start with. The cells provide that armature.

So, although the Model may have broken things down differently than you might otherwise do in your organization, it's been for a purpose. Please consider the cost and difficulty of breaking the processes down in this way, the Model's way, as you answer the questions.

We need to go from however you understand your process to an act-based understanding of a few elements of that process.

[We inserted here a one-page description of the process.]

Actual Questions

For each process that you identified, please tell us on a scale of 1 to 5 how difficult (meaning costly) it will be to get the information we noted. Five is very costly. Remember that you need to include suppliers in virtually all of these processes. (Please give us a rough order of magnitude how many dollars per process you have in mind for the 1 through 5 assignations.)

Please let us know for each process whether the chief cost is in:

- Sufficiently educating all parties involved
- Understanding the agents (actors)
- Understanding what the agents do

Extra Questions

The process of engineering agility follows the same steps of engineering other enterprise attributes, such as lean or quality. In all cases, the steps include explicitly representing your processes in some way. It's widely recognized that great value comes from that step alone, even discounting further steps in the formula. Just exposing the workings of the enterprise to managers in a comprehensible way has significant power.

Quite apart from the whole process of engineering agility into your enterprise, do you think this perspective provides new insights into your processes? Would it make sense to you to deliberately use this type of system-level view of coupling (across the larger customer/supplier chain) to offset a reporting bias of other analytical views that might slight the *dynamic coupling* of processes?

Questions (Short Version)

Please review the example cells of the model (or cells which you select) and let us know which of these could anchor a workable agility strategy, given the scope of the agility problem.

- Please note these few cells and the candidate processes that might support them.
- If it is interesting, tell us why the others aren't viable.

For each process that you identified, please tell us on a scale of 1 to 5 how difficult (meaning costly) it will be to get the information we noted.

- If it is interesting, give us an indication of the major difficulties which make it expensive.
- Quite apart from the whole process of engineering agility into your enterprise, do you think this perspective can provide new insights into your processes?

Results of Cost and Effectiveness Studies

The following was learned:

1. Although the benefits of agility and effectiveness of metrics are assumed to be reasonably well known at this point, devising an agility strategy is not trivial.

- Agility usually costs money which could be put to other strategic investments; relationships of agility to other tactics need to be evaluated.
- Agility in some dimensions counters agility in others, so the general shape and likelihood of the threat needs to be identified.
- An agility strategy needs to function in conjunction with other elements of strategies within the Virtual Enterprise (market dominance versus immediate profitability, for instance).
- An agility strategy needs to leverage natural strengths in the current and possible partners' collective and individual core competencies and management philosophies.
- There are few preexisting rules of thumb. General motivational frameworks by others working in agility are not very useful in detailing a strategy. It is difficult to separate distinct pure agility from more general, weaker definitions.

2. Evaluating cells of the Reference Model is costly, but that cost is in line with other (equally costly) strategic evaluations.

•Parties to be interviewed will be unfamiliar with the goals and purposes of the effort; processes to be surveyed will focus on traits that seem unfamiliar.

•It will be easier, faster, and cheaper to model the process elements of interest from *scratch* than to try to convert from existing models. In part, this is because the details of verifying correctness and completeness in the source model are difficult; and the mechanics of translating among model formats, styles, and methods are inadequate. In any case, the information desired will not exist either in computable models or in a readily available recorded form; the modeling process will involve the cost of raw information collection in essentially all cases.

•Though one can narrow the Reference Model down to a few key cells, responsible strategic planning demands that many options per cell be examined.

•The actual costs of modeling for our scenario were between $500,000 and $1 million, with an hourly breakdown per cell as shown in Table 12.5.

Table 12.5 Hourly Costs per Target Cell

	A.e Depth of Customer Relations	B.b Risk/Reward Contracts	C.c Work Breakdown Structure	D.a Human Collaboration
1.3 Targeted Market	40	80	80	40
2.3 Partner Search	40	80	40	80
3.6 Risk/Reward Strategies	120	40	40	80
4.1 Performance Metrics	120	80	80	120
5.1 Identify Need for Change	120	120	120	80

3. We uncovered no hidden barriers, no deal killers in the basic approach.

- However, it is clear that this method, or any other strategic agility planning approach, is in need of production-quality tools.
- In the military case, these should be integrated with the weapons planning and evaluation process known as Cost and Operational Effectiveness Analysis (COEA). Probably Virtual Manufacturing simulations will be involved.

Discussion

It was a surprise that the modeling costs what it does, relatively the same as ordinary modeling. In retrospect we feel this is because the community has an idea of quality metrics which can be applied at a fine level of granularity without regard to strategic issues. Having a high level of quality is the strategic goal that is served. Agility metrics require a strategic vision and vice versa.

Lacking knowledge on modeling costs of similar strategic tasks, we turned to a major consulting firm (of several thousand employees). That firm performs many strategic modeling tasks, *discoveries* they call them. The typical strategic discovery can be as much as $1 million, apart from analysis and the actual planning.

Clearly, there is a business case that can be made for an enterprise to do such an analysis. No small firm would do this on its own. It would have to be done from the point of view of the entire AVE. In the defense case (our scenario) agility benefits go to the DoD customer, so it is an apt function for them to sponsor.

Chapter 13

Trust

AN EXAMPLE OF THE PROBLEM

Sirius-Beta's second introduction to enterprise engineering was the role it played in automating shipboard logistics for the U.S. Navy. The problem was simple, or so it was thought. Until the mid-1980s, ships kept records about their spare parts and manuals in pencil on index cards stored in huge rolodexes. For all the obvious reasons, the records were poor and difficult to track at the fleet level. The result was that few ships had what they needed, and some had many things that they didn't need. On the whole, there was a vast waste in obsolete parts in the system, which not only cost the taxpayer money (hundreds of millions), but took up valuable space and weight on the ships.

The solution, it seemed logical, was to install modern computers on-board to perform record-keeping. This was accomplished at some cost, generating along the way many stories. The one cogent here is that the computer systems were vehemently fought by ship's officers, and that in the first decade after installation, fleet spares readiness went way down. It took substantial effort to discover what was going on.

What had happened was that there were two spare parts distribution networks. The official one, which was, then and now, broken, and an unofficial one—remember Radar on *M*A*S*H?* The unofficial one, which was the primary channel for key items, depended on the slack accountability of the official one. Ships' officers developed communication networks based on *trust*. Those networks were an underground barter system for trading parts, which had evolved the ability to adapt while in extended cruises.

We understood the need to improve trust in one part of the system, the information support to the decisionmaker. It was a good thing to improve the quality of the knowledge about—and trust in—what each ship had, and this was true for both the shipboard officers and the shore-based fleet logistics planners.

But we misunderstood the nature of the communication channels between nodes. Indirectly, we empowered the official communication channels, the ones that allowed shore-based clerks to carefully control what went where. These were not then, nor now, trusted to the job correctly. We failed to appreciate the power of the trust-enabled adaptive federation, agility, among officers that made the system function by applying local knowledge and domain skills.

This understanding, that there is one kind of trust in *nodes* (agents) and another in *communication* channels between nodes, is captured in the sections that follow. It would have been far better for us to improve the collaboration technology first, perhaps turning a blind eye to the unofficial parts bartering, then later have responded to increasing the confidence of official accounting systems.

Incidentally, this isn't just about spare parts. Naval warfare is a highly distributed affair, and trust among ships (especially their officers) is essential in combat strategy. We found that the primary way this multipurpose trust was maintained and tested was through this huge, unofficial parts network, which was highly personality-oriented. We actually hurt the ability to collaborate adaptively in combat, perhaps in a significant way. Fortunately, the combat system hasn't been really challenged.

The approach we took for measuring agility can be generalized from this situation. In this chapter, we extend the method to indicate the level of trust among participants in an enterprise. We do this because trust is often the key stumbling block to innovative business methods. It is especially so in the interesting and profitable cases where the VE does not wholly depend on conventional buyer-seller business boundaries and contracts.

Unfortunately, many people think that interesting VEs can be supported by electronic commerce (EC) alone. But EC merely makes more efficient the static marketplace where businesses advertise and deliver certain things. It has scant infrastructure for close collaboration over what is made and how. We will look back at today's enthusiasm for EC as an inhibitor to advanced VEs because it puts a few extra years of life into a seventeenth-century business paradigm, one which collects all support for trust in the *legal* infrastructure, rigidly and unagily instanced as contract-insulated business boundaries.

A more interesting model of VEs is where people, resources, and intellectual property are temporarily more intimately intertwingled (our newly coined word) to address a common opportunity. A simple example of a difficult issue of trust in the VE is when a partner enters into the intimate VE with certain expectations, but those expectations are modified by an unexpected process breakthrough. Let's say we have a partner who was brought into the VE to develop and supply an aluminum wing for an airplane, and it is discovered late in the design (and process) development that a composite wing will be better for the customer. Let's further say that the partner cannot make a composite wing, so it makes sense for the VE and the customer to switch partners. And let's further suppose that the original partner has significant sunk costs in developing the opportunity for the VE, in addition to developing some part of the composite design. This is similar to the example in the previous chapter.

In the "old" business system, each partner suboptimizes for its selfish goals, which in this case would produce a suboptimal product, a plane with an aluminum wing. A better business system will agily adjust to the customers' need, and at the same time reward the aluminum-wing partner for essentially putting itself out of the VE. In such cases, that partner has to have *trust* that the VE will deal with it fairly whether it is fully in the VE or out. And the VE has to have *trust* in each partner that they will strive to optimize the enterprise, even when it reduces or eliminates its own role. Moreover, this type of trust has to be inexpensive; that is, it has to be intrinsic to the system—it cannot be gained by a ready platoon of lawyers and consultants.

As with many elements in the management of enterprises, understanding this type of trust is usually handled as a matter of intuitive experience. But the understanding of trust instead should be an elucidatable, measurable, engineerable tool in the enterprise engineer's toolbox.

INDUCTIVE AND DEDUCTIVE TRUST

In common usage, the term *trust* means confidence through experience. By this criterion, if I buy a car, and start it successfully for 100 mornings, I have trust that it will start. We propose to call this *inductive trust*. This type of trust (common confidence) is what dominates both ordinary life and its extension, business.

But suppose there is an unexpected, unseasonable overnight freeze. I will wake up that morning and not expect my car to start. The reason I will not trust my car is that I understand how a car works. I understand the physics associated with a cold battery decreasing the available power, and on the higher viscosity of oil increasing the need for power. In this more knowledgeable state, I would have trusted the car 100 days straight and not on the 101st day because I understood the key mechanics involved. We call this *deductive trust*.

Deductive trust is what we need in the AVE; it can be modeled, analyzed, and measured. It is what we need because inductive trust assumes that things will always be the same as they were, that your experience with a person, company, or process is unchanging. Inductive trust is fine in those few situations where things don't change. But the world is not so kind to most of us. Figure 13.1 shows the relationship.

What we need is deductive trust, but what we have is inductive trust. In the enterprise, we manage inductive trust by seeking out senior managers who have deep, inductive experience, and perhaps paying them excessively for their intuition. Then we get surprised when they perform badly when faced with unfamiliar circumstances. We also use probabilistic methods to quantize trends and hedge those we cannot see with often expensive insurance.

But these are the crudest of agility strategies. Worse, in current versions of the VE, we base inductive trust largely on personal relationships, even friendships, and we try to facilitate that through cultural and ethical alignments. The bad news is that we know this scales poorly in high value complex VEs and ones in which the world constantly shifts.

We *do* use deductive trust in the VE to some extent today: our free market's basic dynamic is self-interest. We understand that driver and expect people and companies to follow the basic principle that they will usually act in their obvious self interest. Our way of incorporating that simple deductive trust into management tools is to create thick shells around companies and to negotiate deals that are essentially of this type: "You do something for us, and if we find it acceptable, then we will pay you."

In other words, we tie our own interest to what we will pay for. Since we presume that getting paid is in the subcontractor's best interest, we trust them to do what we want. But as we all know, these thick legal barriers hinder the intercompany collaboration we seek in the VE and the costs of adapting them counter our desired agility. That's because your processes and theirs cannot interact, collaborate, and change.

For instance, this "suboptimization" would have produced the aforementioned airplane with an aluminum wing instead of the better composite wing, because the aluminum wing design had been tentatively selected, and the supplier had been contracted and had put skin in the game. That whole early decision became frozen in business relationships and the selfish perpetuation of a status quo built on early wrong design guesses. Incidentally, this problem is endemic in the defense, automotive, and aircraft industries where product development cycles often exceed the innovation cycles for key component technology, but they are locked into building the now-obsolete design anyway.

The one modern intercompany trust technique that is deductive concerns *quality*. Large firms send quality auditors into their suppliers' operations to understand their processes sufficiently enough that they can deductively trust the quality of their product. Also, there is a trend, at first look healthy, to employ a universal quality standard to support deductive trust in quality. But on examination, the evaluation techniques used in such audits are based on

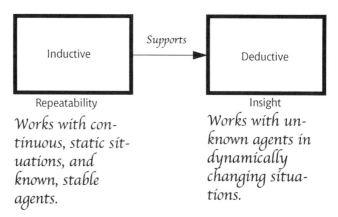

Figure 13.1 Two Definitions: Inductive Confidence Supports Deductive Trust

long, repeatable trends, hardly the stuff to settle the concerns of a manager in a highly turbulent environment. An additional problem: Quality is a strange thing to measure. You don't measure it or what causes it directly; you measure what quality is *not*: (in terms of defects and such) and use those as pointers of where to look for improvement. There is not an elegant, formal connection between the measure of quality and what causes it.

MITIGATED INDUCTIVE TRUST

Our vision of Agile Virtual Enterprises allows for intimate collaboration, perhaps some mixing of resources, and certainly some risk (and speculative reward) sharing. Sometimes, such AVEs can be supported by the less difficult inductive trust if there is a sufficiently robust arbitrating agent, like what we found in Hollywood (and the whaling industry). Remember that we found three key principles of an advanced VE:

1. There needs to be a technique to define and focus the VE. In the movie business, this is a highly developed art of the High Concept definition.
2. There needs to be a set of agents to perform the many tasks of binding, operating, and dissolving the VE.
3. There needs to be a legal/cultural mechanism for quickly forming agreements among partners.

All three of these rely on inductive trust in the normal, non-agile case. In this case, trust is supported in two ways. The first is by the predictable mechanism: An extremely homogenized culture. A member of the VE can to a significant extent trust its partners to behave to cultural norms for ethics, because it always has been so. The penalty for not conforming is at least ostracism. Many VEs function this way today.

But what made the whaling/movie example so interesting was the role that case law plays, bringing deductive trust into the equation. Case law is originally a Saxon system, now firmly embedded in English law and inherited by the United States. In code, the prevailing system worldwide, when a legislative body makes a law, it creates the specific language of that law. That language is always the reference for interpreting the law. But in case law, every court decision that employs a law becomes part of that law with the same force as the original language created by the legislators. This means that for every law, a wide variety of specific applications exist, at the same level as the law itself.

In the whaling industry, many small businesses bonded quickly using extremely lightweight contracts, typically the voyage, the partner's name, and its planned percentage of the gross take. In the three years or so of each voyage, there were always some factors that modified the contract; for instance, a cooper might be ill for an important period.

Yet each member had a high degree of trust in the contract system. This was because over time, every unexpected event that could happen had, the case had been taken to trial, or, in the whaling case, a similar adjudication. The results of these cases became part of the law and were implicit in every small whaling contract, just as if lawyers had been convened in every negotiation, foreseen every unexpected event, and prenegotiated the outcome. In effect, this extended the small, fast contracts with a very comprehensive set of *if-this-then-that* qualifiers for a very large set of unforeseen circumstances. As a result of this extensive contract by inference, each partner had a high degree of trust in the fairness of the system because they knew how it worked.

As a matter of fact, the costs of the continuous litigation are on orders of magnitude smaller than the cost savings in negotiating contracts under this system. As we discussed earlier, a similar lightweight, case-based contract agreement forms the basis of the Hollywood AVE. An interesting side comment: We found that the case-based defense VE infrastructure that was so important during World War II has been replaced by a system of *code*. This single factor nearly doubles costs and creates great delays in the defense supply chain.

An institutional system for trust, similar to case law, can be found in Iran; the Chapter 5 example of their food distribution system. In the U.S. food passes through many hands from the grower to the consumer, each party getting paid along the way. This is made possible by a system of lending capital, which essentially guesses how much value will be in the final product.

In fundamental Islam, usury is outlawed, so this system for funding the growing and distribution of food cannot be supported. What we have instead is a novel sort of virtual enterprise where every party is in for a percentage of how much the final product sells for. Money is advanced for sure, but with the intent of funding the VE, not with the intent of actually making profit on capital. Contracts that bind the VE are lightweight. If a partner does particularly well or poorly, or if some unexpected event occurs, their share is adjusted accordingly. The authority for all adjustments are the Islamic religious arbiters that function surprisingly like English case law.

An amazingly complex accounting system must be maintained to support the Iranian VE. In fact, the arithmetic that we all use today was created in the Islamic world to support just this purpose. And, to our surprise, we discovered that the cost of the Iranian infrastructure was significantly less than the complex accounting system of lending, guessing, certifying and monitoring that is used in the loan-based western food distribution system.

In Iran, business can build VEs based on trust in the religious arbiters. In general, however, the VE is sustained by inductive trust in selfishness. A partner is always presumed to function in its best interests. If the selfish goals of the VE are brought into congruence with the selfish interest of the partners, then there is trust in the system. The novelty in Iran is a real irony since—as we've noted—the U.S. food distribution system was a model for Japanese just-in-time manufacturing processes after the war.

There are other examples of intuitive trust being institutionalized in novel ways to support some elements of an AVE. It is no surprise that many such cases exist; unexpected change has been a business reality for a very long time, and so have both agile practices and the virtual enterprise. What's new with the agility movement is that we want to understand the principles involved, engineer, and measure them so that we can have modern environments. In such cases, inductive trust needs to be supplemented and in some cases supplanted by deductive trust.

Deductive Trust

Another, better notion of trust is based on deductive criteria. On the face of it, this is what we would prefer in engineering agile business systems (as with nonbusiness systems). Using this notion, an agent is trusted if he/she is:

Accountable: This is another way of saying that the agent is causally coupled into the processes in a tight, understandable way. (We expand this one issue below in talking about channels.)

Timely: The agent's insights are based on the current situation.

Accessible: The agent, specifically the agent's insight, information, or knowledge is accessible to you at your convenience.

Accurate: The agent's insight is correct. It's the truth. More about truth in a moment.

Complete: The agent's insight has all the necessary context and qualifiers to allow you to perform your system-level analysis.

Uncorrupted: The agent's insight does not have junk mixed in with the truth.

For example, take a supplier's marketing representative. (Note, all mainstream examples would involve agents as people.) We could really like this person, appreciate his/her ethics, and have had nothing but good experiences so far, and still not have trust in the company under an unusual situation. (Not having trust is simple neutrality as opposed to negative trust: trusting that the company will screw up.)

For the marketing agent to be *accountable,* he or she would have to know fully and represent honestly the capabilities of the supplier to your preferred level of detail. The information would be *timely* if it represents the current state, not an extrapolated, perhaps hoped-for state. It will be *accessible* if you can get what you need when you need it. Your trust in *completeness* and *uncorruptness* means you're getting the whole truth and nothing but the truth. If all these things are true, you have a *trusted agent* as a collaborator in engineering your supply chain.

Incidentally, our definition of deductive trust includes the requirement that the information be accurate, complete, and uncorrupted. This same notion is captured in the oath that witnesses take in U.S. courtrooms in order to establish trust. The witness swears to "tell the truth, the whole truth, and nothing but the truth." Why all three? What's the difference?

The truth means that what will be conveyed will accurately reflect what is known. The *whole truth* means that the statement will be complete. An omitted but essential qualifier or context, for example, could completely change a *true* statement's meaning. While the witness told the truth, it could be missing key ingredients which have the effect of making the true statement less true.

Nothing but the truth is the reverse, where the witness adds statements which, while not untrue in themselves, add false qualifiers or context.

Toward a Science of Deductive Trust

A central problem in modeling the mechanics of trust is that in general, we have inadequate means of formally modeling any interesting behavior in the enterprise. Instead, we have a collection of informal methods and techniques developed for other problem spaces and inappropriately grafted on to the enterprise.

Informal notational methods. These are methods of capturing and structuring information about the process in a codified form. The purpose is not to have a deeply formal model for algorithmic analysis, but to make it easy for a manager at least to understand what is going on. The early IDEF (Integrated Computer Aided Manufacturing Definition Language) family are the most well known of this class, but it includes the large category of what is lovingly termed, post-it note modeling. These techniques are graphic notations for representing activities or processes (and their related factors), largely without an underlying logic.

The problem of creating foundations for modeling is being addressed by the noble efforts of the Manufacturing Engineering Lab at NIST in sponsoring the Process Specification Language (PSL) (Schlenoff, Knutilla, & Ray, 1998). The effort will result in a formal axiomatic basis for modeling languages to be used in the enterprise. This will at least provide the first formal foundation for being able to capture not only the outcome of an action, but the causal physics behind it. The reinvention of IDEF3 should be the first PSL-compliant methodology (Menzel & Mayer, 1997), but it won't help with higher-level phenomenon like trust.

Database methods. These methods grew up with the computing business itself. Unfortunately, the applications were unrelated to control and dealt with relating items of data, for instance, going through a payroll and computing (from all the relevant data) a payroll. Much attention is given to the structure of the data, and none to its underlying physics. You have a model of the structure, a so-called data model, but no model of the underlying process that produced this data. The problem is not so severe in similar methods from the artificial intelligence community, but enterprises do have legitimate needs for databases, so that thinking dominates the modeling process. What currently passes for commercial enterprise modeling (Enterprise Resource Planning) is a tailoring of database modeling to enterprise needs; but that is insufficient for understanding and engineering simple enterprise dynamics, much less something interesting and critical like trust.

Object Oriented (OO) methods. This collection of techniques is being highly celebrated (and employed) as a revolution in enterprise modeling. But consider that OO techniques were developed to solve a particular problem: the difficulty of creating application software. The complexity of problems is simplified by OO. Also, the ability to reuse code, to modify easily existing code promises to create, perhaps sometime soon, feasible coding by semantic-based "annealing" of validated components from diverse sources. But consider how OO solves the problem: By hiding, encapsulating, the details of processes. This is exactly the opposite of what we want to do, since advanced model elements must reveal the underlying physics. A key result of the workshops of the recent International Conference on Enterprise Integration and Modeling Technology was that OO methods should not be confused with real enterprise (and enterprise component) modeling, and that in many respects, they make the problem worse (Hollocks, 1997).

Much of what we have found runs counter to prevailing wisdom, but this stance on OO especially so. It is possible to build objects whose internal mechanics are visible, and some novel OO tools are leveraging this idea to build useful business modeling environments. But OO depends on abstracting the behavior from the mechanics and encapsulating the mechanics. This encapsulation places causal barriers in the way of those, like us, who would like to analyze models where cause and effect are at the same logical level. There is a new trend in OO that may avoid the problem. Dynamic object languages, such as the new Dylan (described in the next chapter), allow a mixed mode, where some classes can be "sealed" to get the benefits of OO, while other segments are open to the kind of analysis we need. This is a by-product of the language's design. The capability was engineered to allow fundamental development (not just analysis, as we would do) on some parts of a program (model) while others are actually running.

Graph/Petri Methods. The most currently leveragable modeling techniques are those that employ graph theories. Graphs, in this context, are collections of nodes and connections. Usually an activity is a node and the connections are dependencies and relations of some type. Graph-based methods are nice because there is a underlying computable formalism which allows the use of algorithmic methods.

Nearly all process modeling methods are a blend of these methods. For example, some implementations of IDEF1X (and its cousins) use graphs as the user display to organize information and as a data structure for the information assigned to nodes and lines. Some significant utility can be squeezed out of these workarounds, which borrow from more than one foundation. But the fundamental problem remains that they are not formal in the way that supports true enterprise modeling requirements. We mention this because without true support for enterprise modeling, we cannot support metrics for trust. Among the key requirements currently missing is the need to model soft elements of the enterprise and to support metrics as native citizens, integrated participants.

TRUTH

Trust is decomposable into two main threads: Trust in the agents themselves and trust in the integration of those agents into the enterprise. In the first case, for instance, you may deductively trust the partner who tracks the customer's psychology and determines an advertising campaign to support the goals of the VE. In the second case, the VE may not buy off on the advertising strategy, or it may but not support it in some key dimension, or it may support it, but some partners may not harmonize with the VE strategy, instead holding to a different, partner-centric strategy.

We call the first case trust in the *agent* proper and the second trust in the *communication/integration channel*. The bad news is that there is no underlying set of mature techniques to support the first. So we'll address some brand-new science for this in the discussion that follows. The good news is that there is quite a bit of mature thinking about the channel notion of trust. This is because the second problem is embedded in the larger problem of secure systems, which the defense establishment calls "trusted systems."

These trusted systems all focus on the channel, not the agent. Trusted systems control access to the channel to determine (in this discussion, we substitute partner for agent to keep things simple) three elements:

1. Whether what comes through is *true*. This is a real challenge in the VE since the values of the target partner may be different from those of the sending partner. It may be required that certain characteristics of the message be changed by the channel so that the perception at the other end appears true. This is a well-known problem: Photographs in magazines are altered in tones, contrast, and sharpness so that they look more like the real thing; actors in the theater cannot act as they do in normal life. They have to amplify some parts of their actions unnaturally so that they *appear* natural—true—to the audience. Similar problems occur in many walks of life.

The receiving agent has to have a deductive knowledge of how the channel changes what it sent, so that it can correctly trust the information. For instance, in the military combat supply chain, most depots may get a message: "send 50 bags of stuff as soon as possible." But certain other service units get a translated command: "send 75 bags of stuff immediately." The intent is that the first group can be told the "truth" about what is needed, whereas the second group, as a matter of culture, needs to be told 75 in order to get 50, and needs to told "immediately" in order for it to get any priority at all.

It is not a lie so much as an enhancement of the message so that the recipients "get" the truth. When an actual high priority need occurs (there really is a need for 75 immediately), the commanding officer avoids that communication channel because she or he cannot trust the enhancement mechanism to adequately present the truth. (A personal visit might be made instead.)

2. Whether what comes through is *complete*. This is also a challenge in the VE because of the problem of tacit information. When you send a message to one partner, it may have sufficient knowledge from the message when added to other knowledge it may have to act correctly. But another partner may lack this secondary information (called tacit) and thereby get a correct and true message, but still act incorrectly.

3. Whether what comes through is *minimally complete*. Instead of lacking tacit information, this case has additional information which puts a new and unintended spin on the message. This is also a problem in the VE. VE partners tend to want all the information they can get about strategic rationale and operational details. But it is often the case that additional information is noise

that is interpreted differently in the context of the core message than it should be.

These three elements are the three expressed in "the truth, the whole truth and nothing but the truth."

In the domain of military trusted systems, there is a means of certifying systems inductively by use of a capability model. The idea of a capability model is powerful, and there is a body of mathematics which exists to underlie the discipline of testing by behavior. What they test is the outcomes. It doesn't matter how it works, or why it is supposed to function, only that it does. But that's useless to us in *deductive* trust. However, there is also a special literature on understanding the *channel* deductively, that is, by mathematical methods to determine the state of truthfulness. Unfortunately, that literature is largely classified. (This is because it also bears on the problem of extracting the truth, the semantic meaning, from a message which is encoded.)

In the domain of legal trusted systems, there is a large body of research on trust. Legal specialists exist who understand how to tell the truth but tell it in such a way that the truth is not conveyed. Unfortunately, the research behind this study is useless to the VE, since it is aimed at avoiding rather than enhancing trust.

But the news is not all bad, because information management practitioners have practical means for working with trusted channels. The hard part is the agents.

AGENTS AND CHANNELS

We've mentioned the distinction to be made between the agent and the channel through which you communicate with the agent. Each has its own type of trust. You have to trust, for instance, that the sales manager of your supplier knows what's up, as well as having to trust that the email that you got from him/her is of sufficient fidelity. One is trust in an agent, one trust in a communication channel.

Agents

We delved into this somewhat because the focus on the communication seems to be the second main distraction in this whole dialog (the first being trust as inductive confidence). Trust in communication is where a lot of VE effort is being placed: Assuring fidelity and controlling access through the channel, the whole Electronic Commerce diversion. But those are relatively simpler issues; the key payoff is in whether the agent is a trusted one.

We've broken the agents down into three types (see Figure 13.2). Often two roles, but rarely three, are played by a single person. There are three types of agents and three criteria by which they become trusted agents.

1. The *Sensor:* This agent is alert to all the factors that are in its assigned domain. Trust in this type of agent means that the signal is true, as we outlined. If kids stop buying white sneakers in favor of blue ones, you want to be able to

trust that your market researcher detects the trend (and doesn't signal false trends).

2. The *Analyzer:* An agent who determines whether a change (or other input from the sensor) is important to the enterprise and in what way. Trusted analysts are rare unless they stick to the most mundane of factors (cost, quality) and stay close to home in terms of existing products and strategies. This agent is the target for the agility metrics project, the metrics intended to increase the ability to audit reasoning about strategies of change, thereby increasing trust.

3. The *Actor:* The agent who triggers and controls the process, which in the agility sphere is a process of change. A trusted actor is one that takes the right action and does it effectively.

Channels

The agents are connected to each other by communication channels. *Horizontal* channels provide links among sensors, analysts, and actors; and *vertical* channels link agents among functions to form a VE, or any enterprise for that matter. All these channels are of the same type regardless of what agents they connect. All are subject to the same problems and probably all are addressable by the same policies and technologies.

Usually, the vertical links in a VE involve only actor agents. If many of those actors are not connected to analysts, the system cannot be agile. What might make an enterprise better, including more agile, is if there are not only many channels, but also if they link across all three types of agents; they cross functional and company boundaries; and there is a high level of trust in the agents (and, of course, the channels too). Therefore, a rule of thumb for AVEs is to have high connectivity and trust among agents.

In most cases, a network of agents operates at the lowest level of trust of any of its components, unless there exist some metrics to evaluate the trust of specific agents and to annotate messages from that agent accordingly. Current metrics—not ours—deal only with some elements of the channel and the simple notion of trust we noted above called (inductive) confidence. Horizontal and vertical channels are shown in Figure 13.3.

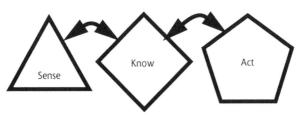

Figure 13.2 Three Types of Agents in the Enterprise

TRUST METRICS

It was not within the scope of the metrics project to address trust metrics directly, just metrics of agility. But it is entirely possible that much of the research on agility metrics can be leveraged to develop metrics for trust.

Our new agility metrics are based on the information-theoretic idea that the more complex a communicative (functional) network is in certain ways, the more resistant to change it is. Among all the complexity metrics that exist, we've distilled some that indicate this resistance. These themselves are functions which we can manipulate in mathematical ways that are being explored in the tool strategy described in the next chapter.

The information-theoretic view depends on breaking business processes down into agents and communicative acts. Agents in that view are the same as the agents we already described. Communicative acts also follow the channels we described. In fact, the agility metrics deal with measuring the *connectedness* of agents, but depend on a single level of trust among all agents.

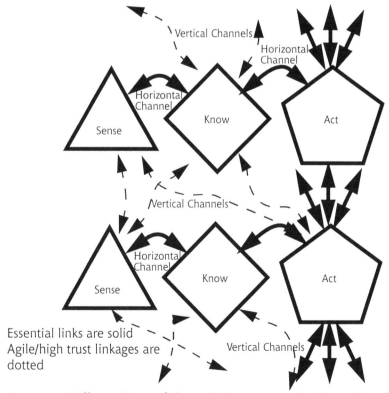

Figure 13.3 Different Types of Channels Interconnect the Agents in an Enterprise

However, this breakdown of agents and channels is just what we've been using in our trust discussion. It's likely that much of the dynamics of our project can be used by someone looking at trust metrics:

- The mapping of business processes to agents in a practical way (via the AVE Focus Group Reference Model).
- The understanding used to map theoretical complexity metrics into specific business strategies.
- The anticipated advances in modeling *soft* (social and cultural) processes which come from the marriage of communicative acts and situation theory
- The clustering, or clumping of agents across functions. Figure 13.4 shows such clustering.

How Trust Metrics Might Look: A Possible Test Case

The most interesting and profitable VEs are those that stretch the envelope of conventional business models. An advanced VE can be highly dynamic, changing configuration in response to customer needs or technology develop-

We decompose agent packets and measure topology of communicative acts

Trust metrics would be top down, and leverage different topology complexity measures.

Figure 13.4 Our Decomposition of the Enterprise into Conversations among Agents can Support Clustering for Trust Metrics

ments; partner constellations and internal processes would be reinvented often.

We are just beginning planning for a very advanced VE experiment that leverages trust and trust metrics. This VE experiment will be in Brazil. Brazil is an interesting country, among the world's largest and most populous. We chose it as the most fertile location for advanced VE research. Some reasons are:

- Brazil is large, has a fast-developing economy, has a promising domestic market, and is physically close to major markets.
- It has in the last 10 years emerged from military rule; as a result, it has greatly eliminated trade barriers and is in the midst of a massive privatization program. So all Brazilian businesses have encountered massive change of a type not seen in the U.S. or Europe in generations.
- There is an ethos that was celebrated 100 years ago in the U.S. as "Yankee ingenuity," and exists in Brazil as "jeito," the ability to make things happen where there is no reason or precedent. It is one of their most-used words.

But those are not the most significant advantages. More fundamental are:

- When Brazil moved to democracy 10 years ago, they reinvented their legal system. It is now what is termed a third generation system, the only such one in a significant nation. This sets a legal infrastructure that is very streamlined for corporate agreements of the type that VEs rely heavily upon. Previously, we noted that U.S. case law was helpful to the whaling VE and still is to the movie VE. But the industrial U.S. enterprise instead labors under a ponderous mix of code, case law, and a burdensome tort system. We believe that the advanced AVE will be a way of life soon in the U.S. but that the first large interesting cases will have a more friendly legal system in Brazil.
- Almost everyone knows that Brazil suffered under the oil shocks and that their massive debt was rescheduled under the guidance of the International Monetary Fund (IMF). Brazil is the only significant nation with IMF oversight that has a promising economy. Citizens of nations under IMF scrutiny consider them vexing interlopers, but IMF involvement has an effect that greatly aids us: it imposes a rationality on the valuation of enterprises.

One of the problems that VEs have is their capitalization. Large enterprises are our current strategy for managing complexity. The capital investment communities in the U.S. and Europe are skeptical of new strategies for handling complexity, regardless of efficacy. This is not so in the IMF valuation. There, if a VE makes good money serving customers, its current and future valuation properly reflects it. The importance of this factor for important VEs in the near term cannot be overestimated. A rational valuation system for enterprises in

Brazil, somewhat lacking in the U.S. and Europe, goes a long way to make the trust management problem easier.

About the VE and Trust

We intend to build a VE of component VEs. One component VE will be in the agricultural/bioengineering sector and consist of small material growers and breeders, and the research agencies and device suppliers that support them. A second VE component will consist of material engineers and processors to supply the new materials. Finally, another VE will design and manufacture small batch, high value products, probably electromechanical assemblies for export worldwide as components in larger products. The novelties in this test case are:

- the three levels of VE trust within each component VE, the larger VE, and the VE to the primary contractors;
- the ambitions of the VE in size, product complexity, and innovation; and
- the intent to engineer the enterprise overall and to manage decentrally using new infrastructure, new models, and new trust and agility metrics.

For this project, modeling will be done in the newly-restructured IDEF3, which conforms to the Process Specification Language. It is easy to use and employs relatively familiar modeling conventions. We believe that the agility strategies for the four or five interrelated VEs will all be different. In other words, each of the VEs will focus on different cells in the agility model. But all the strategies will depend on maintaining a minimum level of trust for the targeted processes (cells of the model). Therefore, the steps we will follow will be:

1. Evaluate the threats and opportunities and devise the VE structure and agility strategy accordingly. A novel strategy will be made possible by our use of trust metrics.

2. Build the VEs, using the VE life-cycle and infrastructure model framework. We will have some key cells selected in each framework as a result of the agility strategy.

3. Model each of those key cells using IDEF3 expanded by Situation Theory to support soft modeling of social collaboration mechanics. We will model each activity at the level of individual speech acts. As with the agility metrics, this technique is to ensure that all elements of the IDEF3 model are at the same level of "granularity."

4. Calibrate that the complexity of vertical connections among agents of different types is proportional to the level of trust in the system.

Chapter 14

Summary and Tools

Well, this has been an interesting voyage. I hope that you've gotten an understanding of the problem and some methods that can—for the first time—help you engineer an optimized response. But methods aren't quite tools, the actual product that you somehow acquire and use operationally. So before we leave you, we should indicate how the methods incarnate into specific tools, as drawn from our own experience.

STRATEGY ("THREAT" AND OPTIONS)

We found three scenarios at the very front of the enterprise engineering food chain. One is the situation that our examples address, where you build agility directly into your strategy, possibly treating certain types of agility as a competitive asset. In every situation where we have encountered this, it is in enterprises that have a competent strategic awareness. They already have strategic planning and evaluation tools employed.

The common medium of these tools is universally *cost* and *benefit*, though we found a surprising diversity among tools in underlying philosophy and method. Not so incidentally, there never seemed to be any strategic vision in the selection of strategic tools. Instead, they were bought and implemented in a haphazard manner, depending largely on the presentation skills of the consultants involved.

But that's another matter. In this, our base case, we assumed that strategic planning tools already existed, that agility was already recognized as valuable, and that the need was to evaluate options.

But we found a second condition much more frequently than we expected. These were enterprises that separate out the response to problems from the strategy. In this case, certain managers plot the strategy, assuming that there will be a certain amount of turbulence which must be tolerated. A second group, usually more junior, is tasked with creating an infrastructure to deal with those problems. Here, agility is not is a strategic weapon, rather a means to keep the strategy from being perturbed by unexpected events. This turned out to be typical of the defense industry, as well as mature industries like the automobile business.

Surprisingly, this created a tool challenge. Since the process was not linked with enterprise strategy per se, a whole different tool set was used, one which tries to guess the risks and the potential damage. It turns out that there is a complete industry that deals with this, whose heritage is in the insurance (and, at arm's length, the investment) community. Tools exist, to be sure, but they are statistically-based tools, of the restrospective type.

The existing tools can tell you how likely you are to face something which has happened before (say, a regional flood), and how likely it is to be damaging. But in many industries it is the things that have never happened before, or that affect you in new ways, that are the killers. We were often asked for tools to identify the unexpected threat, in addition to our commitment to produce decision support tools to address the known threat.

Since this was so common, we had to address it. We did so under the guidance of the AVE Focus Group, and with the help of Sandia National Labs and the Automation and Robotics Research Institute of the University of Texas at Arlington. The result is a "structured brainstorming" tool, designed to uncover general types of unexpected strategies.

This tool is imperfect. It is not formally complete, in that you cannot ever know if what you've produced is correct, but it has been demonstrated to be a useful tool in answering the questions about possible unexpected events or effects.

We also found a third situation concerning how the evaluation of "threat" was handled. This is the VE situation where the unexpected event is the opportunity that triggers the formation of a partnership. In other words, it is not a threat at all that is being tackled, but instead a positive opportunity to leverage.

This is a different beast, requiring a different strategic toolset. It differs from the other cases in two important ways. First, in the other cases, agility is an intrinsic part of the enterprise. Either the enterprise has the ability to respond or it does not. The formation of the enterprise was guided by factors unrelated to the changes being addressed. But in this case, there is only one change of interest, that which triggers the VE. Back in Chapter 7, we noted that this is a different kind of agility, the agility of formation rather than operation. It is quite possible (in fact usual) to have a VE that is agile in formation, but not in operation. Second, also in the other cases, the motivation for the enterprise is independent of its agility, with the latter a component of the strategy. With the AVE, the agility of interest is a prime mover in the motivation of the enterprise. The strategy is centered on agility.

You can see how this presented a different set of tool requirements. People would come to us with certain assets and capabilities at the ready and they need to know several aspects.

- How to model and evaluate other potential partners for their capabilities to address tasks that perhaps they do not currently do, at least in the way they do it now.
- How to model and evaluate the potential capabilities of different combinations of yourself and these partners. In other words, what could you make, if only you had some complementary processes?
- How to model and evaluate the customer for hidden niches or fresh trends.

The problem is that each of these dimensions has unexpected elements. That's the point. You want to identify and match these one to another, so that a new or unexpected market need can be exploited by a hitherto new set of processes that result from perhaps unconventional (perhaps temporary) combinations of competencies from partners.

You may also want to know how to change yourself (or others) to better facilitate this *promiscuous* partnering.

And that's not even the worst, there are a large number of what-if's that you might want to cheaply and quickly look at. And as you go along, some of those need to be looked at in more and more detail, until you are in effect simulating. Combine the many dimensions, the many cases, and the independent or unknown linkages and you have a horror.

It turns out that this is a familiar problem, quite apart from the business world, that the intelligence community often faces. We created a prototype computerized tool to help with this problem, and it is worth spending a few pages describing how it works.

Turnip

There are two parts to this problem, and a third aspect that brings those two parts together.

First and foremost, there is the problem of just plain finding out stuff, stuff about yourself, your potential partners, and your potential customers. We don't help with the essence of this, the discovery and modeling part. This is because in all the cases we encountered, either this knowledge, or the ability to get it, existed or it did not. Where it did not or cannot, there is little for us to do.

Ultimately, you have the problem of looking among vast amounts of information (the stuff you know) to find fits that make sense. The most unconventional fits of capabilities to needs could be the most valuable. A free application that we created, Turnip, helps with this.

In between the two, you have another problem. It is generally easier to look for patterns and such if everything, all you know, is poured into a specialized knowledge pool, using representation techniques that make the job easier. The bad news is that this is the real world, and no one can afford to do that. The stuff you know may be in dozens of different forms, and it is just unrealistic to validate and translate it all so you can do your opportunity browsing.

What to do? You need to *federate* the information. Here at long last is the definition of a concept roughly introduced in Chapter 5. Federating means you just provide some rudimentary communication links among your puddles of information in various formats, and it magically can be browsed as if it were all the same kind of liquid.

We've known how to do this for some time. The old way to do it was to have a neutral format into which you translate on the fly. The problem with this is that every new format needs a translator, and it is hard to keep up with the evolution of each representation format. The better way to handle this is to have each source convey two messages when it communicates: The data itself and a message which tells you (in a way you can understand) how the data is structured into models (or some other representation). This allows the recipient to map elements based on their meaning at the last minute and only as required.

The advantage of this method is:

- you only make a "translation" when required and only on the parts of the models that are of immediate interest, which are small most of the time,
- you don't have to keep track of the various modeling methods and versions, since that is done "at the source," and
- you don't have to worry about keeping two copies of the data current and synchronized: the source copy and your own local, translated copy.

The problem is that, to start with, you have twice as much stuff to keep track of: The data itself and also the information about the method used to structure and index that data. But you also have (for speed's sake) information stored that relates the two in terms of which rules apply where. Most enterprises are already choked by complexity in their information infrastructure. In fact, they pull all kinds of tricks to simplify things just to get through the day, so this method is not widely used today. But it will be soon.

We'll show you in a minute how this complexity can be reasonably managed by the machine. But first, what got us into this was a slightly different problem, how the human user, the analyst/manager, can deal with the huge number of possible combinations of partners, stretches of various processes in combination, and potential changes and opportunities. We're talking about trying to stuff huge universes of colorful birds (and some buzzards) through the very small keyhole which our cognitive abilities allow us.

Visualization of Patterns

The problem is one of abstraction. If you ask a shepherd how many sheep he has, he doesn't physically show you the flock and say, "this many." He uses an abstraction of a number to say 500 sheep. Or perhaps he abstracts further to say that he has a potential 5,000 tons of wool, and 200 ewes per year, with a growth rate of 15% a year. Or he can abstract yet further to the number of sweaters, or a notion of improved warmth in the world, or even improvements in his own standard of living from the wool's income.

Abstraction is a multilayered practice, and one can abstract in many dimensions, often simultaneously. This is the basic miracle of consciousness. Abstraction has several purposes; you do it to make things clearer, to make things easier to store (to remember), or to make them easier to analyze and understand (a process that depends on the former two).

Here we have a problem where we want to create abstractions of this complex universe of VE possibilities so a planner can identify the very few high payoff combinations among all the things that don't make sense. It's almost as if we were looking for the great poetry among the output of millions of monkeys typing randomly.

But wait! Fortunately that is not the case, because the business world is not random. There are all sorts of common threads because we are all human, certain aspects of group dynamics are universal, and there are economic laws in play. There are some built-in self-organizing principles in this system. What we want to find are the combinations that not only make sense (the Shakespearean plays among the monkeys' gibberish) but also are inherently stable. In other words, if conditions were right, they would tend to get together anyway and function together without problems.

Moving beyond the monkey analogy, where word linkage is random, imagine that there is soup of all the possible words and they bump and link together according to their built-in affinities. In non-childrens' story English anyway, this means that "red" (or any color) and "firetruck" would have a greater affinity to each other than the pair of "unhappy" and "firetruck": and that the relation is unsymmetrical: "red firetruck" is a stronger bond than "firetruck red." (However, "firetruck red" may make great sense if your situation is a manicurist! More about situations soon.)

The trick is to abstract the many different types of these *natural* bindings so patterns can be seen. Fortunately, there is a mathematics that supports just this phenomenon.

First, you put all of your representations in an ordered representation space of a specific type, where all of the statements are entities called vectors. You can envision a vector literally. In physical life, vectors are often used as little arrows to describe flow (as in the flow of air over a wing), or stress (as in the direction and strength of forces within that wing). In this simple representation universe, the direction of the arrow is the direction of the force or flow, and the length is the strength of the force or speed of the flow.

Then you change the *topology* of the representation space from one which is handy for seeing where the relations come from to one in which it is easier to see one type of pattern or another.

The notion of topology is easy. Imagine space being defined like a donut, and you are on the outermost surface. If you walk around the equator of the donut, you will return back to the same place. If you turn 90 degrees and walk, you'll go through the hole in the donut and also end up where you left. The topology of this space is toroidal (donut-shaped).

Now, if the donut was a rubber tire, you could cut, twist, and reglue the surface to have different topologies with amazing results (especially if you are in a computer world where physical limits don't constrain you). Then it would be possible for you to return to the same place, but be a reflection of yourself, or experience some other weird transformation!

If you pull some tricks with this topology, the world will make a great deal more of a certain kind of sense. Aerospace modelers use this to look for patterns among the complex vortices that make up the flow over hypersonic wings. Nuclear weapons engineers can no longer test bombs, so they use this technique to simplify simulations. Medical researchers are employing it to recognize patterns in epidemiological data.

Using the technique for knowledge vectors is new, but rather well understood. (The intelligence community uses it to make sense out of huge amounts of apparently disordered information, and this is the foundation we "repurpose.") Because we use speech acts as a language for modeling, and also to define how the model is built, making knowledge vectors is easy. The loop's arrow is simply the vector's arrow.

As this is such an important need, we prototyped a tool, which we call *Turnip*. We assume that the federation of data that we describe in the next section is already done. Turnip is a tool to look for patterns among millions of combinations, and this specific edition looks for agility patterns. The input will be federated information about the environment, processes, and processes-that-could-be by either association or extending an existing capability.

In this version, we address multidimensional spaces. For instance, a primitive version of Turnip works in five dimensions, each dimension representing one of the five intermediate agility metrics, described back in Chapter 12. But we've found it much more useful to double or triple these dimensions by adding other characteristics. Granularity is the property we use in these screenshots, because working with granularity provides us with two advantages: it provides us with the variables for the Layered Formalism and Zooming technique (Devlin, 1997). And, since granularity is the level of clumping of processes, it suggests contractual units. Since most of our strategies include the best selection of contacting units as a key strategic lever, we find this useful.

At any rate, we have a ten dimensional universe plus the measure for density, which is the vertical dimension in the figures. When you transform the topology the way we do, the source information gets boiled down in specific ways; the units go away and the result (called a *fiber bundle*) can be measured in terms of density. The process we described to evaluate the agility metrics by counting loops and nodes is a (very simple) density measure.

What we have in Figure 14.1 is two windows, one each for a VE under consideration. Enterprise option 2 is at the top and option 3 at the bottom. The left-hand axis is the value of the intermediate metric. The right-hand axis is the measure of the granularity, of the process. Closer to the axis is a coarser granularity with the origin being the whole enterprise. The vertical axis is a measure of clustering. Where you see one of the pillars, you see a cluster of processes which are similar according to the topology transformation employed.

The proof-of-concept demonstration assumes only one transformation, that which clusters trust, using the topology features of the previous chapter. But the idea is to employ any of the possible topological transforms that exist. The same mathematician/programmer who prototyped Turnip (Dr. Jeff Weeks) also wrote SnapPea, which surveys all possible topologies. It is downloadable from the University of Minnesota's Geometry Center. The discovery of which functions cluster around which properties in the enterprise is the topic of our future research. We believe that there will be a new science of metamodeling these representation topologies by experts, so the modeling tools themselves will be easier for managers to use.

One would usually use Turnip by having a VE configuration loaded. This represents one possibility of partnering, a specific breakdown of processes without regard to monitoring, contracting, and managing those processes. By clicking the buttons, you can see each of the five three-dimensional graphs that show the clusters that maximize trust. If the clusters are toward the left, that trust supports agility.

Usually, the pillars do cluster at a certain level of granularity. That level tells the manager how best contractually and managerially to cluster the pro-

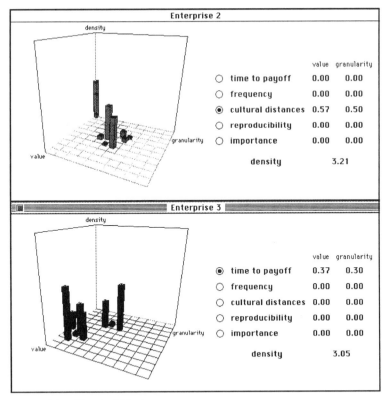

Figure 14.1 Two Turnip Windows

cesses, so as to leverage their natural trust mechanisms. For instance, one might choose to contract responsibility for QA together with the product or service, if that supports trust (and supports agility, if that is your goal).

This mode of operation assumes that Turnip is just a browser of information fed into it. But the user can try new configurations by moving pillars around, changing height, and seeing how that changes processes. This assumes that there is a handbook or library of processes from which you can reverse engineer. You might do this if a set of processes which is key to the strategy does not have a sufficiently high level of trust or agility. By sort of mandating the trust (or agility), you can reverse engineer the necessary processes required, or at least their general characteristics.

Turnip can also be a comparative calculator. Figure 14.2 shows two enterprise configurations, though any number can be specified and saved. You would then pull up the calculator window as shown in the figure Every enterprise you've configured will be listed in both lists. You select one from each list and the calculator tells you how much more agile (under the condition you used in the transformation) the one on the left is than the one on the right. But the calculator also can be configured to show the time and cost (the learning distance) of changing from the configuration on the left to that on the right.

COMPLEXITY

Well, we jumped the gun; we showed you a tool that supposed you had the processes of interest known and modeled. More importantly, we assumed that this unified input was achieved accurately and cheaply. We've already said that in the real world, we think this can only happen when you federate what information pools you have. Federation is costly, in that it greatly increases the complexity of the system. Now, complexity is already killing enterprises just doing mundane matters.

If we employ model federation, it will really be over the limit. Also, if we are looking at many cases of many partners (and many market possibilities), and if we are simulating some cases, the complexity is orders of magnitude greater. What to do?

This is one of the hard issues that must be resolved before even small progress can be made (see Chapter 8). Fortunately, the general problem is well

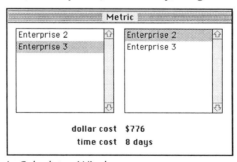

Figure 14.2 Turnip's Calculator Window

known. In fact, it qualifies as one of the grand challenges in all of information science. Once again, the manufacturing enterprise will lead the way, because the problem is at once more critical and results in greater monetary reward than in other domains. (The manufacturing enterprise, especially the VE, is the most challenging of information infrastructure problems because it involves a more explicit requirement for support of *state* than other significant domains.)

Also, once again, we'll harness some mathematical theory which was developed for related problems in other domains. But first a word about the method. In every case, we're taking some pretty strong positions among great philosophical debates about fundamental approaches, and a careful choice of these underlying philosophies is what is allowing us to make progress.

For instance, in the whole discussion over federation, basic religious wars were fought between those who advocate a model as the basic reference and those who promoted a language. Now, in a way this controversy is a little silly, since all models must be described in some language, and all languages must be represented in a model (the grammar). The controversy is not over which is right, but which is more elegant and useful. All are right in the sense that matters, but elegance is directly related to effectiveness and lowered costs. You've already seen that we come down on the side of language, which is at once a paradigm for modeling (the speech acts), and also a means for describing how the models are built.

There are similar, basic controversies over a few other topics. You've encountered one in the previous section. There is a camp of modelers who hold that the best models are those most like familiar (read: physical world) experiences. Thus we have the Macintosh desktop (and the Windows copy). On the other side are those who submit that the clearest expressions of models are those that abstract most cleanly for the use at hand, perhaps using abstractions that take the user far from the physical origin of the model. Turnip is an example of our commitment to this compelling side of that debate.

But back to complexity. The philosophies of how to represent structures in a computer are simple reflections of a larger debate in science over the way the laws of the universe are best represented. This is an argument between the geometricians and the probabilists, and the primary battlefield is the "hardest" of sciences, physics.

The probabilists have a vision of the world that has a certain amount of indeterminism and fuzziness. Events are driven by certain laws of probability. One of the most spectacular successes in the history of theory comes from, *quantum mechanics*. Tightly related is the collection of complexity theory and chaos theory promulgated by the Sante Fe Institute, headed by a physicist clearly (it can be argued) from this school.

The other denomination of believers have a feeling that the universe is deeply geometric, or rather that the laws of the universe become more clear as they become more geometric. The entries on this side are equally solid hits: General relativity and the standard model of particle physics (quarks and such).

This is not a trivial schism; it goes as deep as any belief can go. But it definitely seems that in the real cutting edge of physics, the geometry-based thinkers have convinced most people. So the new grand, unifying ideas, which attempt to swallow quantum mechanics, like superstring theory, are strongly geometric.

The problem is that almost all the rest of the world, and most particularly the elements used in management, are solidly in the other camp. This includes most software engineering. And the reason is clear: The theoretic abstractions are well supported by the type of abstraction we call numbers. This is to say that bean-counters deal with inelegant abstractions. But we knew that, right?

Our problem is not to fix that, but to fix the problem of representing structured knowledge in our infrastructure without the complexity eating us alive. The way this is done now, the information-about-the-information you need to store is significant. As the complexity of this information grows, the meta-information grows more quickly. You can envision this as a library of knowledge. As the library becomes larger, and you strive to make the collection more accessible, the card catalog grows in complexity. The way we do it now, the card catalog's complexity grows faster than that of the library.

The reason is that we treat metainformation as if it is the same type of information. This is where the model-language distinction helps us. We choose to have the models be represented in model terms and the *metamodels* (all that catalog information) in something quite different, a language. Languages can be engineered so that a few rules can be employed in very rich expressions.

Now, here's where we come back to the geometric view of the world. Many of us believe that the most elegant way of decomposing concepts is into primitive elements based on symmetry, remembering that elegance equals affordable effectiveness. In fact, once again we find a marvelously useful mathematics. (For the non-technical manager—essentially all of us—I highly recommend the International Society for the Interdisciplinary Study of Symmetry[1].

One doesn't have to use this geometric perspective, or the metrics, or anything else we've mentioned for VE. But we find it a promising approach to managing complexity to support model federation, and the resulting savings make advanced AVEs a real possibility.

We use concept lattices (Wille, 1985, 1992), which is a very practical expression of the geometric perspective. The idea is simple: Representation systems are generally composed of things and relations that structure those things one to another. The rather simple way is in a hierarchical tree structure, but usually the world isn't so clean. In that case, we use *hetarchies*, where more types of connections are made. Usually, the graphs (the shape of the connections) from such relations are unordered in terms of their underlying structure.

A *concept lattice* is a structured graph for representing knowledge, so that the structure can be used in the representation system. Consider Table 14.1 which has ten items and four characteristics. Each of the items has some of the characteristics or not. The first three characteristics are binary—either you have them of you don't. We've included a fourth that has some scale, so you can see how that would function. In that column you have no speed, a slow speed, or a fast one.

Now look at Figure 14.3. to see how this could be put into a concept lattice. The one we've constructed is actually periodic. You can see two cells, which in the general case could go on forever. So as not to clutter the diagram, we use the item numbers instead of their names. The structure has an origin at the bottom. Note the four arrows to the right; they show that moving in a direction conveys a certain property. For instance, moving up and to the left means the item "has four legs." Moving to the left means it is "brown." Moving forward (to the right on the drawing) one cell gives you the property of being slow; moving two clicks means fast.

One reads the lattice by starting at the origin at the bottom. If an item is brown and has no other characteristic, then it has only one vector, the one to the left. Number 8 (mud) is at the node just one movement left of the origin. Number 10 also has only one characteristic, that of moving fast, so it is two clicks forward from the origin. Item 1 has all four characteristics.

Even though this is a very simple example, it's still easy to see how a great many properties can be "vectorized" and represented. One can also see how properties will cluster. It's not as obvious that any group can be easily characterized as a collection of movements, reflections, and such. Transforming from any group to any other group is accomplished by functions composed of simple symmetry operators. Plus, there is a revolutionary algorithm that allows com-

Table 14.1 Concept Lattice Data

Item Number	Item	Is Brown	Has Four Legs	Makes Noise	Moves
1	Dog	Yes	Yes	Yes	Fast
2	Snake	No	No	No	Slow
3	Bell	No	No	Yes	No
4	Plane	Yes	No	Yes	Fast
5	Table	No	Yes	No	No
6	Tricycle	No	No	No	Slow
7	Turtle	Yes	Yes	No	Slow
8	Mud	Yes	No	No	No
9	Rabbit	No	Yes	No	Fast
10	Car	No	No	No	Fast

plex combinatorial problems to be quickly solved, leveraging this geometry (Karmarkar, 1984).

It turns out that symmetry operations are incredibly efficient for computing, and, when they are performed on regular lattices, they can be easily decomposed for parallel processing. Here's the real payoff: It costs a fair bit to set up the mechanics of regular lattices and the symmetry operators over them. But once you do, the complexity of what can be represented does not increase as new orders of abstraction and recursion are added. All of a sudden, federation doesn't look so expensive, nor the representation of many options of many potential partners and many possible future conditions.

Here's another advantage: We humans are used to looking at two- and three- dimensional structures, but computers have no such limits. We can have as many dimensions as we like. Even better, we can use the representation system to represent the same collection of information indexed in higher dimensions. We can do this because the information about the lattice and associated system is just information. While we are working with multiple dimensions, we can manipulate multiple, simultaneous symmetries. Now this is cool, because the laws of abstraction seem to be related to describing symmetry with symmetry (Goranson, 1996: Lalvani, 1982). Some of our experiments bear this out.

But the big advantage is that the information now has a well-defined topology as well as the representation space. Now, the ability to perform topological transforms to look for concept clusters à la Turnip is now built in. A tool like Turnip, or even the several similar tools out there, can manipulate native data, constantly browsing and shifting information. This is big stuff. Someday, sooner or later, it will likely affect your business.

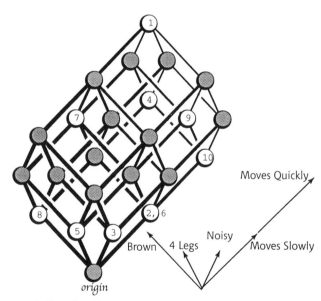

Figure 14.3 A Simple Concept Lattice

SOFTNESS

Complexity is a killer. But it's not the biggest information bogeyman threatening the enterprise. The inability to represent *soft* stuff is. Soft stuff is stuff you don't know much about. We've mentioned it before. You find this condition in situations you cannot fully model because of expense. Or maybe you just don't know how it really works. Social and cultural interactions are of this type. Or maybe you are trying to do some modeling of the future, and you just cannot predict in detail. These are all soft stuff.

We have a conceptual war again, between the logicians and the probabilists. The latter dominate the scene today for the simple reason that, until recently, probability was the only way we knew how to model soft stuff. We have a variety of methods that fold probability into logic in various ways. Perhaps the most familiar is so-called fuzzy logic, but there are many much more common methods. All of your prediction methods are based on this.

But that is an unsatisfying method. Logic is the basis of the scientific method because it allows us to both explain and predict. When we add nonlogical elements into the logic in order to help explain things, we compromise the ability to predict. (Many pseudosciences have plausible, or at least consistent, explanations, but no ability to predict.)

The problem is that the added-in probabilistic elements are second-class citizens in the logic. Think of it this way: only nouns can act in logical statements, so only nouns are first-class citizens. When you add probabilistic stuff into logic, you add it in as adjectives that modify nouns. They only color; they cannot act. There are theoretical reasons why this is bad if you want a real science. If you don't have real science, you cannot have a solid way of predicting the future, and without that, you're always at risk of going out of business.

The solution is to fix logic so that it can have soft objects as first-class citizens. Now you are probably thinking that logic is logic—no one has complained before. Does this guy not know? But this is not as silly as it sounds. In fact, there is an historical precedent. The foundations of modern logic come from Descartes; he based his formalism on an algebra provided by Thomas Harriot, but simplified it by removing the soft object because it was too complicated. The later giant in logic, C. S. Peirce (1960), decried the lack of this object, and his contemporary, Lewis Carroll (actually, the Oxford logician Charles Dodgson) made great fun of its lack.

In 1983, two Stanford mathematicians published a book (Barwise and Perry, 1983) which proposed a new first-class object in logic, the *situation*. Since then, situation theory has worked out the details of this expanding logic. It puts back in the piece that Descartes threw out. But the problems they were trying to address were relatively esoteric issues of linguistics and information.

In 1996 Sirius-Beta cosponsored (with Steelcase, Inc.) a workshop on Business Applications of Situation Theory (BAST). It was held at the Automation and Robotics Research Institute in Dallas-Fort Worth and facilitated by the Industrial Technology Institute of Ann Arbor: it included key representatives from Stanford's Center for the Study of Language and Information (the developers of Situation Theory) and Washington DC's Work and Technology Institute (which sent work-force anthropologists).

In that and subsequent BAST workshops, we worked out, in a preliminary sense, how situation theory can solve the worst of the soft problems. It has already been used for the simplest of these, the problem of tacit knowledge, where you assume that someone knows something that she may not (Devlin and Rosenberg, 1996).

Situation Theory works in this way: In logic (the purest kind, called first order logic), the basic unit is the *fact*. Facts are things you know, either you know to be true or that you know to be not true. These are collected in groups of facts that they call *infons*, the basic units of information.

You reason over these infons to make conclusions, which is just manipulating what you know in a careful way. Into this system, we introduce the *situation*. Situations are open things, in that you nearly never know completely everything about a situation. For instance, you may know that a cube on a table is red, and that it is on the table. But there are lots of things about the situation you don't know, like whether the table is in a falling elevator or whether for sure there is not a bomb in the cube. Some of these you may not need to know right now, but it would be nice to note in case you come back to your notes later and want to ask more questions about the cube. At least the note indicates that there is a situation will prompt you to check about the elevator bit if that is relevant. If you find out that the table is not in an elevator, then you have some hard fact about part of the situation. That soft part has been made hard.

It turns out that Descartes was right; the mechanics of this are quite tricky. But the concept is incredibly powerful. Now, we can reason about things for which we only know a little, and the reasoning is real, not a trick of numbers. This kind of reasoning produces provable results.

But the details of what has been worked out aren't very friendly to enterprise managers, simply because the kinds of problems addressed are fundamentally different. The progress of developing a managerial vocabulary for situation theory has been slow, a victim of the Republican revolution, as sponsored research has been refocused to reduce long term work. But we do have the agenda pretty well scoped out.

That vision includes a new formulation that employs both the situation and the infon. At root, managers are concerned about two things, *what causes what* and *what state are things in* (which is the same as asking what has been caused so far). The first of these is not so easy to know, given the way the logic is set up with infons (facts). We've developed the idea of an *acton* as yet another first-class object. An acton is a unit of action, specified by the set of infons before it happens (essentially what the situation has to be in order for the event to occur) and the set of infons after it happens (which is the resulting situation).

Mostly, actons are just a reshuffled notation which presents infons in a way that we are concerned about. After all, processes are how we as enterprise engineers and managers see the world. But there are some details about state that need to be formally investigated to wring this out well. The state mechanics will keep it straight whether the action has happened, could happen, or will happen.

Actons are the special item that brings situation theory right into the mainstream of what we are concerned with, because the acton can be mapped directly to the *process*. The acton can be defined directly from our communicative act model, so that the calculator we describe later can output both the Dooley graph and the acton expressions. Besides, the way logicians would write an acton, it would serve as executable code in an agent-based simulation environment.

Soft modeling is the Achilles heel of any enterprise modeling project and is crucial to dynamic AVE modeling. Situation theory-based soft modeling will soon be in your future, and that of your competitor.

STATE

There's a final big tool issue; it relates to the notion of *state*. The manufacturing enterprise is the most difficult of all, because nowhere else do we have such an explicit coordination of states of components that must coalesce in some result, the product. All the states in the enterprise must potentially be trackable; managing the enterprise means knowing the state, the future state, and the component causes.

The problem is that the information infrastructure is part of the enterprise. The information infrastructure plays a dual role: It is at once the mechanism the enterprise uses to model itself, and also part of what is being modeled. This is particularly tricky when it comes to the issues of state.

It's as if you were playing chess, but the rules of the game were determined by the location of pieces on the board. Every move would change both the state of the game and the state of the rules. Information scientists have been scratching their heads about this for a few years now (Goranson, 1998b) and have some ideas and possible solutions.

The key behind both ideas is the notion of "late binding," which is the idea that variables in the model, especially state-related variables, are evaluated as late in the game as possible, right before they are needed. This is contrary to what computer people usually want to do because the more you can pin down early and freeze, the better performance you can get out of your system. Late binding costs a lot of cycles when you don't know how to do it well.

Until recently, we really didn't know how to do it. The two areas of concern deal with programming languages and execution environments (basically operating systems).

Language

On the programming language side, a consortium of interests (including ARPA), led by Apple Computer, invested heavily in the technology of dynamic languages, which are languages with the ability to adjust themselves when basic definitions are changed late in the game. This could be done by using

LISP (and similar languages), but they are difficult languages to master, and performance was seen as a problem.

A new language was created called Dylan (for dynamic language) which has many modern features, but particularly dynamism (Shalit, 1996). The advertised advantage was that one could use loose binding for rapid application development, and later provide more (binding) information to the compiler to improve speed.

The hidden advantage is the ability to have the language redefine its internal state very late in the game—just the ability we need for models that need to "see themselves" and adapt based on the current state. Dylan is slowly growing in popularity, but a more profound influence is in how Dylan has affected the drive for such facilities in Java, a widely used and promising language.

Operating Environments

Dylan's dynamism is a revolutionary capability, but it is not enough by itself. What is needed is something much deeper in the operation of the information environment. The old way of hosting an infrastructure put a solid barrier between the state of applications and the state of the machines themselves. The barrier was the operating system "on" which the application run. The advantage was the application was made relatively independent of the environment, but the absolute inability to query and change the state of the hardware was a problem.

Beginning in the 1980's ARPA sponsored research, called Mach, toward a solution to this problem, a "microkernel" with specific properties around which one could build a modern operating system. Among the goals of the project was to provide a way for applications services to monitor and control the machine's state at the lowest level.

The sexiest use of this capability is the ability to have machines collaborate in a multiprocessing mode. But the real power is just the ability we need that exposes state control to the application (actually, application services). Apple also is responsible for bringing this technology to the mainstream in servers, and IBM also is active in this space. Apple has released this technology, now known as Darwin, as open-source software.

Our prototypes employ these ideas, and we can predict with some confidence that you soon will be using dynamic models in your applications which will interact with your infrastructure in an intimate way.

DOOLEY GRAPH CALCULATOR

Pomegranate is our Dooley Graph calculator. One guiding principle in the overall design is to use a visual metaphor all the way down—everything is based on graphic relationships. We divide the design space into three layers and have a graphic paradigm for each of these (see Figure 14.4). Because of fundamental differences among the layers, the graphic paradigm is not exactly the same as you go down, but some key relationships and principles do convey.

At the highest layer, we use Dooley Graphs. At the programming language level, we've chosen to use Prograph CPX (Schmucker, 1994; Shafer, 1994; Steinman & Carver, 1995), as opposed to a more mundane language like C or C++. Here are some reasons for our choice. It is an object-oriented language, which helps with designing components that are modular and reusable by others in a sensible way. But many languages are object oriented; more important, it is the first thoroughly mature graphic programming environment. It's graphic all the way down; there's no text code involved. Graphic languages are much like the graphical models that enterprise modelers use, and we want the modeler to be able to tailor the program to integrate with their existing tools.

Also of primary interest is that CPX uses a *dataflow paradigm*. We are dealing in an area where we've had to make basic decisions about how we deal with time, events, causality, and sequence. The dataflow paradigm somewhat neutralizes these confusing issues. It doesn't matter what happens when, only what the pre- and post- conditions are. This also makes the code cleaner, easier to follow, and incidentally closer to the acton communication/agent state paradigm that we would like to further leverage.

Finally, at the bottom level, we have the *concept engine*. This is no trivial effort. A functional programming approach (as opposed to procedural or object-oriented) is required, meaning at root a LISP. However, all of our research has been in instancing concepts in a graph (or lattice) grammar. In effect, this is also a graphic way of programming, or manipulating concepts. If someone wanted to tinker around at the concept level (and we trust there are those who do), this is the dimension in which they would function. We intend to leverage leitmotifs, conventions, styles, and a few operators across all three levels since all three can use the same concept lattices. We include the term *graph figure* not because we're going to muck about in its details, but merely to show how concept-lattice-ready it appears.

The purpose of Pomegranate is to provide a means to capture a conversation as defined by its utterances and participants, evaluate the conversation using the Dooley Graph algorithm, and then ultimately to provide a mechanism to compare Dooley Graphs. The goal is to provide a framework to measure the Agility of a conversation. Here's how it works.

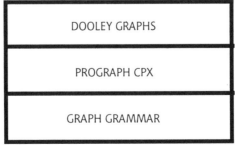

Figure 14.4 Three-Layered Graphic Interface Paradigms

Project Window

The Project Window manages a set of conversation files or documents (see Figure 14.5). The window is designed so that related conversations can be grouped within a project in order to compare the metrics of the conversations. The window provides the ability to create new conversation files, add existing conversation files, remove conversation files, duplicate conversation that exists in the project, and to edit conversation files in the project. The Project Window also provides a way to sort the conversations using any of the available metrics.

Conversation Editor

The Conversation Editor provides the means to add and delete actors and utterances in a conversation. It also provides the function to calculate the Dooley Graph for a conversation. This window is shown in Figure 14.6.

Utterance Editor

This editor allows for detailed specification of utterances. The sender of the utterance can be specified along with the actors that receive the utterance. The utterance type is also specified. In addition, the window provides functions to select other utterances in the conversation for editing.

As can be seen in Figure 14.7, the Utterance Editor window provides several functions for specifying the nature of each utterance:

•The sender of the utterance is specified. Once this selection is made, the sender actor is removed from the selection list for specifying who is to receive the utterance.

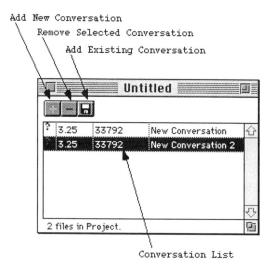

Figure 14.5 Project Manager Window

• The recipients of the utterance are then specified by double-clicking selections in the left hand scrolling list in the window. Each selection will then be added to the recipients list on the right-hand side of the window.

• The type of the utterance is then selected from the *Type* pop-up menu item.

• Then—and this is crucial for proper operation or calculation of the Dooley Graph—are the selections for *Reply To, Resolve* and *Completes.* Each of these selections defines which utterance the current utterance Completes, Resolves, or is a Reply To.

Dooley Graph Window

This window can be opened only from the Conversation Editor. It is opened when the *Do Dooley* button is pushed in the Conversation Editor and displays the Dooley Graph graphically. The window also provides buttons for display of each Dooley metric (Figure 14.8).

Tailoring the Dooley Graph Engine

The whole application is user tailorable, but we especially wanted to make the Dooley Graph Engine tailorable so that expert modelers could employ other introspective metrics, like the Trust metrics of the last chapter.

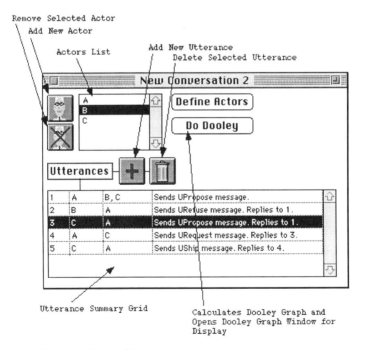

Figure 14.6 Conversation Editor

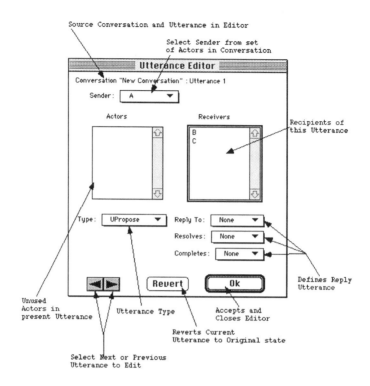

Figure 14.7 Utterance Editor Window

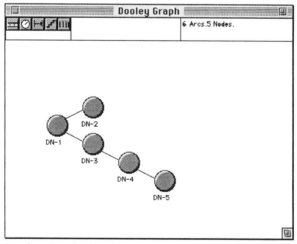

Figure 14.8 Dooley Graph Window

The key to all this is in our selection of a graphical programming language and the way we set up the class structure of the application. We used a conversation paradigm in the program so that the program itself could be modeled by whatever method the user wants, and we also stored in the same concept lattice as the enterprise's processes. An example of what the graphical programming elements look like is shown in Figure 14.9.

CONCLUSION

The Problem

The need for agility has been with some businesses for many years; it's not a new need at all. But it is becoming more of an important factor and for more and more businesses. In the past, enterprises became agile by accident or luck, but now we have the ability to engineer agility into the system. We should be able to make an enterprise optimally more agile, just like we now can make it more lean.

We've found that agility is different from other management techniques, like lean manufacturing and activity-based management. In many cases, following one of those techniques may make an enterprise less agile. Even worse, what makes one enterprise more agile may not function for another. And, similarly, the ability to be agile in one business situation may not be effective, or may even counter the ability to respond to another.

Agility is an essential strategy for some enterprises where market needs move unexpectedly, technology developments are rich, or some unexpected events could be fatal. Agility needs to be engineered to be just the right kind for the type of enterprise and threat, and not too much. Most agility will have

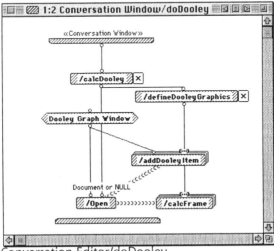

Figure 14.9 Conversation Editor/doDooley

costs, either directly or by compromising some other strategic advantage, so the ability to engineer is particularly important.

The problem is exacerbated by a couple of factors. The first is that we cannot rely on the most basic of managerial skills, intuitive experience—by definition, we are addressing events and dynamics that are outside of such experience. Another problem is that the best terms we can use, like "agility," have become blurred by consultants and researchers with different agendas or timid thinking. We like to have universal solutions, so there is a tendency to hope for simple, standard agility techniques.

We spent some time pinning down the definition by straightforward definition, by illustration with examples, and by contrasting the specific notion of an agile enterprise with other philosophies (most of which will be employed side-by-side with agility).

What is needed is an extension of current modeling and analysis techniques. This extension will address and evaluate risk associated with the uncertain and unknown and will characterize the peculiarities of the specific situation and competitive strengths. It will be insertable in existing strategic methods and tools, but be based on solid principles. Such a grounding will ensure that the decisions regarding agility are correct.

Despite the absolute need for agility, it is widely ignored because the problems are so very hard. We need both new business approaches and new analytical techniques. Just one or the other won't be sufficient.

The Business Approach

New ways of doing business will be required, ways that allow fast and cheap temporary acquisition of capabilities and resources that can be managed as if they were part of the organization all along. At root, the Virtual Enterprise is the model for this way of doing business, though even the VE has manifold types of instances. We've defined these into four extreme types of which all cases are comprised. The standard vision of these types is the federation of small firms under the leadership of a larger coordinator. But the large prime contractor is not required, and the vision is just as valid when assembling resources from within a large corporation.

The enterprise, virtual or not, is a fabric of different infrastructures. Some can be modeled simply and logically, while others don't have such nice tools. The idea of managing is to understand and mold these infrastructures, a problem that is particularly difficult when the infrastructures are dynamic, wholly synthetic, and often abandon traditional models. Unfortunately, there is no way around the fact that managers have to understand infrastructure principles in general, and particularly when they are addressing agility concerns.

We have provided a simple framework, a Reference Model that allows one to understand how their infrastructures support key processes which serve the strategic goals of the enterprise. This has been well tested and has been proved to be useful in the general context, beyond agility.

We were surprised to find that successful agility strategies were quite different, each peculiar to the situation and specific strengths of the organization.

But a few common elements emerged. Trust among the members is the key parameter. This relies heavily on the contractual infrastructure; or more precisely, problems in trust are a consequence of brittle, stable business structures that evolved for reasons unfriendly to agility. Therefore, we spent some time looking at the evolution of the business infrastructure, and especially in the context of the movie industry which does well at agility in this sphere.

We've extracted three principles for an agile business structure which likely will be of interest to any agility planner. Best trust in the AVE is accomplished by a network of trusted agents who help screen, preselect, and vouch for the appropriateness of the VE's potential members. It needs a way of relying on pre-existing contract templates or adjudication mechanisms to allow members to operate in an atmosphere of confidence so that they will not be disadvantaged in a sea of change. In particular, we showed you the advantages of case law for this (though the Brazilian model of specific instant contracts is promising as well).

Finally, the VE requires a means of illuminating each member and all its constituent parts as to the strategic goals of the new, temporary enterprise. This includes some elements of business culture. We described the mechanism in Hollywood which uses a sort of culture-based High Concept mission statement. Because of the dependency of this on specific cultural terms and industry styles, it's not applicable to the general case, so we generalized the idea using the results of a workshop on future needs for the enterprise. In this case, we need specific technology and method examples, but the basic idea is the same: How does player knows what its part is and why so that as requirements change, it can adapt its role in the VE to optimize the VE.

Technical Approach

Which brings us to the technical challenges. It is not enough to give you the business side, we must also give you the new tools and methods you will require. The most basic of these is to evaluate the effectiveness of various infrastructure and processes to change. Using this tool, one can cast the agility benefits of specific configurations in the same strategic space as other benefits (like lower product cost and higher quality) and compare them against the costs of those configurations. This simple cost-benefit analysis, especially those in the trust/contract contexts, can only be done with agility metrics.

We leveraged some research in mathematics and computer science that require only the most superficial of adjustments to be used in the business world. One technique involves analyzing models of processes to evaluate the intrinsic adaptability of that process in a specific context. Another involves extending logic to handle what we call soft elements: Unknowns in the environment and unknown mechanics, such as social mechanisms.

In the former case, the method is to break processes into standard units and model some of them. The standard units of our examples were defined by the Reference Model, though any taxonomy would do. Then, justified by fairly sophisticated math, we have the ability to judge adaptability by simply counting certain features of the model. The addition of soft elements into modeling logic is somewhat more painful for tool suppliers since it involves some extensive replumbing of internal details. However, there are essentially no modeling tools for soft phenomenon, so little reworking is required. Tools based on the expanded logic can function alongside tools based on the more restricted logic. Because nearly everyone will be interested in actual tools, not just the new methods, we spent energy developing prototype tools and describing how they and others will fit into a variety of scenarios.

We believe that agility only makes sense as a strategic weapon in addition to many others, so agility tools need to integrate into many different types of planning systems, supplementing rather than replacing them.

NOTE

1. The ISIS-Symmetry is a group of artists, physicists, dancers, psychologists, crystallographers, mathematicians, and so on. A great many disciplines as well as countries are represented. The informal goal is to engage in cross-discipline encounters to transplant symmetry-based insights into one's own tasks. Their excellent quarterly is *Symmetry: Culture and Science.)* Contact info is: ISIS-Symmetry, Budapest, P. O. Box 994, H-1245 Hungary, http://members.tripod.com/vismath.

Bibliography and References

Agility Forum. *Agile Customer-Supplier Relations.* Bethlehem, PA: Agility Forum, 1994.

Agility Forum, MIT Leaders for Manufacturing and Department of Energy's Technologies Enabling Agile Manufacturing. *Next Generation Manufacturing Project: A Framework for Action.* Bethlehem, PA: Agility Forum, 1997

Alexander, Christopher. *Notes on the Synthesis of Form.* Cambridge, MA: Harvard University Press, 1971.

Alexander, Christopher. *The Timeless Way of Building.* New York: Oxford University Press, 1979.

Alexander, Christopher, Sara Ishikawa, and Murray Silverstein. *A Pattern Language: Towns, Buildings, Constructions.* New York: Oxford University Press, 1977.

Ashley, Clifford W. *The Ashley Book of Knots.* New York: Doubleday, 1944.

Asperti, Andrea and Guiseppe Longo. *Categories, Types, and Structures.* Cambridge MA: MIT Press, 1991.

Augustine, Norman R. *Augustine's Laws.* New York: Penguin, 1983.

Austin, J. L. *How to Do Things with Words.* London: Oxford University Press, 1962.

Automation & Robotics Research Institute. *A Consensus Process Model for Small Manufacturers, An IDEF3 Model.* Fort Worth, TX: Automation & Robotics Research Institute, 1991.

Automation & Robotics Research Institute. *Perform Continuous Enterprise Improvement.* Fort Worth, TX: Automation & Robotics Research Institute, 1991.

Barwise, Jon. *The Situation in Logic.* Menlo Park, CA: SLSI Publications, Stanford University Press, 1988.

Barwise, Jon and John Perry. *Situations and Attitudes.* Cambridge, MA: MIT Press, 1983.

Beck, John Christopher. *A Schema for Constraint Relaxation with Instantiations for Partial Constraint Satisfaction and Schedule Optimization.* Master's thesis, University of Toronto, 1994.

Bloom, Howard. *The Lucifer Principle: A Scientific Expedition into the Forces of History.* New York: Atlantic Monthly Press, 1995.

Bowers, A. F. and C. A. Gurr. "Towards Fast and Declarative Meta-Programming." In Apt, Krzysztof and Frannco Turini, eds., *Meta-Logics and Logic Programming.* Cambridge, MA: MIT Press, 1995.

Brodie, Richard. *Virus of the Mind: The New Science of the Meme.* Seattle, WA: Integral Press, 1996.

Brown, Peter Harry and Pat H. Broeske. *Howard Hughes: The Untold Story.* New York: Dutton, 1996.

Buderi, Robert. *The Invention that Changed the World: How a Small Group of Radar Pioneers Won the Second World War and Launched a Technological Revolution.* New York: Simon and Schuster, 1996.

Carvalho-Rodrigues, F. and J. Dockery. "Defining Systems Based on Information Exchange: Structure from Dynamics." *BioSystems* 38 (1996): 229-234.

Cavedon, Lawrence. "A Channel Theoretic Model of Situated Default Reasoning." *Proceedings of the Second Conference on Information-Theoretic Approaches to Logic, Language, and Computation,* London Guildhall University, 1996.

Cohen, Philip R. and Hector J. Leveseque. "Communicative Acts for Artificial Agents." *Proceedings of ICMAS,* 65-72, 1995.

Collier, John. "Information Originates in Symmetry Breaking." *Symmetry: Culture and Science,* 7, 3, (1996): 247-256.

Conrad, Michael. "Cross-scale Interactions in Biomolecular Information Processing." *BioSystems* 35 (1995): 157-160.

Conrad, Michael. "Cross-scale Information Processing in Evolution, Development and Intelligence." *BioSystems* 38 (1996): 97-109.

Conrad, Michael. "Organisms, Machines, and Societies: From the Vertical Structure of Adaptability to the Management of Information." to appear In *World Futures, Proceeding of the 2nd Foundations of Information Science Conference,* 1997.

Coplien, James O. and Douglas C. Schmidt, eds. *Pattern Languages of Program Design.* Reading, MA: Addison-Wesley, 1995.

Cotter, Sean and Mike Potel. *Inside Taligent Technology.* Reading MA: Addison-Wesley, 1995.

Crole, Roy L. *Categories for Types.* Cambridge: Cambridge University Press, 1993.

Davidson, Janet E., Rebecca Deuser and Robert J. Sternberg. "The Role of Metacognition in Problem Solving." In Metcalfe, Janet and Arthur P. Shimamurain, eds., *Metacognition.* Cambridge, MA: MIT Press, 1996.

Dawkins, Richard. *The Selfish Gene.* New York: Oxford University Press, 1976.

Dawkins, Richard. *Climbing Mount Improbable.* New York: W.W. Norton, 1996.

Devlin, Keith. *Logic and Information.* Cambridge: Cambridge University Press, 1991.

Devlin, Keith. *Goodbye, Descartes: The End of Logic and the Search for a New Cosmology of Mind.* New York: John Wiley and Sons, 1997.

Devlin, Keith and Duska Rosenberg. *Language at Work: Analyzing Communication Breakdown in the Workplace to Inform Systems Design.* CSLI Lecture Notes 66, Stanford, CA: Center for the Study of Language and Information, 1996.

Dooley, Robert A. "Repartee as a Graph." In Longacre, R.E., *An Anatomy of Speech Notations,* Appendix B in (Longacre, 1976) pp. 348-358. Lisse: Peter deRidder, 1976.

Dornheim, Michael A. and David Hughes. "U.S. Intensifies Efforts to Meet Missile Threat." *Aviation Week and Space Technology,* 16 October 1995, 36-39.

Dove, Rick, ed. *Best Agile Practice Reference Base.* Agility Forum Agility Report Series, Bethlehem, PA: Agility Forum, 1995.

ESPIRIT Consortium AMICE. *Computer Integrated Manufacturing: Open Systems Architecture.* Berlin: Springer-Verlag, 1991.

Feinberg, Neal, Sonya E. Keene, Robert O. Mathews, and P. Tucker Withington. *Dylan Programming.* Reading MA: Addison-Wesley, 1997.

Finin, T., R. Fritzson, D. McKay, and R. McEntire. "KQML as an Agent Communication Language," In *Proceedings of the Third International Conference on Information and Knowledge Management.* New York: ACM Press, 1994.

Fulton, James A. *Technical Report on the Semantic Unification Meta-Model.* International Standards Organization TC184/SC4/WG3N175, 1992.

Gamma, Erich, Richard Helm, Ralph Johnson, and John Vlissides. *Design Patterns.* Reading, MA: Addison-Wesley, 1995.

George, Joey F., Suzanne Iacono and Rob Kling. "How Do Office Workers Learn About Computing?" *Information Technology and People,* 6,4 (1994): 249-269.

Godin, Robert and Hafedh Mili. "Building and Maintaining Analysis-Level Class Hierarchies using Galois Lattices." OOPSLA (1993): 394-410.

Goldman, Steven L, Kenneth Preiss, and Roger N. Nagel. *Agile Competitors and Virtual Organizations: Strategies for Enriching the Customer.* New York: Wiley. 1997.

Goranson, H. T. "The CIMOSA Approach as an Enterprise Integration Strategy." In Petrie, Charles, ed. *Enterprise Integration Modeling,* pp. 167-178. Cambridge, MA: MIT Press, 1992a.

Goranson, H. T. "Dimensions of Enterprise Integration." In Petrie, Charles, ed., *Enterprise Integration Modeling,* pp. 101-113. Cambridge, MA: MIT Press, 1992b.

Goranson, H. T. "The Integration Domain and the Application Architecture." In Petrie, Charles, ed., *Enterprise Integration Modeling,* pp. 47-55. Cambridge, MA: MIT Press, 1992c.

Goranson, H. T. "The Integration Domain and the Enterprise Characterization." In Petrie, Charles, ed., *Enterprise Integration Modeling,* pp. 23-34. Cambridge, MA: MIT Press, 1992d.

Goranson, H. T. "The Integration Domain and the Execution Environment." In Petrie, Charles, ed., *Enterprise Integration Modeling.* pp. 56-66. Cambridge, MA: MIT Press, 1992e.

Goranson, H. T. "Metrics and Models." In Petrie, Charles, ed., *Enterprise Integration Modeling.* pp. 78-84. Cambridge, MA: MIT Press, 1992f.

Goranson, H. T. "Metrics in the Sirius-Beta Integration Domain." In Petrie, Charles, ed., *Enterprise Integration Modeling.* pp. 430-444. Cambridge, MA: MIT Press, 1992g.

Goranson, H. T. "Services in the Sirius-Beta Inter-Integration Domain." In Petrie, Charles, ed., *Enterprise Integration Modeling.* pp. 341-355. Cambridge, MA: MIT Press, 1992h.

Goranson, H. T. "The Suppliers' Working Group Enterprise Integration Reference Taxonomy." In Petrie, Charles, ed., *Enterprise Integration Modeling.* pp. 114-130. Cambridge, MA: MIT Press, 1992i.

Goranson, H. T. "Knowledge Representation by Metastructures." *Symmetry: Culture and Science* 7, 1 (1996): 91-96.

Goranson, H. T. "Design for Agility Using Process Complexity Measures." *Agility and Global Competition* 1, 3 (1997a): 47-55.

Goranson, H. T. "ICEIMT in Perspective." In Kosanke, K., and J. G. Nell, eds., *Enterprise Engineering and Integration: Proceedings of ICEIMT '97, International Conference on Enterprise Integration and Modeling Technology,* pp. 167-174 Berlin: Springer-Verlag, 1997b.

Goranson, H. T., R. Borowsky, G. Colquhoun, A. Molina, G. Morel, J. Nell, C. Reyneri, H. Synterä, F. Vernadat, M. Walz, and M. Winkler, "Research for Advanced Enterprise Integration Standards." In Kosanke, K., and J. G. Nell, eds., *Enterprise Engineering and Integration: Proceedings of ICEIMT '97, International Conference on Enterprise Integration and Modeling Technology,* pp. 117-122. Berlin: Springer-Verlag, 1997c.

Goranson, H. T. *Agility Measures: Engineering Agile Systems.* Wright Laboratories Technical Report 97-8053, U. S. Air Force Manufacturing Technology Directorate, 1997d.

Goranson, H. T. "Soft Mathematics and Information Dynamics." *Biosystems,* 46 (1998) 163-167.

Goranson, H. T. "Agile Manufacturing." In Molina, A., J. M. Sánchez and A. Kusiak, eds., *Handbook of Life Cycle Engineering; Concepts, Tools and Techniques.* Boston: Kluwer Academic Publishers, 1999a.

Goranson, H. T. "Architectural Requirements of Commercial Products." In Bernus, P., K. Mertins, and G. Schmidt, eds. *Handbook on Architectures of Information Systems*, pp.711-732. Berlin: Springer-Verlag, 1999b.

Griffin, Nancy and Kim Masters. *Hit and Run: How Jon Peters and Peter Gruber Took Sony for a Ride in Hollywood*. New York: Simon and Schuster, 1996.

Haegeman, Liliane. *Introduction to Government & Binding Theory*. Oxford: Blackwell, 1991.

Hagstrom, Robert G., Jr. *The Warren Buffet Way: Investment Strategies of the World's Greatest Investor*. New York: Wiley, 1994.

Hilfinger, Paul. *Abstraction Mechanisms and Language Design*. Cambridge, MA: MIT Press, 1988.

Hollocks, B. W., H. T. Goranson, D. N. Shorter, and F. B. Vernadat. "Assessing Enterprise Integration for Competitive Advantage." In Kosanke, K., and J. G. Nell, eds. *Enterprise Engineering and Integration: Proceedings of ICEIMT '97, International Conference on Enterprise Integration and Modeling Technology*. Berlin: Springer-Verlag, 1997.

Hurwitz, Roger and John C. Mallery. "The Open Meeting: A Web-Based System for Conferencing and Collaboration." *Proceedings of the 4th International Worldwide Web Conference, Worldwide Web Journal* 1, 1: (1995)

The IDEF Framework. Dayton, OH: The IDEF Users Group, 1991.

Jarboe, Kenan Patrick and Joel Yudken. *Smart Workers, Smart Machines: A Technology Policy for the 21st Century*. Washington: Work and Technology Institute, 1996.

Johnson, M.E., L. Meade and K. J. Rogers. "Partner Selection in the Agile Environment," *4th Agility Forum Conference*, pp.496-505. Bethlehem. PA: Agility Forum, 1995.

Jordan, James amd Jerry Rosser. "Modeling Agility in Virtual Enterprises." *Proceedings of the Sixth National Agility Conference*, Bethlehem, PA: Agility Forum, 1997.

Kahl, Wolfram. "Internally Typed Term Grammars." In *Graph Theoretic Concepts in Computer Science*, 24th International Workshop, Working Group 1998, Smolenice Castle, Slovakia, June, LNCS, 1517, Berlin: Springer-Verlag 1998.

Kaminski, Michelle, Domenick Bertelli, Melissa Moye, and Joel Yudkin. *Making Change Happen: Six Cases of Unions and Companies Transforming Their Workplaces*. Washington: Work and Technology Institute, 1996.

Karmarkar, N. "A New Polynomial-time Algorithm for Linear Programming." *Combinatorica*, 4 (1984) 373-395..

Katarani, Kojin. *Architecture as Metaphor: Language, Number, Money*. Cambridge, MA: MIT Press, 1995.

Kidd, Paul T. *Agile Manufacturing: Forging New Frontiers*. Reading, MA: Addison Wesley, 1994

Kidd, P. T. and W. Karwowski, eds. *Advances in Agile Manufacturing: Integrating Technology, Organization and People (Advances in Design and Manufacturing, Volume, 4)*. IOS Press, 1995.

Kosanke, K., and J. G. Nell, eds. *Enterprise Engineering and Integration: Proceedings of ICEIMT '97, International Conference on Enterprise Integration and Modeling Technology*. Berlin: Springer-Verlag, 1997.

Lalvani, Haresh. *Transpolyhedra: Dual Transformations by Explosion-Implosion*. Privately Published. 164 Bank Street, Apt 2B, New York 10014, 1977.

Lalvani, Haresh. *Structures on Hyperstructures*. Privately Published. 164 Bank Street, Apt 2B, New York 10014, 1982.

Lalvani, Haresh. "Continuous Transformations of Subdivided Periodic Surfaces." *International Journal of Space Structures*, 5, 3&4 (1990) 255-279.

Livingston, Charles. *Knot Theory*. Washington, DC: Mathematical Association of America, 1993.

Longacre, R. E. *An Anatomy of Speech Notions*. Lisse: Peter de Ridder, 1976.

Lynch, Aaron. *Thought Contagion: How Belief Spreads Through Society.* New York: Basic Books, 1996.

MacLane, Saunders. *Categories for the Working Mathematician.* Berlin: Springer-Verlag, 1971.

Marijuán, Pedro. "From Computers and Quantum Physics to Cells, Nervous Systems and Societies." *BioSystems* 38 (1996): 87-96.

Marijuán, Pedro. "Gloom in the Society of Enzymes." *BioSystems 38* (1996): 163-171.

Malone, Thomas W., Kevin Crowston, Jintae Lee, and Brian Pentland. "Tools for Inventing Organizations: Toward a Handbook of Organizational Processes." Center for Coordination Science White Paper 141. Cambridge, MA: MIT, 1993.

Matsuno, Koichiro. "Being Free from Ceteris Paribus: A Vehicle for Founding Physics upon Biology Rather than the Other Way Around." *Applied Mathematics and Computation* 56 (1993): 261-279.

Mayer, R. J. *IDEF0 Functional Modeling.* College Station, TX: Knowledge Based Systems, Inc., 1990.

Mayer, R. J., T. P. Cullinane, P. S. deWitte, W. B. Knappenberger and M. S. Wells. *Information Integration For Concurrent Engineering (IICE) - IDEF3 Process Description Capture Method Report.* College Station, TX: Knowledge Based Systems, Inc., 1992.

McCullough, David. *The Path Between the Seas: The Creation of the Panama Canal, 1870-1914.* New York: Simon and Schuster, 1977.

Menzel, Christopher and Richard J. Mayer. "A Situation Theoretic Approach to the Representation of Processes." *International Journal for Concurrent Engineering Research and Applications* (1997).

Mooney, Robert F. and André R. Sigourney. *The Nantucket Way: Untold Legend and Lore of America's Most Intriguing Island.* Garden City, NY: Doubleday, 1980.

Morita, Akio and Shintaro Ishihara. *The Japan that Can Say No: Why Japan Will Be the First Among Equals.* English Translation: New York: Simon and Schuster, 1988.

Nagel, Roger N. and Rick Dove. *"Principle Investigators with 15 industry executives."* Goldman, Steven L., and Preiss, Kenneth, eds. *Twenty-first Century Manufacturing Enterprise Strategy: An Industry-Led View.* Iacocca Institute at Lehigh University. Bethlehem PA: Agility Forum, 1991.

Oleson, John D. *Pathways to Agility: Mass Customization in Action.* New York: John Wiley and Sons, 1998.

Panko, Raymond R. and Susan T. Kinney. "Dyadic Organizational Communication: Is the Dyad Different?" *Proceedings of the 25th Hawaii International Conference on Systems Sciences,* pp.244-253, 1992.

Parunak, Van. "A Linguistic Approach to Modeling Virtual Enterprises." Unpublished paper available from the Industrial Technology Institute, Ann Arbor, 1996a.

Parunak, Van. "An Introduction to Speech Acts and Dooley Graphs." Unpublished paper available from the Industrial Technology Institute, Ann Arbor, 1996b.

Parunak, Van. "Measures and Projections." Unpublished paper available from the Industrial Technology Institute, Ann Arbor, 1996c.

Pearlman, Wolf. "Toward a General System for Knowledge Fusion." *Kybernetes,* 25, 7/8 (1996): 135-140.

Peirce, C. S. *Collected Papers.* ed. Charles Hartshorne and Paul Weiss, Cambridge: Cambridge University Press, 1960.

Petrie, Charles J. "Agent-Based Engineering, the Web, and Intelligence." *IEEE Expert: Intelligent Systems & Their Application.* pp.24-29, 1996.

Petrie, Charles, ed. *Enterprise Integration and Modeling: Proceedings of the First International Conference on Enterprise Integration Modeling Technology.* Cambridge, MA: MIT Press, 1992.

Petroski, Henry. *Engineers of Dreams: Great Bridge Builders and the Spanning of America.* New York: Knopf, 1995.

Pictorius, Inc. *Prograph CPX ABC Reference.* 1994.

Porter, Michael E. *Capital Choices: Changing the Way America Invests in Industry.* Executive Summary, Council on Competitiveness, Washington, DC: 1992.

Pree, Wolfgang. *Design Patterns for Object-Oriented Software Development.* Reading, MA: Addison-Wesley, 1994.

Preiss, Kenneth, Steven L. Goldman, and Roger N. Nagel. *Cooperate to Compete.* New York: Van Nostrand Reinhold, 1996.

Presley, A. R., B. L. Huff and D. H. Lilies. "A Comprehensive Enterprise Model for Small Manufacturers." Paper presented at the 2nd Industrial Engineering Research Conference, Los Angeles, California, 1993.

Presley, A. R., M. E. Johnson, J. Weddle and D. H. Liles. "Enterprise Excellence: Small Manufacturers and Continuous Improvement." Paper presented at the 2nd Industrial Engineering Research Conference, Institute of Industrial Engineers, Atlanta, Georgia, 1993.

Rhodes, Richard. *Dark Sun: The Making of the Hydrogen Bomb.* New York: Simon and Schuster, 1995.

Rich, Ben R. *Skunk Works: A Personal Memoir of My Years at Lockheed.* Boston: Little Brown, 1994.

Rogers, K. J., L. Whitman and D. R. Underdown. "The Enterprise Integration Issues Encountered with Agile Process Introduction." In *Flexible Automation and Intelligent Manufacturing* (FAIM98), pp. 51-59. New York: Begell House, 1998.

Schlenoff, Craig, Amy Knutilla and Steve Ray. *A Robust Ontology for Manufacturing Systems Integration.* Proceedings of the 2nd International Conference on Engineering Design and Automation, Maui, August, 1998.

Schmucker, Kurt. "Prograph CPX- A Tutorial." *MacTech* 10, 11 (1994): 69.

Shafer, Dan. *The Power of Prograph CPX.* San Jose, CA: The Reader Network, 1994.

Shalit, Andrew. *The Dylan Reference Manual.* New York: Addison Wesley Developers Press, 1996.

Spencer, Andrew. *Morphological Theory.* Oxford: Blackwell, 1991.

Steinman, Scott and Kevin Carver. *Visual Programming with Prograph CPX.* Greenwich, CT: Manning, 1995.

Thom, René. *Structural Stability and Morphogenesis.* Reading, MA: Benjamin/Cummings, 1975.

Tyler, Patrick. *Running Critical: The Silent War, Rickover, and General Dynamics.* New York: Harper and Row, 1986.

Walker, Lois E., and Shelby E. Walker. *From Huffman Prairie to the Moon: The History of Wright-Patterson Air Force Base.* Washington, D.C.: U.S. Government Printing Office, 1983.

Wille, Rudolf. "Tensorial Decomposition of Concept Lattices." *Order,* 2 (1985): 81-95.

Wille, Rudolf. "Subdirect Product Construction of Concept Lattices." *Discrete Mathematics* 63 (1987): 305-313.

Wille, Rudolf. "Concept Lattices and Conceptual Knowledge Systems. *Computers and Mathematical Applications,* 23, 6-9 (1992): 493-515.

Winograd, T. and F. Flores. *Understanding Computers and Cognition.* Reading, MA: Addison-Wesley, 1988.

Wyatt, Justin. *High Concept: Movies and Marketing in Hollywood.* Austin: University of Texas Press, 1994.

Index

Aerospace Agile Manufacturing Research
　Center. *See* Organizations: Aerospace
　Agile Manufacturing Research Center
Agents
　actons defined, 240
　actor, 222
　analyzer, 222
　change monitors in partners, 142
　communicative acts, 102
　emergent behavior as agility, 163
　federatable executables, 163
　horizontal channels, 222
　late binding, 241
　notion of action, 162
　open agent enterprises, 46
　opportunity identification, 115, 132
　partner search, 140
　sensor, 221
　shop floor, 131
　trust, 43
　trusted agent, 220
　trusted agent channel, 221
　using communicative acts, 161
　vertical channels, 222
　virtual enterprise organizer, 72

Agile Virtual Enterprise Focus Group. *See*
　Research projects: Agile Virtual
　Enterprise Focus Group
Agile virtual enterprise reference
　model, 109 - 144
Agility
　agility budget, 189
　and activity-based costing, 91
　and business process re-
　　engineering, 91
　and concurrent engineering, 93
　and enterprise integration, 94
　and enterprise resource planning, 91
　and flexible manufacturing, 90
　and modeling, 101
　and object orientation, 97
　and product data management, 96,
　　186
　and rule-based technology, 147
　and total quality management, 91
　as creativity, 68
　best agile practice survey, 107, 144 -
　　155
　costs, 203 - 209
　defined as capabilities, 104

defined as evolution, 105
definition, 3, 68
information infrastructure
    definition, 127
legal certifiers, 129
legal/explicit infrastructure
    definition, 128
limits, 102 - 107
metrics defined, 74
modeling, 102
partner search, 119
physical infrastructure definition, 130
research needs, 48
second-order agility, 103
social/cultural infrastructure
    definition, 127
three principles, 43
types of change, 73
Agility Forum. *See* Organizations: Agility
    Forum
AIM-9X. *See* Research projects: AIM-9X
    missile
Apollo mission, 32
Apple. *See* Companies: Apple Computer
ARPA. *See* U.S. Government Agencies:
    Defense Advanced Research Projects
    Agency
Augustine, Norman, 33
Automation and Robotics Research
    Institute. *See* Organizations: Automation
    and Robotics Research Institute

Brazil, 225

CALS. *See* Research projects: Computer
    Aided Logistics Support, 34
Carroll, Lewis, 239
Case law
    agility environment, 83
    and oil industry, 13
    and privateers, 17
    and trust, 215
    English influence, 29 - 33
    Federal Acquisition Regulations, 36, 82
    in film industry, 12

influence of Quakers, 14, 53
inheritance of comman law, 35
Iranian food distribution system, 216
Russian substitute, 24
Soviet Union not follow, 30
Uniform Commercial Code, 35
Center for the Study of Language and
    Information, *See* Organizations: Center
    for the Study of Language and
    Information
Chomsky, Noam, 172
Communicative acts, 158 - 171
    see also agents
    and agents, 161
    and reference model, 177
    as utterances, 178
    assert defined, 168
    background, 166
    commit defined, 168
    complete dynamics, 171
    defined as speech acts, 163
    dynamics defined, 167 - 171
    example, 176 - 179, 180 - 186
    inform defined, 168
    pay defined, 169
    question defined, 168
    refuse defined, 168
    reply dynamics, 170
    request defined, 168
    resolve dynamics, 170
    respond dynamics, 169
    ship defined, 169
    solicit defined, 168
    speech acts, 163
Companies
    2 Technologies, Inc., xv
    Agile Web, xv
    Andersen Consulting, xv
    anonymous
        airline, 151, 155
        automaker, 25
        electronics manufacturer, 149
        railroad, 144, 154
        shipyard, 152, 155
        telecom, 157
    Apple Computer, 61, 154, 241, 242
    Arthur D. Little, Inc., xv

Associated Fiberglass, xv
AT&T, xiv, xv, 57, 61
Atari, 8
Ben Franklin Institute, xv
Boeing
   Commercial Airplane Group, xv
   Military and Space, xv
   Rocketdyne, xv
Burger King, 6 - 8
Casio, 71
Caterpillar, 72
Ceco Corp., xv
Chrysler, 4
Columbia Pictures, 39
Competitive Technologies Inc., xv
Conduit Electronic Delivery
  Systems, xv
Contemporary Design, xv
Creative Artist's Agency, 43
D'Ancona & Pflaum, xv
Deere & Co., xv
Digital Equipment Corp., xiv, 57
Dow Corning, 88
Dupont Advanced Material Systems, xv
Eastman Kodak, xv
Electronic Data Systems, xv
Enterprise Agility International, xv
Executive Action Group, xv
FKW Incorporated, xv
FlexCell, 24, 146
Ford Motor Company, xv, 4
Gaudiouse and Associates, xv
Gemini Industries, xv
General Electric, 3, 27
General Motors, 4, 54
Global Strategic Solutions, xv
Goodyear Tire and Rubber, xv
Gunneson Group International, Inc., xv
H. R. Textron, xv
Hall & Associates, xv
Hehr Power Systems, xv
Hewlett-Packard, 57, 61, 154
HighTech Marketing, xv
Hughes
   Aircraft, 54
   Missile Systems Co., xv
IBM, xiv, xv, 3, 57, 61, 154, 242

Industrial Light and Magic, 43
Intelligent Systems Technology Inc., xv
Jim Bronson, xv
Kavco Industries, xv
Knowledge Based Systems Inc., xv
Levi Strauss, 16, 71, 72, 90
Lider and Associates, xv
Lockheed Martin, xv
   Missiles and Space Co., xv
   Palo Alto Research Center, xv
   Vought Systems, xv
Loew's, 38
Mack Truck, xv, 71, 90
Mantech International, xv
Manufacturing Application Center, xv
Martin Marietta, xv
Matsushita, 22, 39
Mattel, 8
MCA, 39
McDonalds, 6 - 8
McDonnell Douglas, 8
Menlo Park Ass., xv
Metropolitan Edison Company, xv
MGM, 38
Microsoft, 8, 19, 39, 61
Netscape, 61
Newport News Shipbuilding, xv
Northrop Grumman, xv, 34, 150
Paramount, 38, 39
Philip Morris, 27
Process Consulting, xv
Rally's, 7
Raytheon, xv, 3, 33
RCA, 3
Rheaco Inc., xv
RKO Studios, 38
Schnader, Harrison, Segal & Lewis, xv
Seagram, 22
Sega, 8
Sherpa Corp., xv
Sikorsky Aircraft, xv, 147
Sirius-Beta, xiii - xvii, 6, 211
Sony, 8, 39
Steelcase, xvi, 239
Strategic Business Management, xv
Sun Microsystems, 61
Sylvania, 3

Symbiotic Resources, xv
Taligent, 154, 155
Telart Technologies, xv
Tex Direct, xv
Texas Instruments, xv
The Schraff Group, xv
Toyota, 2, 39
Twentieth Century-Fox, 38
U. S. Steel, xv
Unisys, 61
VFD Consulting, xv
Virtual Learning Center, xv
Wang Laboratories, 3
Web Pipeline, Inc., xv
Westinghouse, xv, 34, 150, 155
Concurrent engineering, xii, 186
Cost and operational effectiveness
    analysis, 209

Darius, 35
DARPA. *See* U.S. Government Agencies:
    Defense Advanced Research Projects
    Agency
Darwin, 242
Defense acquisition reform, 197 - 203
Descartes, René, 239, 240
Digital Equipment Corp. *See* Companies:
    Digital Equipment Corp.
Dooley graph, 164, 176 - 195, 242
Dylan, 242

Enterprise engineering, xii
Enterprise integration
    capability model, 95
Enterprise modeling
    see also agents
    see also communicative acts
    abstraction methods, 230
    category theory, 159, 172
    collaboration theory, 167
    complexity theory, 234, 235
    concept engine, 243
    concept lattices, 236, 243
    concept topology, 231

conceptual clustering, 234
enterprise reference model, 109 - 143
federatable executables, 163
federatable representations, 164
fiber bundles, 232
fuzzy logic, 239
granularity, 232
graph theory, 172
graphic representations, 164, 219
group theory, 172
IDEF3, 226
information theory, 158, 223
Karmarkar algorithm, 238
linguistics, 171
metamodels, 236
model federation, 230, 234
modeling trust, 218
multiple representations, 164
parametric representations, 164
reference model, 199, 208
sentential representations, 165
set theory, 172
situation theory, 171, 226, 240
soft modeling, 239 - 241
state, 241
tabular representations, 164
trust, 211 - 226
ESPRIT. *See* Research Projects: European
    Strategic Program for Research in
    Information Technology

Film industry, 12 - 13
    and Howard Hughes, 54
    as a source of the virtual enterprise, 53
    development of the virtual
        enterprise, 40
    Flashdance, 41
    influence of food distribution, 39
    Jurassic Park, 40
    monopoly, 39
    packet-unit system, 40
    Rocky, 41
    Schindler's List, 40
    Waterworld, 21 - 22, 39

Gates, Bill, 19
Gold rush, 16

Hammurabi, 35
Harriot, Thomas, 239
High concept, 40 - 51, 203
   and agents, 42
   and case law, 42
   defined, 41
   feature based modeling, 44
   feature driven enterprise, 50
   in film industry virtual enterprise, 42
   in missile enterprise, 197
Hughes, Howard, 54

IBM. *See* Companies: IBM
ICAM. *See* Research projects: Integrated
   Computer Aided Manufacturing
Industrial Technology Institute. See
   Organizations: Industrial Technology
   Institute
International Conference on Enterprise
   Integration Modeling Technology, *See*
   Research Projects: International
   Conference on Enterprise Integration
   Modeling Technology
intertwingle, 89, 98

Java, xiv
Jefferson, Thomas, 31, 53
Jeito, 225

keidanran, 39, 56
keiretsu, 39, 56
kisha club, 39

Lean manufacturing, 1
   in film industry, 38
   not agile, 4 - 5, 7, 77, 85
LISP, 242, 243

MacArthur, General Douglas, 38
Mach, 242
ManTech. *See* U.S. Government Agencies:
   Manufacturing Technology Directorate
Mass customization
   not agility, 71
Meme
   defined, 32
   self-perpetuating enterprise, 53
Metrics
   and benchmarking, 77
   distance, 183, 194
   Dooley graph complexity, 183
   downstream, 76
   dynamic, 77
   frequency, 185, 195
   heritage component, 81
   importance, 185, 195
   moveability, 195
   questionnaire, 204 - 207
   response component, 79
   rules of thumb, 83
   time delay, 184, 194
   topology match, 184
   trust, 223
   upstream, 76
microkernel, 242
Moby Dick, 14
Morita, Akio, 39, 57, 197
   see also Companies: Sony
   The Japan that Can Say No, 39, 57
Movies
   See film industry; whaling industry

National Cash Register. *See* Companies:
   AT&T
National Research Council. *See*
   Organizations; National Research
   Council

Oak Ridge National Laboratories. *See* U.S.
   Government Agencies: Oak Ridge
   National Laboratories

Object Management Group. *See*
   Organizations: Object Management
   Group
Object request broker, xiv
Oil industry
   see also whaling industry
   first oil well, 16
   Rockefeller, J.D., 18
Organizations
   Aerospace Agile Manufacturing
      Research Center, xv, xvi
   Agile Manufacturing Research
      Institutes, 71
   Agility Forum, xiv, 5, 71, 106
   American Association for the
      Advancement of Science, 32
   Arizona State University, xv, 71
   Automation and Robotics Research
      Institute, xvi, 228, 239
   Center for Manufacturing
      Competitiveness, xv
   Center for the Study of Language and
      Information, xvi, 172, 239
   Chinese People's Army, 27, 31
   College of William and Mary, 31
   CommerceNet, xv
   Consortium for Advanced
      Manufacturing International, xv
   Cornell Theory Center, xv
   École Polytechnique, 30
   École Ponts et Chaussees, 30
   Georgia Institute of Technology, xv
   Harvard College, 31
   Illinois State University, xv
   Industrial Technology Institute, xv, xvi,
      239
   Institute of Advanced Manufacturing
      Sciences, xv
   Institute of State and Regional Affairs
      (PA), xv
   International Monetary Fund, 225
   International Society for the
      Interdisciplinary Study of
      Symmetry, 236, 250
   MIT, 25, 32, 71, 167
   National Center for Manufacturing
      Sciences, xv

   National Research Council, xvii
   Object Management Group, xiv
   Pennsylvania MILRITE Council, xv
   Pennsylvania State University-
      Harrisburg, xv
   Rensselaer Institute, 31
   Russian mafia, 24, 27
   Sante Fe Institute, 235
   Society for Manufacturing
      Engineers, xv
   Stanford University, 25
   Suppliers' Working Group
      market study, 59
   University of Alabama, 31
   University of Indiana, xv
   University of South Dakota, xv
   University of Texas - Arlington, xv
   University of Texas - Austin, xv
   University of Virginia, 31
   West Point Military Academy, 31
   Western Kentucky University, xv
   Work and Technology Institute, xv, xvi

Panama canal, 32
Peirce, C.S., 239
Pomegranate, 242 - 247
Prograph CPX, 243

Railroad industry, 31
Research projects
   Agile Virtual Enterprise Focus
      Group, xiv, 12, 109
   AIM-9X missile, 33 - 34, 187
      Israeli response, 33
   benefits study, 60
   Business Applications of Situation
      Theory, 172, 239
   Computer Aided Logistics Support, 34,
      88
   computer integrated
      manufacturing, 59
   distributed automotive
      manufacturing, 25 - 27
   early knowledge representation, 15
   Energia very heavy launch vehicle, 24

European Strategic Program for
  Research in Information
  Technology, xiv
Integrated Computer Aided
  Manufacturing, xi
Integrated Manufacturing Technology
  Roadmap, xvii, 44
International Conference on Enterprise
  Integration Modeling
  Technology, xiv, xvii
invention of can opener, 11
invention of pocket watch, 13, 18
invention of tin can, 11
Knowledge Query Markup
  Language, 167, 168
Lean Aircraft Initiative, 59
Next Generation Manufacturing, 44
numerical control of machine tools, 59
Process Specification Language, 226
SEMATECH, 56, 94, 105
software collectives, 23
standard for the exchange of product
  data, 96
Strategic Defense Initiative, 29
Suppliers' Working Group, xiv, 57, 94
  detailed report, 64
Rogers, William Barton, 31

Selective ignorance, 23
SEMATECH. *See* Research projects:
  SEMATECH
Semiconductor industry
  virtual enterprise, 56
Sirius-Beta. *See* Companies: Sirius-Beta
Spielberg, Steven, 40
Spruce Goose (aircraft), 54
Steelcase. *See* Companies: Steelcase
Structured brainstorming, 228
Suppliers' Working Group. *See* Research
  projects: Suppliers' Working Group
Systems engineering, 58

Trust
  communication channels, 212
  deductive trust, 213

deductive trust defined, 217
  inductive, 213
  metrics, 223
  mitigated induction, 215
  nodes, 212
  trust agent. *See* Agents
  truth, 219
Turnip, 229 - 234

U.S. Government Agencies
  Air Force, 33
  Army Corps of Engineers, 32
  Defense Advanced Research Projects
    Agency, xiii, 58, 59, 241, 242
  Department of Commerce, xvii, 44
  Department of Defense, xiii, xvii, 44,
    89
  Department of Energy, 44
  Manufacturing Technology
    Directorate, xi, 54, 58, 59
  National Aeronautics and Space
    Administration, 24
  National Institute of Standards and
    Technology, xv, xvii
  National Science Foundation, xiii, 44
  Navy, 211
  Oak Ridge National Laboratories, xvii
  Sandia National Laboratories, xv, 228
  Special Operation Forces, 106

Virtual enterprise
  see also agility
  and electronic commerce, 87
  definition, 65
  four types, 66
  infrastructure, 110, 126 - 136

Washington, George, 31
Weapon systems, 2
  example, 180 - 186, 187 - 197
  similar to commercial products, 32
  wrong the first time, 187
Whaling industry, 13 - 19
  attempts to steal, 16

   culture of, 17
   shift to baleen, 16
   shift to gold exploration, 16
Work and Technology Institute. *See*
   Organizations: Work and Technology
   Institute
World War I
   virtual enterprise, 58

World War II
   and case-based trust, 216
   postwar demonstrations, 59
   virtual enterprise 59

zaibatsu, 39

About the Author

H. T. GORANSON is senior scientist for Sirius-Beta, a research firm in Virginia Beach, Virginia. He has been engaged in cognitive models and representation for collaboration, and has served as principle investigator-technical monitor for major projects sponsored by the U.S. Defense Advanced Research Projects Agency.